KEY CONCEPTS IN THE PHILOSOPHY OF EDUCATION

What is education, and why does it matter? Philosophers from Plato onwards have addressed these questions. However, finding your way through the vast corpus of their writings is a daunting task. For those who want a modern guide, this book is the answer, offering a clear and lively survey that guides the reader through the key terms and concepts and opens up the interest and relevance of the subject for today. Over 150 concepts are described and analysed, and, together with an extensive bibliography, the work provides an unparalleled guide and reference resource.

Christopher Winch is Professor of Philosophy of Education at University College Northampton. Previous publications include *Quality and Education* (Blackwell, 1996) and *The Philosophy of Human Learning*, (Routledge, 1998). **John Gingell** is Head of Philosophy programmes at University College Northampton.

KEY CONCEPTS SERIES

KEY CONCEPTS IN THE PHILOSOPHY OF EDUCATION

Christopher Winch
and John Gingell

London and New York

First published 1999
by Routledge
11 New Fetter Lane, London EC4P 4EE

Simultaneously published in the USA and Canada
by Routledge
29 West 35th Street, New York, NY 10001

Typeset in Bembo by The Florence Group,
Stoodleigh, Devon

Printed and bound in Great Britain by Clays Ltd, St Ives plc

British Library Cataloguing in Publication Data
A catalogue record for this book is available from the British
Library

Library of Congress Cataloguing in Publication Data
A catalogue record for this book has been requested

ISBN 0–415–17304–3 (pbk)
ISBN 0–415–17303–5 (hbk)

CONTENTS

ACKNOWLEDGEMENTS

In writing this book we have benefited greatly from numerous conversations with colleagues over the years. Our particular thanks go to various participants at the West Midlands Philosophy of Education Society Annual Conference at Gregynog Hall, Powys with whom we have discussed many of the issues dealt with in this volume, and who have ensured that erudition has always been accompanied by enjoyment.

We would also like to thank Alison Winch for commenting on a draft of this book.

KEY CONCEPTS

A

aesthetic/artistic education
accountability
achievement
action research
advising
affirmative action
aims of education
apprenticeship
assessment
attention/attentiveness
authority
autonomy

B

behaviourism

C

censorship
co-education
cognitivism
common good

common sense
communitarianism
compensatory education
competence
competition and cooperation
compulsion
concept formation
conservatism
constructivism
creativity
critical thinking
culture
curriculum

D

definition
democracy
deschooling
development
discipline
discourse
discovery learning
diversity

E

education
effectiveness
elitism
emotions
entitlement
epistemology
equality
erotetic
essentially contested concepts
excellence
existentialism

experience
experts
expression (free)

F

feminism

G

genre
giftedness
good practice

H

health education
Higher Education
homosexuality
human nature

I

idealism
ideology
imagination
individuality
indoctrination
inspection
instrumentalism
intelligence

J

judgement
justice
justification

K

knowledge

L

leadership
learning
leisure
liberation
literacy

M

markets
Marxism
means and ends
memory
metanarratives
metaphysics
mixed ability
moral education
motivation
multiculturalism

N

narrative
nationalism
nature/nurture
needs
neutrality

O

objectivity
open learning
oppression

P

paradigm case arguments
parental
paternalism
pedagogy
philosophy
physical education
play
pluralism
political economy
postmodernism
practical education
pragmatism
prefiguration
process
progressivism
psycholinguistics
public schools
punishment

Q

quality

R

racism
rationality
reading
reconstructivism
reductionism
reflective teaching
relativism
Religious Education
research
rights
rules

S

schools and schooling
scientific method
selection
self-respect
sex and gender
sex education
skills
social cohesion
socialisation
sociolinguistics
sociology of knowledge
special education/learning disabilities
spiritual education
standards
stereotypes

T

teaching
theory and practice
tolerance
training
transcendental arguments
truth

U

utilitarianism
utopianism

V

virtue theory
vocationalism

W

work
writing

INTRODUCTION

Key Concepts in the Philosophy of Education is an in-depth glossary which, it is hoped, will provide students and teachers of philosophy of education and other people interested in the subject, with a useful reference book on key theoretical terms and, where appropriate, the various debates surrounding them. The glossary also gives historical overviews of key debates. The entries vary in length according to the importance the authors have attached to each topic. They have been selected through the authors' experience of what is needed for a comprehensive course in the philosophy of education, through comments and suggestions from Routledge referees, colleagues and students, and, finally, to a careful survey of the literature in the philosophy of education over the past forty years.

All cross-references are in bold. Sometimes the actual concept referred to may not be in the precise form in the entry . Readers are advised to read an entry that interests them and then to use the cross-references as a means of further exploring the area of controversy that they are interested in. Bibliographical citations within entries actually refer to the bibliography at the end of the book.

Although the book is jointly authored, the final text is the result of close cooperation and discussion between us. However, one author took primary responsibility for each entry and, although (for philosophers) we are in remarkably close agreement on most of the issues discussed in this book, there are inevitably

1

differences in emphasis and outlook, which are reflected in the tone of the entries themselves. We have decided not to eliminate completely the authentic 'authorial voice' of the two authors as we feel that an individual point of view and style of approach are an intrinsic feature of philosophical writing. We do not mean that it is impossible to co-author extended pieces of philosophical writing, since this has been done very successfully by many philosophers. However, given the range of topics that we discuss, it would have been little short of a miracle for such a commonality of views to have emerged in every entry. What we have striven to do, therefore, is to arrive at entries that both of us are, philosophically speaking, reasonably comfortable with in a small minority of cases and very happy with in the great majority.

Finally, instead of a list of contents in the traditional style, we have provided a list of the concepts dealt with in this book. Cross references are provided within the text.

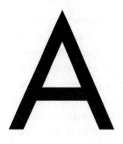

aesthetic/artistic education   On surveying the titles of books and articles within philosophy of education concerned with the topic of aesthetic or artistic **education** there seems to be, initially, a large body of work dealing with this area. There is a series of books by Best (1978, 1985, 1992) a substantial literature on **creativity** and important articles by Hepburn (1960, 1972). However, closer scrutiny of this material shows that very little of it has either to do with aesthetic or artistic education. Rather, it has to do with using the arts as a way of educating something else. Thus, Hepburn argues (1972) that the arts – and especially literature – are of importance in the education of the **emotions**. Best holds that the value of the arts is in their contribution to our understanding of 'the human condition and other aspects of life' (1985: 186). The literature concerning creativity, although it may touch upon aesthetic or artistic appreciation only does so in the context of teaching people to produce works of art. What we have in this literature is either an emphasis on practice or the embodiment of a tradition that goes back at least to Plato which insists that the significance of the arts must be cognitive or moral. And these attitudes are reflected in the **curriculum** in schools. So, for instance, music education is essentially about learning to play an instrument or to sing. Literature functions as a part of learning a language and tends to be approached as if it was essentially didactic and art-history has trouble finding any place

3

on a curriculum. (Before the introduction of the National Curriculum in England and Wales in 1988 there was little if any art-history taught before children were 16. At present there is *some* concern to see that children appreciate, say, paintings but it is a concern that looks like vanishing almost before it has been established and it stops far short of offering art-history as a distinct subject on the pre-A level curriculum).

But all of this is terribly odd! Whilst it may be perfectly true that lessons for life may be learned from art – if you want to understand human beings, then reading Jane Austen or Henry James is a better bet than perusing the latest **behaviourist** textbook – it is also true that Austen and James are novelists not psychologists and have to be appreciated as such and that the vast majority of art simply does not have this kind of cognitive or moral loading. It is difficult, for instance, to see what moral messages music is supposed to deliver and the notion that it functions as an articulation of human feelings has been much criticised (Beardsley 1958; Dickie 1997). To see art as simply instructive both makes mysterious our approach to it – the person listening with rapt attention to a Mozart concerto for the hundredth time must be seriously stupid if they have yet to get the message – and trivialises it – because it treats works of art as if they are simply containers for something else. If we think that the value of Monet is that he enables us to look at the countryside in a different way then we are doing a grave disservice to both Monet in particular and painting in general.

This is not to endorse either a purely formalist view of art – which seems just as open to criticism as a purely expressive or mimetic view of art (see Beardsley 1958; Dickie 1997) – or to hold that art is merely entertainment. It is to insist that art is, in and for itself, serious (so serious that many people can spend their lives concerned with it in various ways) but its seriousness is not as a means to other (e.g. educational) ends, but rather as an end in itself. Artistic achievement is one of the great forms of human achievement – perhaps, the greatest and it is, as such, that it ought to be studied.

accountability 'Accountability' refers to a moral relationship that is created when someone gives to someone else an undertaking to do something. This second party is either someone in **authority**, who trusts the first party or someone who has committed resources for the act to be carried out. **Education**, whether carried out by the state or privately, fundamentally involves accountability relationships. Resources are committed to build schools, large amounts of time and energy are committed by children and teachers, and promises and contracts are made to provide educational goods and to strive to achieve them. However, unravelling the nature of accountability relationships in education is more difficult than merely stating that they exist.

One problem is the number and variety of interested and involved parties or *stakeholders*. The other is the long-term nature of most educational projects and the consequent difficulty in ascertaining when a promise made has in fact been kept. The difficulty becomes particularly acute in relation to publicly-funded education because the stakeholders include: children (who commit trust, time and energy); parents (who are the primary custodians of childrens' interests); taxpayers both private and corporate (who commit resources); governments (who deploy resources raised from taxation) and teachers (who commit time and energy). It is generally accepted that there is a moral obligation on the part of teachers to be accountable to the various elements of society who have a stake in education, but there is far less agreement as to how that obligation is to be discharged. One extreme would suggest that there are almost no circumstances in which a teacher should not be trusted to carry out his or her duty. Another extreme, advocated by Chubb and Moe (1990) and Tooley (1995) is that market relationships, largely unmediated by the state, can do this job.

Beyond this large dispute there are other issues that publicly-funded education systems have to deal with, in ensuring accountability. The first is that of ensuring that the mix of **aims** adopted by the system is actually met and, if so, to what extent. The second is the question of whether one seeks to assess the effectiveness of the system *as a whole* or whether one seeks to assess individual units of educational activity, like schools and teachers. Answers to the first question will be compromised if there are no clear aims for the system, or if the stated aims do not reflect the wishes of some of the stake-holders. Different answers to this latter question will lead to different forms of **assessment**. Pure market-led systems of accountability will mean that the impersonal forces of supply and demand will determine whether schools remain in business. Even market systems need indicators of effectiveness and there is not much consensus as to which are the best. The major alternatives are *customer satisfaction* (raising the question as to who exactly are the customers), *assessment results* (raising issues about whether results reflect effectiveness); *value-added measures* (which have their own epistemic problems) and **inspection** (which poses issues about subjectivity).

achievement The outcomes of education are usually charac-terised as the achievements of those who have been educated. These may be expressed in terms of whether or not the **aims** of education were fulfilled in relation to those individuals and to what degree. In order to find out what has been achieved one requires some form of **assessment**. Most non-educators tend to think of educational achievement in terms of scores achieved in tests or examinations and, maybe, they wish to compare educational achievement against educational **standards**. Some have argued (e.g. Pring 1992) that, although achievements can be compared, standards cannot. The distinction between the two rests on the observation that in comparing achievements, or in assessing them, one is some-times comparing them against a standard. Thus, if a student achieves 50 per cent in a test and 50 per cent is the score needed for grade C then that student meets the standard for the award of C.

However, low raw achievement does not necessarily imply a lack of educational success. A student may transform him-self educationally to a great extent by starting from a low base and moving to a high one compared to where he was before but a low one compared with, say, national norms. Such a student has, in a real sense, achieved much. It is, however, much easier to assess achievement through the calibration of a test score than it is through a measure of transformation (see **effectiveness**) and measures of transformation are logically dependent on measures of achievement since they measure the gap between two measures of achievement. However, if testing is not adequate then the possibility of assessing achievement is also compromised. The main threat to adequate measures of achievement lies in their providing adequate validity. While this may seem like a technical problem in relation to some subjects like mathematics (but see Davis 1995, 1996) there are more daunting difficulties in measuring the achievement of other, less easily quantifiable, aims, such as **spiritual** awareness. There are further questions concerning the long-term achievements realised by education. Should one, for example, measure pre-school achievement in terms of adult social success and can this be done with any degree of accuracy (Schweinhart and Weikart 1980)?

Other issues arise concerning what is meant by achieving high standards. Is it better to eliminate low achievement than to raise high achievement? If one opts for high achievement does one mean by this that the achievement of some students should meet high standards, or that it is enough that one student meets very high absolute standards (see Cooper 1980, Winch 1996). Or again, does high achievement mean high rates of transformation for the most able students or for all? Is it worthwhile measuring achievement in terms of transformation or should one be more bothered about whether indigenous achievement meets standards accepted internationally? These questions suggest that simply claiming that an education system is achievement-oriented is not claiming very much. Questions about how achievement is to be conceptualised and which conceptualisation is to be given most weight when evaluating educational activities are not only philosophical matters but political problems of some complexity.

action research   It is argued that teachers need research that tells them how to improve their classroom practice. Large-scale projects carried out in contexts remote from their own will not help them. In addition, the invidious model of teacher as practitioner and researcher as dispenser-of-**advice** deprives teachers of professional autonomy. The solution is to empower the teacher as a researcher in her own right (Stenhouse 1975). This entails, not just that teachers carry out research according to the suggestions of others, but that they set the research agenda and determine the methodology. In this way they are fully autonomous in directing the research process towards the resolution of their own professional concerns.

The action researcher will identify an issue that needs to be resolved. She will design an intervention and record the effects of its implementation, review the outcome and disseminate her results. She will carry out her research in her classroom, integrating it into her everyday work. The advantages can be seen in the enhancement of professional power that it gives to teachers together with control over the research agenda. In this respect, teachers are emulating the practice of higher-prestige professions such as medicine.

Potential disadvantages concern possible lack of expertise of the teacher-researcher, the limited validity and reliability of results obtained in such conditions, together with a possible waste of resources. However, a powerful coalition is building up against the perceived irrelevance of much academic educational research (Hargreaves 1996), and action research offers a way of addressing practical concerns.

advising   There are some areas of academic concern which say as much about the context in which they originate as they do about the issues they address. Such is a short paper by Douglas Stewart 'An Analysis of Advising' (1978) which defends the giving of advice – in the particular contexts of counselling, moral education and professional guidance but the list could be much extended – against the charge that advisers are seeking to control, dominate or manipulate the person being offered the advice or striving to decide, speak for or get such a person to do something. Stewart's analysis owes much to the analytical tradition of Austin and Searle (Austin 1962; Searle 1964) and his solution to the problem turns upon arguing that in giving advice I am aiming for an 'illocutionary' effect, i.e. to have the person being advised recognise and understand what is being said to him, rather than a 'perlocutionary' effect, i.e. having him actually do what he is advised to do. Unfortunately this distinction does not seem to do the trick. When we advise our students, in their own best interests, to read book X we want, if we are sincere, not merely that they recognise what is being said to them but that they, in their own best interests, actually do read X.

However, the success or failure of the analysis is by the way. Such a defence of such an everyday practice – even when such a practice is extended into professional spheres – is only apposite in a world partly gone mad! Without the giving and taking of advice such practices as child-rearing, education, friendship, training, medicine and much of the everyday commerce between human beings, e.g. 'My sink leaks . . .' 'Ah, what you need for that . . .', would become impossible. Therefore, any rejection or resentment of such a practice – in terms of 'personal space', autonomy or what have you, shows a dangerous alienation from the realities of human life. If we have reached a situation in which some people are prepared to countenance such a rejection or harbour such a resentment we have reached a sorry state indeed.

affirmative action   A strong version of the notion of **equality** of opportunity maintains that it does not obtain unless outcomes of educational processes are roughly the same for all groups. This condition will not obtain so long as they are denied equality of treatment. In order to ensure commensurate treatment it is necessary to change entry conditions so that some groups receive a comparative advantage. Only in this way will historic injustices be righted. Affirmative action could be seen as a group-oriented version of Nozick's (1974) idea of rectificatory **justice**. In addition, it has the advantage of encouraging people to avail themselves of opportunities who would not otherwise have done so, even if they had the potential.

Unfortunately people regard procedural justice as applying to individuals rather than groups and they see affirmative action programmes as a violation of procedural justice (see Flew 1981). There are also problems with the links between equality of opportunity and outcome. There is no guarantee that equality of treatment will guarantee equality of outcome, given uneven distributions of interest, motivation and ability among individuals. If equality of outcome cannot be secured through changes to entry conditions then there is a temptation to intervene to produce inequalities of treatment within the educational process, in order to secure desired outcomes. But this strategy is likely to provoke further opposition as it can be argued that procedural justice is being further violated. Rectification for past wrongs to groups cannot be settled administratively, as educational outcomes are crucially tied to individual effort and talent.

aims of education   The aims of any system of education tell us what it is for. Since they embody the fundamental purposes of **education**, they determine the character of everything else: institutions, **curriculum**, **pedagogy** and **assessment**. To get clear about the aims of education is, therefore, to begin to clarify the rest. Just because aims are not written down, it does not mean that they do not exist. They can be implicit as well as explicit, and can be embodied in the everyday practices of teachers and students, as well as in government documents. Indeed, the printing of aims in a document is neither necessary nor sufficient for education to have aims, since documents can be ignored.

Society consists of different interest groups such as the government, the state apparatus, various groupings of citizens, businesses, children and educational professionals themselves, all of which may have influence over education. Accordingly, aims can be set by different groups within society acting in concert, in conflict, or in a spirit of compromise. The more there is agreement, the more likely that a consensus over aims is likely to be achieved. The less likely there is to be agreement, the more likely it is that aims will either be directly imposed by a powerful group such as the state, or they will in practice be set by those most directly concerned with education, namely teachers.

Education can have more than one aim, so long as aims are not mutually incompatible. It is not possible, for example, to aim to produce citizens who obey the state unquestioningly and at the same time to produce free spirits who are able to question any proposal that they encounter. Many aims are broadly compatible with each other but exist in a certain tension. Partly, this results from the limited time available in any educational process. Partly, it is because some aims can only be *fully* achieved at the expense of others. A society which agrees on the range of aims it is going to pursue still has to agree on the relative weighting of each aim and the degree to which each should be prioritised.

There are different ways of categorising aims of education. One tradition emphasises the importance of education as an individual, liberal good with intrinsic value. Another tradition sees education as a public, as well as an individual good, with **instrumental**, as well as, or in contrast to, intrinsic value. Broadly speaking, the former tradition is called 'liberal', the latter 'instrumental'. Instrumental aims can be further classified into vocational, societal and personal. Seen in this way, there is no necessary incompatibility of these aims with each other, provided that the place of the others is recognised. It seems, for example, that someone could be educated to be autonomous as an intrinsic good for that individual, and at the same time learn to be a citizen and a productive member of the society. It is often thought, however, that at least some of these aims are incompatible with each other. Some are thought to be aims of **schooling** (Barrow 1981) rather than of education, others again are thought to be excessively favoured at the expense of others, instrumental over liberal, for example (Gray 1993). Writers who adopt either or both of these positions generally wish to homogenise the aims of education in favour of their own views.

Specifying aims of education in contrast to aims of schooling is illegitimate unless there is some independent criterion for distinguishing between education and schooling. To categorise aims as belonging to one rather than the other involves an attempt to define the respective spheres of education and schooling. This means that the distinction cannot be used as a criterion for classifying aims until it is properly sorted out. Attempts to show that education is unduly weighted in favour of some aims rather than others are not necessarily fallacious, but they do require argument and evidence in their support. Such arguments or evidence would need to show either that the favoured aims were unobtainable under the current system or that the weightings of different aims were, in some way, unfair.

It is time to look at major educational aims in more detail. There are three, related ways in which this can be done, as illustrated in Table 1. The alternative classifications show us: (a) that there is considerable overlap between different aims in terms of the sets of distinctions; (b) that social, instrumental and vocational aims are at least as, if not more numerous than the intrinsic, individual and liberal aims favoured by most philosophers of education; (c) that none of these aims is necessarily incompatible with each other, although the degree to which they can all be jointly implemented is, no doubt, limited; (d) that classification is often difficult.

These reflections suggest that the tendency to dichotomise aims along the lines suggested above is misguided if it is intended to sharply separate out two contrasting philosophies of education concerning aims which are largely incompatible with each other. Attempts to debate the value of aims which use one-dimensional systems of classification or which see the terms of the debate as *exclusive* rather than *inclusive* either–or are in danger of missing both the diverse interests of those involved in setting educational aims and important philosophical distinctions in their classification.

Table 1 *Major educational aims*

(a) Concern with the needs of society and with the needs of individuals

Individual needs	Social needs
1 The promotion of autonomy	To promote economic development
2 To give the individual a secure cultural background	To preserve the society's culture
3 To give an individual the ability to take part in society through an occupation	To produce good citizens

(b) Instrumental versus intrinsic aims

Instrumental	Intrinsic
1 The promotion of autonomy	The promotion of autonomy
2 To give the individual a secure cultural background	To give the individual a secure cultural background
3 To give an individual the ability to take part in society through an occupation	To preserve the society's culture
4 To promote economic development	
5 To preserve the society's culture	
6 To produce good citizens	

(c) Liberal versus vocational aims

Liberal	Vocational
1 The promotion of autonomy	The promotion of autonomy
2 To give the individual a secure cultural background	To give the individual a secure cultural background
3 To preserve the society's culture	To give the individual the ability to take part in society through an occupation
4 To produce good citizens (?)	To promote economic development
5	To produce good citizens

apprenticeship   Apprenticeship is an ancient institution for **teaching** and **learning** in a **vocational** context. Its practical basis is the need for skills in professions, crafts and trades to be passed on from generation to generation. Its moral rationale rests on the need for the values and outlooks of occupations to be passed on. Typically, apprenticeship has involved a close relationship between the apprentice, or aspiring entrant into a craft and the master, who is not only skilled in the craft, but a custodian of its values and traditions and, importantly, a teacher of those skills and values to the rising generation. Apprenticeship was, in the Middle Ages, the mode of reproduction for those crafts that were practised by associations of tradesmen known as guilds. Some commentators, notably Adam Smith (1981) saw a dark side to apprenticeship, claiming that it was nothing more than a self-serving attempt by guilds to control access to the labour market and to artificially bid up the price of labour.

Unlike the pupil–tutor relationship described in Rousseau (1911a) the apprentice–master relationship relies on the explicit inculcation of values and skills within the customs and rituals of the guild. The development of modern capitalism has undermined the guild system, but the practical and moral advantages of apprenticeship have been thought to be so advantageous to the economy and society in many countries, that apprenticeship has lived on as a means of on-the-job education and **training** in many countries, achieving perhaps its most highly-developed modern form in contemporary Germany (see Streeck 1992). It is important to realise that the apprentice–master relationship as it evolved in western Europe is not one of 'learning with Nellie' or 'learning by osmosis' but of structured didacticism within the context of an established curriculum. Attempts by Frank Smith (1985) and others to promote laissez-faire methods of learning to **read** as 'apprenticeship' are, therefore, misleading.

assessment   Questions about assessment within education typically concern two areas: whether we should have assessment at all within our education system – and, if we are to have it, what type or types we should have. It is *usually* the first type of question that is seen as philosophically interesting, the second being thought of as a technical matter of concern for the practitioners of different subjects.

The idea that we might do away with all assessment within education is likely to be regarded with puzzlement – and, perhaps glee – by the average teacher about to mark, say, the maths exercises of a class of thirty pupils. Glee, because this is a tedious task, puzzlement, because it is a task that most teachers would see as a necessary part of the teaching and learning of mathematics.

This common sense reaction is essentially correct. However, from time to time some theorists have suggested that we abolish assessment either within part of the education system or throughout. Lerner has suggested (1972) that it should be possible to do courses at university without being assessed, whilst the group of theorists called the **deschoolers** have wished to abolish all assessment within the education system. Both suggestions have met with vigorous replies. With regard to the first suggestion Flew, in what is perhaps the authoritative text on the purposes of educational assessment, pointed out that education by its very nature involves **teaching** and **learning** and that to be involved in either – in their usual intentional senses – is to be involved in trying to bring about the mastery by someone i.e. the learner, of some piece of possible **knowledge**. But if someone is *sincerely* trying to learn something or trying to teach someone to learn something then they must, necessarily, be concerned whether, how far, and how well they are succeeding. And they cannot claim to be so concerned unless they take steps to find out the answers to these questions. Such attempts to find out are what we mean by 'assessment' (Flew 1976). Flew's point is perfectly general i.e. it applies to all *sincere* teaching and learning. But it is also open with regard to forms of assessment, i.e. it doesn't imply, for instance, that we must have written, timed examinations. It could be argued that Flew's position can be strengthened here. The sincerity of purpose he bases his argument upon could be thought to justify not merely some form of assessment but some efficient form of assessment. That is, the form of assessment used has to be shown to be likely – within the limitations of assessment generally – to produce a reasonable answer to the questions posed.

The reply to the deschoolers was mounted by Barrow (1978) who convincingly demonstrated that the main force of their arguments is generated by confusing four distinct elements of assessment. These are, first, grading, which is any attempt to distinguish people's competence in any matter by any means. Second, certification, which is the business of making one's grading public by means of certificates or degrees. Third, the use of examinations as a means to grade. Fourth, the use of other means of assessment, for example, continuous assessment or the intuitive judgement of teachers. And he shows that whilst there may be pertinent questions to be raised with regard to each of these areas individually (for example, is there too much certification in society and is it used in a reasonable manner?) there is a strong case for some forms of grading within education, because education must involve standards of competence and we must have ways of measuring progress with regards to such standards. And he makes a case that some certification is useful within society, so that we do need a system with regard to items as diverse as ability at mathematics and car-driving skills which tells us whether people are basically proficient at such things. This point might be made stronger by the consideration that the public education system within any democratic country should be **accountable** to the public at large, and one of the ways that such accountability most easily operates is by examination of the processes of certification (Barrow 1978).

Recent philosophical writing about assessment has not seemed to have the wide sweep of the issues raised above, but has been both interesting and important. It has been suggested that if we want a school system which imparts 'rich' knowledge to its pupils then the ways we currently use to assess pupils, e.g. the standards and tests associated with the English National Curriculum, are either likely to be valid but not reliable, or, reliable but not valid. That is, that such tests will either properly test the 'rich' knowledge that we desire but then not enable us to predict future performance on the part of the people tested, or, that they will enable us to predict future performance but only at the expense of not really testing for 'rich' knowledge (Davis 1996). Whilst such a suggestion seems to raise merely technical problems, it, in fact, again threatens assessment as such and, if accepted, would lead us towards educational nihilism. However, given a reasonable amount of care about the specification of test items and the awareness that there will never be a perfect test and that there will always be a degree of inferential hazard (Dearden 1979) in moving from the results of one test performance to future performances, there seems little reason to accept the suggestion (Gingell and Winch 1996). It would be foolish in the field of educational assessment – such as it would in the law courts and driving tests – to think that we can completely eradicate the possibility of error. Therefore the question is always not whether such and such a means of assessment – in any field – does its job perfectly, but whether it does it in a way that is reasonably successful. And always to be borne in mind when answering such a question is the implication of having no system at all and the fact that, for the people being assessed, such assessment should constitute a form of **justice** (Dearden 1979).

attention/attentiveness Since Descartes's *Meditations* attention has been thought of by many philsophers as a self-focusing on inner mental content. Modern computational theories of mind see this manifested in the taking up of brain capacity (Stainthorp 1989). It is, however, an elementary conceptual point that people, not brains, attend. However, neither of these accounts tells a teacher whether or not a student is paying attention. Wittgenstein, in the early stages of the *Philosophical Investigations* (1953) brings out the connection between individual concern and external manifestation that is characteristic of attentiveness. This is manifested in the fine shades of behaviour and nuances of speech which characterise the way individuals approach a task, and, subsequently, in the quality of what they do or produce. The concept of attention also has important links with two other concepts of great educational significance: that of effort and that of love.

Someone who attends may only be able to do so through making an effort and overcoming distraction. Their attentive efforts assist them in overcoming obstacles. Someone who approaches a subject or a task with love, will, at the very least pay a disciplined attention to it (Murdoch 1992) and, as Wittgenstein pointed out (1967), will be prepared to see that love put to the test. In an educational and learning context, this will involve overcoming obstacles internal to the task or subject and external ones arising from distraction together with a passionate striving for **excellence**. The concept of attention, if properly considered, should remind us of the importance of the affective aspect of **learning**.

authority Authority is often divided into two types: being *in authority* and being *an authority* (Peters 1967). To be *in* authority is to have the entitlement to have one's wishes acceded to. To be *an* authority is to have knowledge which can be relied upon. Traditionally, educators have been thought to be authorities in both of these senses. Teachers have been thought to have the entitlement (and have been awarded the concomitant *power*) to ensure that their wishes are adhered to and they have been appointed partly because of their possession of reliable knowledge to be imparted to their students. In more recent times, the authority of teachers and of educators more generally has come to be questioned. The most prominent source of this questioning has come from **progressive** and child-centred educators, who have argued that the overt imposition of one will on another is psychologically and educationally damaging. Since being in authority does involve the teacher in an overt imposition of will, it is argued that the role of teachers should be changed to a non-authoritarian model as, for example, 'facilitators'. More generally, modern democratic societies have tended to become much less deferential towards professional claims to authority, so that the sources of traditional educational authoritativeness have been steadily undermined.

The Rousseauian objection to authority in education sprang from a belief that the overt thwarting of the pupil's will, while he was still immature, would have long-lasting harmful psychological effects. Rousseau did not, however, believe that the tutor should have no *power* but that this power, which involved controlling the child and the curriculum, was to be exercised without the child's knowledge. If Rousseau's moral psychology is rejected as unproven and implausible, then where does the authority of educators stand? In a practical sense, it is difficult to see how Rousseau's proposals could make sense in a classroom of thirty children; if it was difficult to manipulate Emile, then it will be well-nigh impossible to manipulate thirty Emiles who are all interacting with each other. In such a situation it is difficult to see how a teacher could operate without the conferral of some legitimacy for her exercise of power in the classroom and this would require that she be placed *in* authority over the class.

The question remains as to whether or not a teacher should be *an* authority in the sense of possessing a body of knowledge to be transmitted to her pupils. A generalised argument against the authority of teachers would entail rejecting this role as well, for precisely the reasons that the institutional role of the teacher-as-authority was rejected, that imparting knowledge to pupils would involve the overt imposition of will: in telling them what to believe and informing them when their beliefs were mistaken. Child-centred progressives believe that children are naturally curious (this belief stems from Rousseau's idea of *amour propre* (see **progressivism**) and that, left to their own devices they will carry out their own learning. On this view, the job of the teacher is to become a *facilitator of learning* (C. Rogers 1990) who enables the pupil to learn what he wants to know in the way he wants to learn it. In this way the **pedagogy** of the teacher becomes non-authoritative and the **curriculum** is determined by each individual child. A thoroughgoing non-authoritarianism in education places the teacher in a very different role from that of the traditional teacher, although the distinction between progressive and traditional teacher is a more–less rather than an either–or one.

There are two independent, although related, arguments against authority in education. The first is that authoritative teaching involves **indoctrination**. The second is that it violates a pupil's **autonomy**. In the first case, it can be argued that by presenting information as unquestionably true and uncontroversial, the teacher is indoctrinating the child. Since she cannot do this except by posing as an authority and by brooking no argument against her pronouncements (being in authority), the role of the educator as authority is essential to her role as indoctrinator. Strip away the authority and you strip away the possibility of indoctrination. The ultimate plausibility of this argument is going to rest on two things: first, the extent to which one regards such definitions of indoctrination as plausible and, indeed, on whether one regards indoctrination as undesirable; second, the extent to which indoctrination might be achieved through covert means, through a careful manipulation of the educational environment. If this is possible, then the argument against indoctrination may well militate against Emile-type approaches which rely on covert power rather than authority.

The argument from autonomy as an educational aim gains its strength when *strong* autonomy is seen as desirable. Strong autonomists hold that the aim of education should be to enable pupils to adopt values that are not necessarily approved of by society. If society were to prescribe what values a pupil could be educated to adopt, perhaps among a range of alternatives, then it would be authoritatively imposing values on the child. Strong autonomists would argue that society could not impose such an authority on pupils and yet at the same time expect them to become truly autonomous. This argument is plausible to the extent that one believes that strong autonomy is a desirable educational aim, but it should be noted that it is a more limited claim than that there should be no authority in pedagogy.

Influential as arguments against authority in education are, it is unlikely that authority will ever be completely rejected in educational circles. First, it is practically difficult. Second, the philosophical arguments against authority are contestable and, according to some, implausible. However the trend in society away from authoritative figures and towards the celebration of individualism means that educators, like other professionals, are going to find the task of balancing authoritative with non-authoritative approaches very difficult to achieve successfully.

autonomy Autonomy is regarded as one of the principal educational **aims**, primarily in the liberal tradition. In modern democratic societies it is often claimed that people are not merely free to choose their own governments, but also the way that they wish to lead their lives. There has been a vigorous tradition of thinking of politics as a way of preserving and extending rights at least since the time of Hobbes. J. S. Mill (1974) has probably had the most influence on liberal philosophy of education in the formulation of autonomy as an educational aim. His conception of autonomy is, however, controversial (see below). Autonomy is usually more richly specified as rational autonomy since **rationality** is also thought to be a vital educational aim (cf. J. P. White 1982).

Autonomy can be defined in various ways, relating to different levels of human rationality. If rationality is defined in terms of the ends in life that people may pursue and the means that they adopt to pursue them, then one can identify three possible levels of autonomy. First, society determines the ends of individuals and they are free to adopt the means to achieve those ends that they see fit. For example, society might prescribe that all adults should be in paid employment, but within that specification individuals would be free to choose which employment they should seek. Such a society would give individuals a certain amount of independence in their choices without allowing them to determine the overall aims of their lives. Second, a society might provide a set of aims of which it approved and let citizens choose aims amongst that set, together with the means for achieving them. Such a system is sometimes called 'weak autonomy'. It would, for example, allow people to choose whether they wished to maintain domesticity, engage in voluntary work or seek paid employment. Finally, society might allow individuals to choose any aims that they see fit whether or not society approves, subject only to the constraint that, in doing so, they should not harm any other individual without their consent. This is the kind of autonomy that Mill is thought to have promoted; it is often called 'strong autonomy' and is associated with scepticism about the existence of a common good, even weakly defined. A strong autonomist would defend the right to indulge in, for example, self-destructive behaviour. Contemporary defenders of strong autonomy include Norman (1994) and J. P. White (1997b).

How do the aims of education relate to the values of society? It is frequently assumed that if strong autonomy is seen as a desirable societal end, then it should be adopted as an aim by a public education system. This does not follow; a society might be composed of different currents of opinion, only some of which supported strong autonomy; alternatively, the society might decide that young people, incapable of making fully rational choices about ends, might instead be steered towards approved ends during their youth, with the option of a wider choice in adulthood.

A strong autonomist might argue that anyone seriously interested in promoting rationality would have to approve of strong autonomy. Someone who is rationally autonomous, it might be maintained, should be able to choose amongst ends according to whether or not they were morally acceptable, not just to society, but to *themselves* and be able to do so through a process of rational justification. It could not be sufficient, it might be argued, to rely on the authoritative say-so of others for the choice of something as important as the ends of life. If a necessary condition of rational autonomy is that one can choose ends as well as means, then one must be able to make a meaningful choice from *all* the ends available, not just those sanctioned by society. To allow for anything less than an unconstrained appraisal would be to limit rational autonomy in such a way that a fundamental aim of education would be unachievable, since reason might well determine ends which were not sanctioned by society. To confine oneself to societally approved ends would be to risk substituting submission to authority for rationality as an overriding educational aim.

Against this it could be argued that the resources deployed by society would be misused if strong autonomy were adopted as an educational aim. For if a society were to use its **authority** concerning educational matters in order to promote aims it considered were desirable, and it at the same time adopted as an aim that the desirability of such aims should be questioned and, if necessary, rejected, it could be argued that it had an inconsistent set of aims. In this case one could either jettison strong autonomy as an educational aim or the other aims. The strong autonomist is not necessarily committed to this view; he does, however, maintain that education ought to adopt as an aim that aims should be considered that are *not* desired by society. It could be maintained that this is apparently inconsistent, committing him to the view that both socially desirable and socially undesirable aims should be pursued. That is to say, if he accepts the weak autonomist's view that *only* aims approved of by society should be pursued, he cannot at the same time hold that some aims *not* approved of by society (for example, to lead the life of a drug addict out of choice) can be pursued. The strong autonomist cannot at the same time hold to a belief in weak autonomy, he must define himself in opposition to the weak autonomist. However, his position is not the same as the claim that only socially undesirable aims should be pursued. The strong autonomist is not committed to this view.

Two final points can be made in favour of weak autonomy. First, the argument for strong autonomy rests on a false premise, namely that self-justification is sufficient for the adoption of an aim. This precludes the possibility that one may have to rationally justify aims to society before adopting them. Liberals may be sceptical about a common good but they cannot just brush it aside and also claim that they champion rationality. The weak autonomist is not committed to the implausible view that society can never question its values. All that is claimed is that the education system should pursue aims that are consistent with its current values.

B

behaviourism Behaviourism is a psychological doctrine about the nature of mind. It includes a theory of learning which suggests that the only proper concern of the teacher is that of behaviour modification. The preferred mode of learning for behaviourists is *conditioning*, which involves alterations in the predecessors and consequences of the target behaviour. Although it is difficult to see how, on their own assumptions, behaviourists can say this, some of these alterations are pleasant to the target organism (rewards) and some are unpleasant (punishments). These alterations are repeated until the desired result is achieved. Thus, rats may be conditioned to run through a maze. *Conditioning* is distinct from **training** in that no intellectual activity on the part of the subject is thought necessary in order for the desired result to be achieved. Behaviourist techniques can be applied to animals and humans alike.

What is the relevance of behaviourism to education? As a matter of principle, behaviourists assume that the internal mental life of the individual is irrelevant to their learning. Some behaviourists would even deny that the individual has a mental life. Educators need to ask whether they would be prepared to accept such assumptions. The second point is practical. Since conditioning is distinct from training, an educator committed to the efficacy of training in some circumstances needs to know whether conditioning is an effective substitute. Training very often relies on rewards and punishments to achieve the desired result, but trainers are not necessarily committed to ignoring the thoughts and feelings of learners. Neither are they committed to the rigid behavioural result that the behaviourist specifies as the outcome of learning. For example, a trainer might be satisfied if someone learns to achieve a desired result (say, finding a way to the end of a maze) if necessary, by using thought and ingenuity. Developing thought and ingenuity might even be part of the training process. A conditioner on the other hand would look for a rigid behavioural response, for example having the subjects run down the maze to the exit in a way that their behaviour had been shaped to achieve.

Thus Lieberman (1990) describes how rats conditioned to run through a maze failed to do so when the maze was filled with water. Instead they swam, held their heads up and tried to see where the exit was. This was not the result that one would expect from the application of behaviourist learning techniques. Part of the problem comes from the dogmatic scientism adopted by many behaviourists. Knowledge is to be gained under experimental conditions. These involve repeated stimuli *of the same type* followed by repeated responses also of the same type. But behaviourism makes the assumption that the expression 'of the same type' is to be interpreted strictly so that it can be defined in experimental terms. This is necessary to ensure that findings made in laboratory conditions are reliable, that is, can be replicated in future experiments. It does not follow that they are valid and can serve as general accounts of how the animals learn.

Behaviourist ideas have been adopted through strategies such as the setting of behavioural objectives or through behaviour modification techniques. The former involves setting short-term educational **aims** in terms of target behaviours to be adopted by the student. The idea is that a somewhat vague educational aim, such as the ability to get on with a variety of people, can be made operational in a highly specific way, so that a relatively limited repertoire of behaviour serves as a sufficient condition for achieving that aim. In practice, the behavioural objective is an operational **definition** of the more vague educational aim. Behaviour modification is a form of teaching that has, as its outcomes, behaviours which are aimed for in an educational programme designed around behavioural objectives. Instead of specifying knowledge or attitude as the desired outcomes, highly specific and easily **assessable** behaviours serve as desired outcomes. This approach has greatly influenced the **competence** movement (see Hyland 1993) and the notion of competence is, very often, a slightly richer version of a behavioural objective (for example, to construct a table) or of a modified sequence of behaviours (for example, to measure, plane, saw, join, etc.).

Educational programmes that are *explicitly* based on behaviourism have lost a lot of their appeal in recent years. They can still be found in some varieties of **special education**, where narrowly defined behavioural objectives may be a suitable expression of some educational aims or where behaviour modification in a relatively crude sense (the student no longer abuses or attacks carers) is a realistic objective for a sequence of lessons. Their lack of endurance in mainstream practical educational situations is, however, a testimony to the flawed philosophical foundations on which behaviourist theory rests.

censorship Most liberals accept Mill's (1974) formulation of
the harm principle as the basis for determining censorship
of adult creative artefacts. Nothing should be censored unless
it can be shown to cause harm (not offence) to non-
consenting parties. Since, however, children below the age of
16 are not thought to be fully-fledged rational beings, and
so remain more susceptible to harm than adults, the issue of
censorship for them is somewhat different. One solution is
to take the Lockean (1961c) account of children's rights and
apply it to censorship issues.

On this account, parents or caregivers are charged with
protecting children's interests. This gives them temporary
derivative rights over children in their care, which will include
the control of access to books etc. When they judge that
access is not in the best interests of the child they can, in
the child's best interests, withhold it. Practical problems arise
with the availability of material beyond the direct control of
parents, e.g. in schools and libraries. The role of these institutions *in loco parentis*, adjudicating between the wishes of
different parents, becomes particularly important (Sadker and
Sadker 1977; Winch 1993). Opposition to censorship of
materials for children also comes from child libertarians who
oppose the Millian and Lockean account given above (see
Archard 1993 for a full account). The problem of censorship
of children's material comes in its acutest form in contexts

where value pluralism, public institutions for children and strong advocacy of child autonomy coexist.

co-education Co-education, where boys and girls are educated together, is the norm in the western world. It is usually assumed – not argued for – that it is more 'natural', more conducive to future understanding between the sexes than single sex education. However, there seems to be evidence appearing that these social 'goods' may be purchased at the costs of educational goods. So, for instance, the achievement of girls in co-educational maths and science classes has long been a cause for concern. But now, in England at least, there seems to be evidence, across the curriculum spectrum, that boys underperform educationally in co-educational schools (e.g. Kress 1998).

In an article that addresses the 'crisis' in co-education Laird (1994) argues both that co-education is bought at a social price for girls, for instance, in terms of sexual harassment and decline of self-esteem; and that we should be thinking of modes of co-education which address these educational and social concerns. So, for example, there is nothing intrinsic to the notion of co-education, as such, which necessitates that boys and girls all have to be taught the same things in the same ways and it may be the case that some differentiation of ends and means might address some of the problems being experienced at the moment. Certainly, if these problems continue, we would expect much more literature on such topics.

cognitivism Cognitivism is the philosophical doctrine that thought is essentially both symbolic and internal to the individual human mind. It is customary to oppose cognitivism to **behaviourism** as the main alternative account of the mind, although the two are best regarded as contraries rather than contradictories since both could be false (see **learning**). Cognitivism is important for education because its claims provide the framework for theories of learning that claim it

29

takes place through symbolic activity within individual minds. Nearly all cognitivists are also representationalists; they believe that the mind's symbolic activity takes place in representations which connect with relevant features of the world. Empiricists believe that these representations arise from experience, innatists believe that they inhere in the mind at birth and **constructivists** believe that they are constructed by the mind as a result of the engagement of pre-existing mental structures with experience.

Constructivism and innatism are the most influential forms of cognitivist thinking about learning to be found at present. However, a view influenced by empiricism, called connectionism, is also gaining in influence (Evers 1990, Searle 1992). Piaget and his followers are the best-known constructivist thinkers. Their view is that the mind's constructs go through a process of **development** from birth to adolescence so that they come to be more accurate representations of reality at each stage. Innatists like Chomsky (1988) and Fodor (1975) hold that some mental structures are present from birth, in particular the deep syntactic structure of language and the range of concepts that are available to all humans. The claim that the mind works through the construction and manipulation of mental representations is central to understanding this family of doctrines. The best way of understanding the idea is to think of a map and its relation to the ground depicted. The map consists of a scale, converting distances from the ground to the mapsheet, a key, specifying that certain symbols stand for certain kinds of object and a focus of interest so that some aspects of reality (e.g. transport networks) are represented rather than others (e.g. mineral resources). The symbolism of the map is governed by the scale and the key which are both sets of rules which allow the map reader to interpret reality according to the map's conventions.

Whether representationalism works depends on whether it is intelligible that a solitary mind can operate with rules before it engages with other minds. The answer given by Wittgenstein's private language argument is thought to be 'no' – it is impossible for the mind to operate a private system of symbols only accessible to itself since it would have no means of correctly identifying and re-identifying private symbols. However, this version of the argument only applies to those versions of cognitivism that claim that we form private symbols of reality which only we have access to. Empiricism and constructivism are vulnerable to this kind of argument, but it is doubtful whether modern innatism is. Innatists claim that the mind is nothing more than the central nervous system appropriately configured, and no individual mind is inherently private since neural contents are available for inspection (Fodor 1975). Innatists are, however, committed to the view that the representing mind is, in the early stages of life, solitary in its operation, manipulating the structures and concepts that it was born with and attaching the words of its natural language to them through a process of hypothesis formation and testing.

The innatist picture of the mind is that of a somewhat bare map into which fine detail is filled in and where names are attached to places as learning proceeds. The account depends on whether or not it is possible for a solitary being, from birth, to operate a rule system. This possibility has been hotly disputed. Some, like Rhees (1964) and Malcolm (1989), have claimed that a solitary could not, in principle, be able to distinguish between correct and incorrect applications of rules and so could not have a private rule system. Others, like Baker and Hacker (1990), have argued that there is nothing self-contradictory about such a supposition provided that such rules are shareable. If Baker and Hacker are right, cognitivism survives, since innate representations are clearly shareable. If they are wrong, then the cognitivist programme is in jeopardy. It cannot be saved by making the claim that the rule system should be interpreted naturalistically as a system of physical laws, since rules and physical laws have fundamentally different logical properties. It makes sense to say that one follows a rule correctly, not that one follows a law of nature correctly, for example. Sometimes it is claimed that the mind represents just as a computer does, however Searle (1992) has argued that computers do not represent to themselves, they are so constructed that they represent for humans, and cannot, therefore, be taken as model for the mind.

Connectionism is the doctrine that learning takes place through the impact of the world on distributed neural networks. In some versions such impacts lead the network to build up a representation of the world. This doctrine differs from innatism by denying the existence of pre-existing structures. It is, however, still a representationalist theory. Other, more radical, versions deny that neural networks learn through building up representations, but do so in an, as yet inscrutable, non-representational manner (Searle 1992). Such theories are not cognitivist on the definition offered above, but they lack the intuitive appeal of representationalism and as yet, lack convincing scientific support.

Cognitivism is attractive to many educators because it appears to marry the view of Rousseauian progressivism, that learning best takes place through the solitary exploration of the world through hypothesis testing, with the modern scientific outlook that suggests that the essence of a human is his brain. In one or other of its forms it is the outlook that lies behind most theories of learning apart from the largely moribund **behaviourism** which is only still influential in areas such as **training** and **special education**. Cognitivism now occupies pride of place as an account of mainstream learning.

common good   The idea of a common good is important in considering educational **aims**. Those who argue that there is a common good maintain that society is more than the sum of the individuals composing it and that it has interests of its own, including that of assisting the less fortunate (Reese 1988). Strong conceptions of the common good maintain that there are positive ends to which all members of a society should contribute. Such a conception will be found, for example, in a society bound together by a common religious faith. A weak conception of the common good maintains that there is a set of alternative goals which it is worthwhile for individuals to pursue, any of which is acceptable to society.

This is also sometimes known as the weak conception of **autonomy** (White 1990; Norman 1994).

Many liberals, following Mill (1974) reject any conception of the common good, maintaining instead that individuals should be free to pursue whatever goals they wish, subject only to the constraint that they should not harm other fully rational beings without their consent. This is known as the strong conception of autonomy. A severe problem arises when an education system tries to accommodate the aspirations of both strong and weak autonomists. For the two positions are incompatible. The strong autonomist maintains that some life-objectives may be pursued without society's approval. The weak autonomist maintains that only those life-objectives that meet with society's approval may be pursued. Those who espouse a common good must, therefore, at the very least be weak autonomists regarding educational aims, since they are committed to a minimal form of common good which is nothing more than a list of acceptable life-objectives, without any prioritising within that list.

common sense   This term, used by Gramsci (1971), encompasses the practical wisdom of 'common sense' employed in an everyday context together with the assumptions that underpin it. According to Gramsci, 'common sense' in the ordinary sense is always underpinned, even if implicitly, by a worldview. Since there are different worldviews, it is quite possible that there are different forms of common sense. In the political sphere (Gramsci's main area of interest), different social classes have different ways of conceptualising politics and economics which, in turn, lead to different versions of practical wisdom. Thus capitalists might see human motivation as underpinned by acquisitive individualism and develop a 'folk wisdom' accordingly. The proletariat might see human motivation in terms of the desire to maintain group solidarity and thus develop a different form of folk wisdom.

This account of common sense can be applied to education (W. Carr 1995). Different assumptions about **human nature** and the **aims** of education lead to different ways of organising educational practices. Thus a **progressive** might assume that a child's motivation is intrinsic, while a traditionalist might assume that rewards and sanctions are a necessary part of classroom life. Thus, research which suggests that high expectations, classroom discipline, strong leadership and clear curriculum differentiation lead to effective schooling is 'common sense' (J. P. White 1997a; see also Barrow 1976) only if one operates within a more-or-less traditional worldview. An alternative worldview might reject such findings as common sense and might find them extremely controversial. The question is not an empirical one, but concerns assumptions and values.

communitarianism   The political doctrine of liberalism, both in traditional and modern forms, has been much under attack recently. One of the major targets for this attack has been the notion of the free, autonomous and rational self which is supposedly the ideal liberal citizen. Writers such as Taylor (1979), Sandel (1982) and MacIntyre (1981, 1990) have argued that such a view of the self is (a) is empty of content; (b) violates the ways in which we actually understand ourselves; (c) ignores the way in which we are embedded in the cultural practices of our communities; (d) ignores our need to have our individual judgements confirmed by others; and (e) pretends to an impossible objectivity. Ourselves, argue such writers, can only properly be understood as rooted in the attitudes and practices of the actual communities that we, in fact, inhabit.

The communitarian attack on liberalism has been resisted (see Kymlicka 1989) but whether such resistance has been successful remains to be seen. The debate, however, has obvious implications for education. The communitarian challenge threatens any naive notion of educational **neutrality** and the aim of education as that of creating **autonomous** individuals. In contrast, it seems to support forms of **multiculturalism** which eschew liberal choice in favour of cultural reproduction. Although the debate is educationally important it has only very recently been taken up by philosophers of education (although aspects of the debate, such as, multiculturalism have been long on the agenda).

A recent attempt to synthesise the political and educational debate can be found in Jonathan (1997).

compensatory education   This is the idea, influential in the US and UK in the 1960s and 1970s, that children's education should compensate for the cognitive and affective shortcomings of their culture. Associated with such figures as Bereiter and Engelmann (1966) in the US and Bernstein (1973) in the UK, compensatory education became influential in educational policy as part of initiatives to raise standards and increase equality. Programmes like Headstart were inspired by compensation theorists.

The movement has had its critics. The first line of criticism, owing to Labov (1972), was that it addressed a non-existent deficit in lower-class children. Radicals maintained that the education system failed students rather than *vice versa*. More moderate critics maintained that the nature of the educational problems facing lower-class students had been hastily and carelessly diagnosed (C. Winch 1990). Empirical confirmation was patchy. Those programmes based on the premise that lower-class children suffered from verbal deficit have been largely discredited (Tizard and Hughes 1984). On the other hand, longitudinal studies of programmes like Headstart have indicated that they may have assisted students in avoiding practical problems in later life.

The insight of the compensatory education movement was that there may be a cultural mismatch between the expectations of school and home (Brice Heath 1983). The dangers of their approach are that they encourage a sense of fatalism and low expectations concerning lower-class students on the part of teachers. Extreme pessimists believe that the mismatch is not cultural but genetic and therefore that compensation is not possible (Murray and Herrnstein 1994).

competence Ordinarily, when one is able to do something in a way that satisfies certain minimum standards, one is said to be competent at that activity. Thus, I am a competent swimmer if I am able to swim beyond a certain minimum distance in normal circumstances. The criterion for the ascription of competence is my ability to perform. On this account, it would be meaningless to say that I am competent although I have never performed, or that there are no circumstances in which it is envisaged that I could perform. This account has been challenged by Chomsky (1965) and others, who maintain that competence is, at bottom, an innate neural representational system. It is the presence in my brain of such a system which determines whether or not I am competent.

On this account, the system may not be 'activated' for one reason or another and, consequently, I will not be able to perform the act the statement of competence specifies. Chomsky thinks that this account is essential in order to account for the creativity of human linguistic ability, which involves understanding and producing sentences never previously encountered. This account ignores the plasticity of human ability. Competence in the ordinary sense involves performance in circumstances that, although normal, are almost always novel. Our abilities to swim, drive automobiles etc. are constantly exercised in novel conditions without its ever being presupposed that we need an innate neural representational system for swimming or driving in order to carry them out.

This feature of flexibility in our competences is a problem for those who attempt to specify them so as to provide rigorous 'Competence-based Education and Training' (CBET), such as is to be found in the UK National Vocational Qualification (NVQ) system (Jessup 1991). If competence does not require neural representations, neither can it be taught simply by *conditioning* so as to produce routine responses to routine situations. Competences, like the ability to drive, are exercised in a wide variety of circumstances and require knowledge, judgement and skill in their exercise, all of which may be a result of **training**. CBET programmes aim to break competences down into a series of subskills which can then be inculcated through simple procedures. If, however, competences are greater than the sum of any set of subskills (Hyland 1993) then this approach will not work. Furthermore if they presuppose a range of knowledge in their successful exercise then any **assessment** of them that relies solely on a restricted set of performances is unlikely to be valid, unless it employs some other way of assessing that knowledge (Prais 1991).

competition and cooperation   In dealing with the discussion concerning competition and cooperation within **education** one needs not only a degree of philosophical acumen but also a large measure of robust common sense. It is claimed, for instance, that all competitive activity must be inherently wicked because it involves winners and losers and that any instruction in the rules of, say, games must be indoctrination and must stifle the creativity of children. The first claim demonises the members of chess clubs, football teams and bridge drives to an absurd extent. Whilst it is very difficult to see how such people are harming anyone it is fairly easy to see how such people would be harmed if some Puritan government banned such activities. The other claim simply misunderstands the nature of the key terms used (see **indoctrination**, **creativity**).

Such extravagance of claim and the virulence of some of the dispute (Fielding 1976) reveals this as a political as well as an educational argument where what is seen to be at stake is not simply the state of our schools but the future of society. But again, hyperbole makes bad argument. Whatever one's political persuasion it seems difficult to imagine a society in which there was no competition at all, e.g. for mates, for jobs; and it is equally difficult to see how making a fourth at bridge is collaborating in the suppression of the working class. The classic analysis of 'competition' is given by Dearden (1972). According to Dearden A and B are interacting competitively if and only if (a) there is some X they both want, (b) it is not the case that both A and B can gain possession of X, and

37

(c) the knowledge that by gaining possession of X one would deprive the other of it does not deter either A and B from seeking it. Dearden then goes on to point out that although some things concerned with education may be competed for, e.g. a school prize or a place at a favoured school, some important things such as knowledge cannot be competed for because if one person gains knowledge this does not prevent others from gaining the same knowledge.

Dearden's analysis has been criticised as to detail, for example, is it really the case, as Dearden claims, that it is illogical to talk of competing against oneself? (Kleinig 1982) But there have also been more substantive objections. First, Dearden's account overstates – at the very least – the compatability between competition and cooperation. This is because although, as Dearden points out, engaging in many forms of competitive endeavour involves the mutual acceptance by the participants of the rules of the game, such an acceptance, whilst presupposed by cooperation, is not enough to constitute it because cooperation involves a harmony of ends and this must be missing in competitive interactions. Second, Dearden fails to distinguish being in competition from acting competitively and the latter can come up for assessment as well as the former (Kleinig 1982).

Both charges can be answered in one of two ways. The first is simply to point out that in any team game cooperation within teams is necessary that is, they do have to have harmony with regards to ends, and that therefore acting competitively within your own team will be frowned upon. So cooperation in such games can coexist with competition and acting competitively can be both a good thing, if directed towards the other team; or a bad thing, if directed to members of your own team. The second, and rather more subtle defence, lies in unpacking the notion of the ends that are often – but not always – involved in competition. When I play bridge, I play to win. If I did not do so my playing would neither give pleasure to me nor to my opponents. But I do not play bridge in order to win, I play bridge in order to play bridge, for the joy of the game. Winning and playing competitively are not ends in themselves – all serious games players know the boredom that accompanies playing against incompetent or unserious opponents – they are concomitants of a desire to play the game, and that shared end is served, not impeded by acting competitively. Of course, some play only to win and sometimes do so at any cost, by cheating. But the existence of such people is no more a direct challenge to most competition than the existence of plagiarists is to most scholarship.

There is nothing inherently evil in competition and therefore there is nothing wrong in certain types of competition in schools. There often is something wrong with inappropriate or involuntary competition – there is hardly anything more pathetic than watching children forced to play games they will never be good at and have no interest in playing – but deciding when competition is appropriate or not is a question of judgement not of ideology.

Having said all this, it remains a scandal that in any developed country children are forced to compete for a decent, basic education because of the variability of schools.

compulsion It is a remarkable, but generally unremarked fact that, in Europe and America at least, children are compelled to go to school and when they get there they are compelled to do some things rather than other things. This compulsion to attend a particular institution and indulge in particular institutional activities was strongly criticised by the **deschoolers**. In reply to their arguments (see Barrow 1978) philosophers from the analytical school had little difficulty in showing that the arguments they produced over, say, **assessment** or **curriculum** choice, were faulty and that their general position was badly argued and poorly evidenced. However, very little attention was given to one of their explicit or implicit basic assumptions, namely that, if we compel someone to do something, then we need to provide good reason for that compulsion. The fact that in this case those compelled are children alters the matter somewhat – because we expect children to be the subject of *some* compulsion – but does not affect the basic thrust of the question that concerns compulsory **schooling**.

Little has been written on this outside the realms of the deschooling debate although sceptical positions concerning compulsory schooling have been put forward by Krimerman (1978) and Kleinig (1982). A sustained attempt to argue through these issues was produced by Chamberlin (1989) (and see K. Williams 1990) and hopefully this important issue will now generate continued philosophical interest.

concept formation   Our ability to order elements of the world into different kinds of things in order to further our practical projects and then to talk and make judgements about these orderings, is our ability to form and handle concepts. In making the **judgement** '*a* is *F*' the ability to distinguish between *F*s and non-*F*s is presupposed. Where does this ability come from? *Abstractionists* maintain that we acquire concepts through noticing the similarities between like objects and abstracting the likenesses to form concepts from them (Locke 1961a). Abstractionism is often attacked for presupposing the very ability it seeks to explain (see Carruthers 1992). In noticing that *a*, *b* and *c* are all *F* it is maintained, we must already possess the concept *F*. *Associationists* maintain that concepts are formed through the association of one mental idea with others in a cognate group. Thus, I may associate triangles with the image of an equilateral triangle, whose presence in my mind calls up the other varieties of triangle that I have experience of through the senses (Hume 1958). When I consider the false proposition that all triangles are equilateral, the equilateral image 'calls up' associated images of scalene and isosceles triangles that moves me to reject my original supposition. Associationism appears to depend heavily on mental imagery employed in acts of judgement and is, arguably, subject to the strictures of the private language argument of Wittgenstein (1953).

Some have maintained that all or many concepts are *innate* (Descartes 1966). Modern versions of this doctrine can be found in Chomsky (1988) and Fodor (1975). According to these writers, concepts are preformed at birth and we then learn to match the words of our mother-tongue onto these pre-existing concepts. The main argument for this appears to be that conceptual **learning** can only take place through hypothesis formation and testing, and that, in order to test hypotheses about the meanings of words, one needs pre-existing concepts in order to test. However, if learning can take place through practice, **training** and instruction then there is no reason to suppose that the innatist account is unavoidable. One can then take seriously the idea that concept formation occurs as part of learning one's mother-tongue, through the acquisition of rules for the use of words in social, practical situations which are then extended to uses in mental non-discursive acts (see **judgement**).

conservatism 'Conservatism', a term employed in politics, means different things on either side of the Atlantic. In the UK conservatives wish to halt or slow down change. In the US, conservatives have an agenda of religious or moral funda-mentalism in social policy and neo-liberalism in economics. Given that such political positions have educational implica-tions, what is an educational conservative? In the UK an educational conservative wishes to slow down, or resist, educational change. He will probably be a progressive, since **progressivism** is still the educational orthodoxy to a large extent. In the US, he will perhaps stand for the teaching of religiously based **common sense** in schools, such as creationism, Christian religious doctrine and certain practices such as daily worship. American educational conservatives will also most likely be concerned that citizenship education should clearly espouse the values of a common culture (e.g. Hirsch 1987) and the free market.

Conservatism in the first sense has an important role in edu-cation, which is prone to constant interference and innovation. Conservatives see it as their role to question new ideas and to ask whether they will really lead to an improvement. As well as doing this explicitly they may carry on a less articulated role as resisters of new innovation by, for example, implementing reforms half-heartedly or by redefining old practices in new terminology. There comes a point at which educational conservatism becomes obstruction and that point arguably occurs where a democratic decision is wilfully undermined.

constructivism Constructivism is a set of related doctrines about **learning**. Conceived of by Piaget (1953) as a way of incorporating the best insights of both empiricist and rationalist accounts of learning, it develops the Kantian claim that information from the world is arranged by our psychic constitutions into a form that is intelligible to us. In a sense then, we actively construct what we learn (Kant 1963). This view is combined with a **developmental** theory about the way in which the mind operates on raw data at different stages of human growth. However, the Piagetian version of constructivism has enjoyed a close relationship with **pragmatism** and, in particular, pragmatist doctrines deriving from James and Dewey, that maintain a scepticism about the possibility of achieving objective truth as the proper object of knowledge. The version that openly expresses scepticism about objective truth is known as 'radical constructivism' and is principally associated with the work of von Glasersfeld (1989). Modern constructivists have also been influenced by **cognitivist** theorising. Constructivism is, then, a theory about learning which incorporates different philosophical positions. From cognitivism is taken an account of learning in terms of hypothesis formation and testing – this has become the preferred account of how learning is always active, even if it doesn't involve overt physical activity. Unlike many cognitivists however, constructivism only admits of innate structures and capacities, not innate concepts.

It is easy to see how constructivist doctrines have fitted neatly with contemporary **progressive** and **postmodern** thinking. Progressivists stress the active nature of learning and the role of individual interest in directing it. Postmodernists are sympathetic with scepticism concerning objective truth. The idea that inquiry is directed towards objects of individual interest and that its goal is to overcome obstacles to individual interests is largely congenial to these educators.

However, constructivism has its critics. It is said that the claim that learning is active is less radical than it appears, since all learning (whether physically active or passive) is active in the constructivist's sense. Hence little of pedagogical interest can arise from constructivist claims. Second, critics have noted constructivist scepticism concerning objective **truth**. The idea that truth is nothing more than the viability of beliefs seems to be the result of posing a false dichotomy. Either one must choose between truth-as-viability or timeless, certain and objective truth. This seems to be the position developed by von Glasersfeld. But critics (e.g. Suchting 1992) have pointed out that this is a false dichotomy. One does not have to believe that all truths that have a basis in an objective order that exists independently of human perception must, thereby, be timeless and certain. The great majority of empirical knowledge is objective in the sense above and is also *justified* in the sense that there are objective discipline-specific means of validating knowledge-claims. The goal of timeless, certain, objective truth, perhaps modelled on propositions of mathematics or logic, is inappropriate for most forms of knowledge but this does not make them merely subjective or ready for redefinition in terms of truth as viability.

creativity The analysis of the concept of 'creativity' is one of the success stories of philosophy of education. But it is a success which also shows some of the limitations of the field.

How the teaching of 'creativity' came to prominence as an educational issue is a rather puzzling question. It is not clear whether the educational establishment was reacting to calls from outside education to widen the curriculum in certain ways (Elliot 1971) and that this led educational psychologists to begin investigating creative thinking; or whether it was the psychologists, unhappy with certain aspects of their psychometric tests, who set the whole thing in motion (Hudson 1966); or whether again, it was teachers, frustrated by certain received wisdom about teaching methods, who originally instituted the enquiry. What is clear is that by the late 1960s or early 1970s there was a wealth of material, often confused and confusing (with little attempt, for instance, to distinguish 'creativity' as normally understood from the technical use of the term by psychologists designing 'creativity tests'), which seemed to certain philosophers to demand a response which distinguished the different aspects of the debate and faced the central educational questions.

The main thrust of much of the non-philosophical work emphasised informal teaching methods, free expression and an unwillingness to provide answers for children in schools. Consequently there was a distrust engendered towards teaching children artistic techniques (for instance, how to play the piano), or artistic and aesthetic theory (for instance, discussing the relative merits of different painters, writers or composers). Some commentators went so far as to say (Lytton 1971) that, as schools were necessarily rule-bound institutions, there was little hope that they could foster the spirit of freedom and self-expression necessary for real creative work.

The philosophical reply to this, in some ways a model of its kind, was to insist upon the centrality of our normal notions of 'creativity' and to tease out the governing conditions of such notions. This was done initially by the implicit or explicit use of a **paradigm case argument** where a group of standard and minimally contentious examples of the concept are collected and then a set of necessary and sufficient conditions are derived for the reasonable use of the concept. In this case the examples were writers like Shakespeare and Dostoyevsky, scientists such as Einstein, composers such as Beethoven, painters like Rembrandt and Picasso, etc. The conditions for the use of the concept derived from the collection of such examples clustered around three main conditions. First, that the creative person must be identified by something in the public realm; it is the characteristics of the work that such people produced, which provided the key to creativity. This means that even if the search for the creative mental processes which lead to the production of such work makes sense – and to make it make sense you have to assume (a) that there is a determinate set of such mental processes, and (b) that they are knowable – it must be a secondary investigation which depends upon having first determined objective criteria for what counts as a creative product in the particular field in question. Second, that the work produced satisfied the technical and intellectual standards of its own particular field, i.e. that it is a good play, painting, concerto, or what have you. This assumes that there exist standards to measure such things and that, given we are concerned with the intentional production of such work, the producers of the work understood and were able to work within such standards. Third, that the work did not merely accommodate itself to the already existing standards but also extended such standards in a desirable way, that is, it displayed a measure – at least – of welcome originality (J. P. White 1968; Woods and Barrow 1975). It was also pointed out that, given the individuals whose work contributes to the paradigm, we should not expect that any individual will be creative in more than a very few spheres; if someone is a creative writer this is no evidence that she will be a creative painter. Thus creativity, as applied to persons, does not seem to be some general ability which may be exercised in any particular sphere that the person wills but rather a characteristic which is developed within a particular sphere and may not travel far from that sphere.

Given such conditions it was a fairly easy task for the writers who developed them to show that much of what went on in schools in the name of 'creativity' was either completely beside the point or was unlikely to do anything at all to teach or encourage pupils to produce work of the requisite type, or to even set them on the beginning of the road to such production. What was needed, it was claimed, if we realistically wished to promote creativity, was an emphasis on introducing pupils to, and getting them to understand and work within, the particular fields in which creativity is possible. So, for instance, if you wish to encourage pupils to be creative whilst playing the piano, you have to teach them how to play and teach them the standards appropriate to piano playing. And the latter involves getting them to understand the work of other piano players. A concern for technique and standards and an understanding of what has been done so far in the field are not inimical to the development of creativity, but rather, its very centre.

Thus far, thus good! In their own terms the philosophers who presented the above analyses of 'creativity' mounted a very convincing case. If they were a little too accommodating of notions such as self-expression (see **expression**) which seems to have little determinate meaning, this hardly disturbed their main points. However, some of the more recent literature seems to show that, whilst it may be the case that the excesses complained about in schools have to a large extent disappeared under the pressure of educational reform, the underlying attitudes which produced such excesses are alive and flourishing (Best 1992). The doctrines have slightly changed and their methods of justification have probably shifted from a basis in psychology to a basis in postmodernist theory, but the challenge they present to the type of education envisaged above remains much the same. And this, in part, we suspect represents a failure on the part of philosophers of education to actually get their messages across to other educationalists; a failure for which they may be blameless, but which may indicate an unwillingness to go beyond theorising to the task of popularising such theories.

It is also the case that an analysis based upon a **paradigm case argument** remains vulnerable to paradigm shift (Kuhn 1975). Thus, whilst the elements of the analysis presented above may fit very well the works of previous revolutionary artists such as Picasso or Braque, who were imbued with an understanding of, and reverence for, the artistic tradition they inhabited, it is not at all clear that it fits the work of some contemporary 'creative' artists such as Damien Hirst or Jeff Koons. This is largely because such work does not seem to necessitate the type of education in the arts that the paradigm case argument, as presented, seems to call for. And what this means is that the work mentioned above may only be the opening battles of what threatens to be a long war between different proponents of creativity.

critical thinking The idea of critical thinking has provided the impetus for one of the great growth areas in philosophy of education over the last thirty years, especially in America. From modest beginnings (see Ennis 1962) it has developed into a multimillion dollar industry producing materials (e.g. books, courses, pamphlets) which aim to teach people to think critically whatever the actual content of their thoughts, e.g. history, science, literature or simply the problems of practical life. Whole departments in universities are devoted to the investigation and dissemination of such critical thinking.

Although there are some disagreements among the main proponents of critical thinking about *exactly* how to characterise their field they seem to agree that there is a set of generic thinking skills which underpin all reasonable thought which can be isolated and inculcated through courses concerned with their development. So, for instance, Ennis holds that rational thinkers exhibit certain proficiencies, tendencies and good habits. Under proficiencies Ennis listed: observing, inferring, generalising, conceiving and stating assumptions and their alternatives. Such thinkers tend to offer well-organised or well-formulated lines of reasoning, they evaluate statements and chains of reasoning and are habitually on their guard to detect standard problems (Ennis 1974). If we can teach such skills to students then, Ennis believes, we can improve their general thinking skills and thus improve their performance in whatever domain of intellectual endeavour they are concerned with. Ennis draws an analogy with mathematics which may be learned in a maths class but may be essential, or at least useful, elsewhere, for example, in science. There are two problems here. First, even if one is totally familiar with mathematical procedures one cannot use them in science unless one knows enough science to understand *when* such procedures may be useful and when not. Second, even if one can transfer skills from one familiar domain to another this does not mean that one can transfer such skills to a totally unfamiliar domain. One may understand and be able to define the key terms in, say, a scientific argument but despite this understanding be completely at a loss when faced with, say, an argument in literary criticism because of an inability to identify the key terms and assumed background knowledge. Ennis acknowledges such problems and the questions of judgement they raise and requires that rational thinkers exercise their skills in familiar fields of experience. Ennis's proposals, despite this provision, are not problem-free. However, they are far more problem-free than some of the alternative and altogether more grandiose proposals. So, for instance, Paul (1990) divides critical thinking into 'weak' and 'strong' varieties; strong, which is the favoured version, is self-directed and applied to one's own assumptions and arguments. It develops a sensitivity to different world views, is able to avoid egocentric and sociocentric assumptions and is characterised by intellectual virtues such as honesty, courage and humility.

Apart from the fact, that this seems a version of Plato's unsustainable equation of knowledge and goodness (after all 'Is X a good person?' just does seem to be a different question answered in different ways to 'Is X a good thinker?'), we also have a view of critical thinking which, with its talk of 'world views' threatens to collapse into **cognitive relativism** and therefore to abandon the objectivity for assessing reasoning which the original programme seemed to promise. Or, if this does not happen, it seems to depend upon bringing into play notions such as 'egocentricity' and 'sociocentricity' which have no clear criteria for application in this area and making use of notions such as 'intellectual courage' which seem to have little to do with thinking skills (Siegel 1988).

The divorce between moral and cognitive considerations which we are implicitly endorsing above, has been noted by Martin (1992). Whilst Martin's observations about living in a world in which people often seem able to think even when they lack care and compassion for the human objects of their thought are sound, we do not think this separation is to be regretted in this particular context. First, because education- ists are terribly prone to aspire to unattainable ideas of general excellence at the expense of more modest but valuable and achievable goals, for example, to bring all educational goals under grand schemes for producing 'good people' or 'good citizens', and in so doing to overlook the fact that a large proportion of children have problems with basic literacy. The separation of the criteria for thought from the criteria for goodness is well established. Second, because the discrimi- nation which allows us to distinguish the ethical and the cognitive is, for all its complexities, a result of several hundred years of critical thinking within Philosophy and to deny it is to deny exactly that which critical thinking is supposed to promote.

The main critic of schemes for critical thinking is, without doubt, McPeck (1981, 1992), who has argued vigorously and at length that all thinking, except that on the most trivial level, is subject-specific and therefore relies on subject knowl- edge. Therefore, pupils should be taught by people who have the requisite subject expertise. The alleged transferability of critical thinking skills is largely bogus and, if pupils need a training in thinking for their everyday lives, this is best approached by a training in the separate academic disciplines.

A full analysis of the thrusts and counter-thrusts of this still continuing argument is beyond our remit. In the end, the success or otherwise, of schemes for critical thinking may be a matter to be investigated empirically rather than philosoph- ically. However, if this is so, such an empirical investigation will be exceedingly complex. It would have to investigate the success and failure of pupils given a separate critical thinking course when they approach a new area of knowledge as well as those pupils introduced to critical thinking as part of their training in particular disciplines, i.e. critical thinking *per se* and critical thinking in, say, science. It would have to pay proper attention to what are likely to be marginal improvements. And it will have to find some way of dealing with the likely Hawthorne effect (in a series of studies at the Hawthorne plant in America from 1927 to 1932 it was discovered that people react favourably given attention, despite any changes in their material circumstances) of any scheme designed to improve general thinking skills.

culture   Given that it is clearly the case, as Durkheim claimed, that education is a process of cultural transmission, there is surprisingly little in the literature concerning the precise role of culture in any particular educational package. Questions concerning this role have recently surfaced in discussions about **multiculturalism**. However, given that the general questions relating any culture to any education system have not, as yet, been fully addressed, the inconclusive nature of these discussions is to be expected.

The concept of 'culture' has at least three separate meanings:

1 All the beliefs and practices of a given society.
2 The intellectual and artistic beliefs and practices of a given society.
3 The best intellectual and artistic beliefs of a given society.

What discussion there has been in the philosophical literature has focused on the relationship between (2) and (3) and their respective roles in education (if any), rather than encompassing a discussion of all three meanings. In both Britain and the United States of America there have been spirited, if rather lonely, defences of 'high' culture, as the basis of education. In Britain such a defence was carried out over a period of more than twenty years by G. H. Bantock (1971). Horrified by modern popular culture – as opposed to the 'folk' culture he discerned existing in previous ages – and drawing upon a tradition of argument associated with Matthew Arnold, T. S. Eliot, D. H. Lawrence and F. R. Leavis, Bantock, in a series of books and articles, presents a case for an education based around the development of an artistic – and especially literary – sensibility which unites facts, values and emotions in a concern for understanding 'felt life'. Bantock's analysis and the educational prescriptions which flow from that analysis, whatever their positive virtues, are rather spoiled by certain inadequately supported assumptions, so, for instance, his dislike of modern, popular culture – especially in its commercial aspects – seems visceral rather than intellectual, as if the taint of commerce and popularity never touched artists such as Rembrandt or Dickens. And, because of this he ignores the type of discrimination which might be applied in this field, say, between Raymond Chandler and Mickey Spillane, Louis Armstrong and Acker Bilk, and Cole Porter and the Spice Girls. Second, his conception of 'high' culture – in Arnold's words 'the best that has been thought and known' – with its focus upon literature, completely ignores the vast domain of craft traditions, much of which (for example, the work of designers and makers such as Chippendale, Adam, Wedgwood, Wren, Morris, Mackintosh, Mies van de Rohe) has as much right to be included in the ambit of Arnold's definition as the literary figures that he espouses. Lastly, and connected to the previous point, Bantock's prescriptions for education are frankly **elitist** with only the relatively few able to benefit from the type of education recommended and the majority condemned to a second-rate education (and this, despite the fact that there are cultures, for instance, Russia and Italy, where what is regarded as 'high' culture in Britain and America, for example, classical music and opera, are widely popular).

The situation in the United States is rather different. There have been suggestions, at tertiary level, that students concentrate upon certain key texts (the Fifty Great Books approach), but much of the recent discussion has concentrated on rather different problems. E. D. Hirsch (1987) has argued forcibly that American education is in crisis, that the crisis is associated with an approach to education which emphasises pedagogic processes and the acquisition of skills at the expense of content, and that such a situation will only be overcome when students in elementary schools are presented with a common fund of knowledge. It might be wondered whether such an approach is committed to 'high' culture or simply a common culture for schools. Hirsch's examples for items on a common **curriculum** do not really answer this question.

He surmises that 50 per cent of the curriculum in any developed country will focus on the same material, e.g. all 'educated' people should know about Darwin, the basic facts of maths and geography and texts such as Don Quixote. Such an emphasis must be different from the particularism that seems to typify popular culture. For the rest of the curriculum, Hirsch thinks, it should be possible to secure agreement on 80–90 per cent of the culturally specific items – for instance, that all children in schools in the United States should be familiar with the Declaration of Independence and the American Constitution.

Whilst it is certainly true, as Hirsch argues, that no education at all can go on without some common understanding shared between teacher and learner, it might be wondered whether the type of prescription that he favours will really provide a high quality of education for all, or whether it is likely to encourage a cultural tour approach which is notable for its superficiality.

curriculum What sorts of thing we ought to teach in our educational institutions, that is, not just schools, is a central question for educationalists and consequently one of the main battlegrounds in philosophy of education. It is important to note that the question is one concerning prescription (what ought to be the case), and not merely of description (what actually is the case). And this question is *the* question of curriculum choice.

Unfortunately, discussion of it is sometimes made opaque by an either too wide or too narrow definition of what constitutes the curriculum. So, for instance, we have heard it said – by a Government appointed Inspector of Education – that the curriculum is 'everything that goes on in school' which would make the colour the school walls are painted a question of curriculum choice and bullying a part of curriculum content (see also Whitfield 1971). Conversely a definition such as 'planned, sustained and regular learning, which is taken seriously, which has a distinct and structured content and which proceeds via some kind of stages of learning' (Wilson 1977) would make some activities which children engage in at school but which, arguably, are not taken seriously, e.g. woodwork, not part of the curriculum. The key to understand the question of curriculum choice is to understand the relationship between the curriculum and the **aims** of education. The curriculum is the plan for the implementation of educational aims. As such aims can vary widely and be couched in different terms − e.g. the articulation of **knowledge** (Hirst 1965a), the development of **autonomy** (J. P. White 1973), a preparation for adult life (C. Winch 1996) − and as each term may sustain different interpretations (Kleinig 1982), it is hardly surprising that this is an area of intense controversy. Which is not to say, however, that the same type of item may not appear on different curricula with different justifications, for example, the teaching of science may be justified by reference to its status as knowledge or it may be justified by the fact that people cannot function effectively in large parts of the modern world without an understanding of science.

Given this necessary connection with the aims of education the curriculum is, perhaps, best thought of as that set of planned activities which are designed to implement a particular educational aim − or set of such aims − in terms of the content of what is to be taught and the knowledge, skills and attitudes which are to be deliberately fostered. The curriculum, as a whole, is to be distinguished from the syllabus and the lesson. The first of these concerns the content and structure of some 'subject' within the curriculum, for instance, science. The second refers to the portion of time wherein such syllabus content is implemented.

Despite what we say at the beginning of this section concerning the ideal, prescriptive nature of the question of curriculum choice, it is worth remarking that in practice, the content of the curriculum and the items that thus appear on the syllabus of a particular subject, may not directly flow from an overarching set of educational aims but may, instead, reflect the power of some interest group within society to determine the content of education. Thus, from 1944 until 1988 in England the only legally prescribed subject in English schools was **Religious Education**. Not because this was part of some coherent picture of what education should be, but because of the power of the churches at the time of the 1944 Education Act. Similarly, the fact that a study of Satanism is unlikely to occur on a Religious Education syllabus anywhere in the world or that a text such as Mark Twain's *Huckleberry Finn* is unlikely to be taught in American schools, derives from the power of veto that interest groups in the particular societies have managed to garner unto themselves.

As well as the questions of the curriculum mentioned above there has also been debate over the last twenty odd years concerning the 'hidden' curriculum (Illich 1971). This refers not to those activities which are deliberately planned for pupils and students to engage in, but rather, those unplanned – and perhaps unintended – messages which are transmitted to pupils via the institutional structures of our educational establishments and the – often unacknowledged – attitudes of those, teachers and others, who serve such establishments (see **deschooling**). Such messages have been thought important in the field of **moral education** but they have also been the focus for many critics of the educational establishment (Bowles and Gintis 1976; Kleinig 1982) who see such messages as, by and large, detrimental to the interests of pupils and students and society generally. There are important matters for discussion here which impinge upon many of the other topics covered in this book (see **authority**) but which, perhaps because of the intemperate language and lack of logical rigour of many of the critics (see deschooling) have not been fully addressed by philosophers of education within the analytic tradition.

Since the 1988 Education Act there has been in place in England and Wales a National Curriculum which consists of three core subjects (English, Maths and Science) and six foundation subjects. Such a curriculum, according to its own documents, is 'broad, balanced and relevant' and will provide a proper basis for the education of all children. Unfortunately, there seems no recognition within the documents that such terms are all relative, i.e. 'broad and balanced' as compared to what and 'relevant' to what purposes? Further, given that the curriculum has been subject to continual change since its inception, this initial claim – even if it was once true – seems likely to fall prey to such changes.

Although there has been some reaction to this curriculum within philosophy of education (J. P. White 1990) there has been far less than might have been expected in a country that counts among its philosophical heritage, Mill (1974), with its argument that to deliver up the curriculum to the government is to be in danger of tyranny.

definition   Philosophy of education – like philosophy itself – is largely a question of conceptual investigation. Because this is so there is a proper emphasis on conceptual clarity and thus an emphasis on the definitions of the concepts used in educational discourse. After all, we cannot be concerned to promote, say, creativity or intelligence, unless we first enquire what the concepts of 'creativity' and 'intelligence' mean. Such a search for definition is not merely a search for verbal equivalents – as in a dictionary – but rather a search for the conditions which must be satisfied before we are prepared to call anything creative or intelligent.

Traditionally, this has been thought to be a search for the necessary and sufficient conditions for the application of a concept. A condition is necessary for the application of a concept if it *must* be present before the concept is applied, for example, nothing can be called a square which doesn't exemplify the condition of having four sides; foursideness is necessary – but note, not sufficient – for squares. A condition is sufficient if its presence alone guarantees the application of the concept, for example, if something is a horse then it *must* be an animal: horsiness guarantees animal status. In the sort of complicated areas that philosophy deals with, the usual search was for a set of conditions which were all necessary and jointly sufficient for the application of concepts. So, for instance, a 'square' can be defined as a figure on a plain surface with four equal sides and four equal angles. More interestingly, something like 'punishment' can be defined as

Condition One: The deliberate infliction
Condition Two: Of pain or unpleasantness
Condition Three: Upon an offender
Condition Four: For an offence
Condition Five: By someone in authority

Individually each of these conditions has to be present before we call something 'punishment' – they are individually necessary – and if taken together they are sufficient to ensure that what we have is a case of 'punishment' and not something else, for example, 'revenge'. (Of course, we need to define other terms such as 'offence' and 'offender' before the whole is clear.)

One alternative form of definition is the *operational definition*, in which an abstract concept is defined in terms of key observable features, so that, for example, temperature is defined in terms of thermometer readings. Unlike the approach described above, there is a greater emphasis on various sufficient conditions for fulfilment and less emphasis on necessary conditions. This approach has been taken up by **behaviourists**, who have attempted to define complex action in terms of specific behaviours, so that, for example, hunger in a rat can be defined operationally in terms of various highly specific forms of food-related behaviour, various combinations of which are sufficient conditions for the presence of hunger (for example, agitation and searching, searching and eating, fighting and eating). Following the work of Wittgenstein (see below), the use of rigid operational definitions in mainstream science has become largely redundant. Scientists now prefer to take into account particular aims and contexts when framing operational definitions.

Some modern philosophers – following the work of Wittgenstein – have wondered whether all concepts may be defined in either of these neat and tidy ways. Wittgenstein (1953) noted that if we taken a word like 'game' there seem to be no nice neat sets of conditions which all games satisfy.

Rather we have a complex set of interrelationships which link some games to others but which also serve to distinguish these from others again; for example, some games are competitive, some are not, some require equipment, some do not, some require teams, some do not. Such relationships, Wittgenstein called 'family resemblances' and he seemed to think that the line between what we are and are not prepared to call a game is likely (a) to be fuzzy and (b) to depend on our purposes in seeking such a definition. The problem is, of course, to discern whether a particular concept, say **play** or **creativity**, is to be defined in terms of family resemblance, in terms of necessary and sufficient conditions or operationally.

democracy Democracy literally means 'rule by the people' but the form that it takes varies widely. It is the system of government of choice in many of the wealthiest and most influential countries. Their education systems prepare young people to take part in their system of government. Many, however, are critical of the way in which democracy operates in their own countries. Typical complaints relate to the low degree of knowledge of and participation in the political process; the unrepresentativeness of institutions and the inadequacies of education as a preparation for life in a democracy. One of the strongest currents of thought on this last criticism is due in large part to Dewey, who argued that education for democracy had to begin at school in a practical way. Dewey's own conception of democracy stressed the importance of multiple and freely initiated social interaction rather than the functioning of representative institutions (e.g. Dewey 1916). Nevertheless, even if his conception of democracy is rejected it is still possible to claim that it constitutes a *precondition* of any effective democracy. Others, however, who worry about the consequences of an ignorant citizenry stress the importance of more traditional forms of education (Lasch 1995).

The question then arises as to what extent education should embody these non-authoritarian forms of communication so as to prepare children for adult life in a democracy. Dewey at one time took the view that communication and hence social life was only possible when there were no relationships of authority between communicants (1916: 6). Insofar as schools exist to promote democratic values it would seem that they would have to remove authoritarian relationships from education as far as possible. Education for democracy thus becomes education freed from authoritarian relationships. A similar line of argument can be found in the work of Rousseau who argued that democracy could only exist in a situation where free and equal human beings made decisions on their own behalf. Rousseau, unlike Dewey thought that only direct democracy was desirable, where citizens made direct decisions rather than through the medium of elected representatives. He further argued that authoritarian forms of education would destroy that possibility (Rousseau 1911a). Rousseau's ideas were taken up most notably by the visionary educator A. S. Neill (1965) in the UK.

Much depends here on whether or not **prefigurative education** is necessary to develop democratic attitudes and habits. Although it is true that, in order to take part in a democracy, one must develop dispositions and competences like tolerance, the ability to negotiate and to make informed decisions, it is not clear that the only way in which these can be developed is by practising them in prefigurative form from the outset of education. An alternative model of democratic education might stress the importance of an understanding of the history and culture of the society, gained through instruction, together with a training in the importance of orderly and civilised behaviour when dealing with disagreements. In such an education the role of **authority**, at least in the early stages, might be quite significant. Democrats will agree on the need for democracy, they may disagree about the nature of democracy and will almost certainly do so about the nature of an education for democracy.

deschooling The deschooling 'movement' clustered around the works of Goodman (1960, 1964), Illich (1970, 1971) and

Reimer (1971) and flourished in the late 1960s and early 1970s. Although the members of the 'movement' diverged in their attitudes to contemporary schooling they were united in the belief that the present schooling system has to be removed and replaced by something else, in their dislike of our present-day society with its class-riven nature and reliance upon industrialisation, and in a Romantic optimism concerning human nature and the possibility of societal progress. They were also equally in debt to the educational ideals of Rousseau (see Rousseau 1911a and entry on **progressivism**).

Goodman believed that our schooling was failing both in its own terms and in terms of proper education, which should be concerned with **truth**, beauty, **learning** and **culture**. He also believed that schools both because of their institutional nature and the teaching processes they adopted, for example, instruction rather than **discovery learning**, suppressed **individuality** in their successful attempt to socialise to national norms and regiment to national needs. We should replace contemporary schooling with mini schools for children up to the age of 12, where about twenty-eight children are taught – if this is the right word – by four adults and the curriculum is derived from the childrens' actual interests. Thereafter, formal schooling should be replaced by an apprenticeship system which would cover everything from car mechanics to philosophy.

Illich and Reimer's objections to schooling are rather more focused than Goodman's. Schools fail, according to their view, first, because they try to do too much by serving four distinct social functions: custodial care, social role selection, indoctrination and education, and these things interact in ways that subvert some of the ends such as education, because of the success of others, such as ends to do with social control. Second, schools present a false picture of knowledge and learning, for example, that learning relies upon teaching, and that, at the behest of the education system as a whole, they grade this knowledge in inappropriate ways. Third, the hidden curriculum in schools teaches children to value certain things (such as childhood, the virtue of being taught) which impede their individuality and result in our present, and awful, society (as well as the horrors of Auschwitz). Schools should be replaced by 'networks' and 'learning webs', for instance, record and information systems, and skill exchanges which are centres that provide access to skill models.

A devastating critique of the deschooling movement is provided by Barrow (1978). He shows the wealth of dubious assumptions that the members of the movement share, their arbitrary selection and distortion of empirical evidence, their reliance on anecdote, and the mass of bogus reasoning employed; for example, just because some people become literate outside schools and others fail to become literate in schools this *does not mean* that schooling is not the best way to promote mass literacy. Barrow is fully aware of the social and educational dangers of the prescriptions of the deschoolers. However, he perhaps does not emphasise one aspect of these dangers enough. Our schooling systems, both in Europe and America, do fail a large percentage of the children going through them both in terms of what is on offer in the school and in terms of the potential for curriculum choice. They are also guilty of presenting children with inappropriate messages as far as the hidden curriculum is concerned. In concentrating upon the extreme claims of the deschoolers we may forget these modest but more important claims, or, in seeing the rout of their ideas we may become complacent concerning the success of our school system.

development Development is closely linked with **learning**, and, although the relationship between the two is far from clear, it is connected with the fact that humans grow from babies into adults. There are two kinds of educational development theory. The first is a normative account of how education should proceed through consecutive stages (cf. Egan 1986; Whitehead 1967). The second postulates that the human mind grows through distinct stages at which different *kinds* of learning take place. Authors associated with this type of theory include Piaget (1953) and Vygotsky (1978). Some of these authors see these stages as real structures in the human mind. Other developmentalists see the stages as convenient labels for describing the process of mental growth (Donaldson 1992).The idea of development has received much theoretical elaboration and some empirical support but at the same time it has attracted trenchant criticism.

The first kind of theory prescribes a course of **education**. As such it is neither true nor false but persuasive or unpersuasive. To be persuasive a normative theory needs justification and this is what a psychological theory of development is thought to provide. For example, Rousseau (1911a) develops a normative theory of stages of education based on an empirical account of how the human mind develops. Much therefore, depends on the truth of the psychological development theory. However, these theories have a number of problems. The first is the running together of different claims. Some kinds of learning are logically impossible without prior learning. For example, one cannot learn that all whales are mammals if one has not first learned what mammals are (Hamlyn 1978). But this tells us nothing about what is or is not psychologically possible, it only gives us constraints on learning in general. The second problem is also a logical one, but of a different nature. Developmental theories generally claim that stages follow in an invariant sequence and that one stage cannot occur without its predecessor having first occurred. If item A can only be learned at stage 4 then it cannot be learned at stages 1–3. But it is very difficult to prove this. The fact that no individual has been observed learning A at stages 1–3 does not show that it cannot happen. One instance of its happening is an effective refutation of this part of the theory. One cannot rely on induction to provide support for continued non-observation of the non-validating event in interesting cases. This would be as reliable as someone leaping from the hundredth storey concluding, by the time that he had reached the second that everything was going to be all right, since it had been up to then. Of course there are some growth-related facts whose truth we can rely on through evidence, for example that 6-month-old babies can't run a three-minute mile. But we didn't need a developmental theory to tell us that.

On the other hand, if stage 4 is defined as the stage where items like *A* cannot be learned then that is not going to be refuted, but neither is it very interesting since we are interested in finding out *at what age A* can be learned, and unless ages are related to stages in some way that is not going to be possible. Those who believe in the real development of mental structures as conditions of learning need to consider very carefully whether there can ever be a fully developed and reliable theory of such stages.

There is a further problem with developmental theories in that in either their presentation or reception there is the risk of confusing the normative with the empirical. For instance, if stage 4 is the final stage of a developmental process we might think that this is the stage that we should be aiming for and that anyone who does not or cannot reach this stage is psychologically and educationally underdeveloped. Such a view can have unfortunate effects on whole subject areas (D. Locke 1979, 1980). A subject like Fine Arts, which may be associated with a particular stage of development like Piaget's concrete operational stage, may be thought to be intellectually and educationally inferior to a subject like Mathematics, which is largely associated with a later stage (formal operations).

discipline 'Discipline' at its most basic level, simply means the submission to rules or some kind of order. Given that the aims of schooling – at least in the developed world – are usually thought to include the introduction of children to some of the academic disciplines, e.g. Mathematics, History, Physics, Literary Criticism, and that such things are called 'disciplines' just because they consist, or are thought to consist, of sets of rules, obedience to which determines success or failure within any particular one of these, then the centrality of discipline to **schooling** and **education** is easy to see. (The hesitation about whether this really is so is caused by the fact that whereas in, say, Mathematics it seems a relatively easy task to specify such rules; in something like Literary Criticism – especially in its **postmodernist** phase the rules are hotly disputed.)

However, the task of examining the role of discipline in **schooling** is a far wider one than that of a simple enumeration of the rules to be obeyed if you wish to master academic subjects. And it is a task that touches upon very significant notions for education such as, **authority**, **learning, socialisation**, and **punishment**. There is a vast literature on discipline in schools, much of which either ignores the complexity of the concept and its connections, or which simply begs questions with regard to those connections, for example, it is simply assumed that certain methods of ensuring the submission of children to school rules are justifiable without any discussion of the legitimate limits of school and teacher authority or the **aims** of **education** as such. The complexity of the concept is well brought out in Kleinig (1982) and the practical problems surrounding it by R. Smith (1985: esp. chs 1–6).

The problems come when we move from submission to the rules necessary to engage in academic disciplines to the type of submission to rules that is often supposed to be necessary for learning as such to take place, for example, rules relating to a quiet, well-ordered classroom; those supposed to be necessary in any well-ordered institution such as rules relating to lunchtime behaviour; and the general social rules that many see as part of the school's remit to reinforce.

So, for instance, whilst there seems little problem in relating some senses of authority (for example, being *an* authority on something) to the discipline needed for the study of academic subjects, there are many problems when we consider teachers being *in* authority in those other areas. Partly, these have to do with the widely differing types of rule on offer, for example, do there have to be rules prescribing total silence in the classroom or, if not, what levels of noise are acceptable? and partly with the type of advice offered to teachers by works on school discipline, such as manuals which consists of lists of tricks for keeping a class in order.

With the first of these, there is often a reluctance, on the part of teachers, to confess that the actual rules in place are as much a matter of their own personal preferences rather than something that can be shown to be conducive to learning. With the second, it often seems to be the case that the aim of having, say, a quiet, well-ordered classroom, has supplanted any aims to do with the children's actual learning. With both there is the quite legitimate worry that the processes of social-isation involved are aimed at producing neat, obedient and non-questioning children rather than **autonomous** learners.

With regard to institutional rules and the enforcement of societal rules, the questions are equally complex. Whilst there may be few problems in accepting that all institutions need some rules to function, it is not at all clear that such func-tioning in schools is couched in terms of educational aims and not other, and quite extraneous things. So for instance, rules to do with attendance and class times seem unprob-lematic; rules to do with the compulsory wearing of uniform seem very problematic, because there are plenty of successful schools that do not have uniform rules. The same type of problem occurs with the enforcement of societal rules. Most of us would have little trouble in schools having and enforcing rules concerning stealing but we might disagree when it comes to deciding upon the seriousness of a child swearing in the playground. One of the basic questions here is to do with how far we expect teachers to be experts not only in the subjects but with regard to the mores of society and with regard to morality (D. Carr 1991).

All the above problems are exacerbated by the fact that any breakdown in discipline in schools is often visited by punish-ment and so we have the possibility of schools punishing children for the infringement of system-generated rules which have, arguably, little, or nothing, to do with the children's learning.

The Elton Committee Report on discipline in English schools (1989) made it clear that teachers did perceive disci-pline to be a problem. It also made it clear – especially with regard to primary schools (see appendix to the report) – that the types of indiscipline which caused concern were often of a trivial nature. Teachers, overwhelmingly, saw smaller class sizes as a cure for the problem. However, if such a reduction is justified it may be for other reasons than those given. There is no research that shows that a reduction in the number of pupils in a class necessarily leads to well-behaved classes or better academic outcomes. But it seems obvious that organising a class of twenty children is a less stressful occupation than doing the same with thirty-plus children, and teachers, as well as other professionals, deserve attention to be given to the removable stress of their jobs as well as to its outcomes.

discourse   Discourse theory is associated with the work of Foucault. In a series of books (1970, 1977, 1978) he has attempted to trace the growth of modern bureaucratic society. According to Foucault, such growth is characterised by the growth of discourses which provide conceptual frameworks for practices within the society. Such discourses are prescriptive as well as descriptive and contain not only norms for action but norms for such things as truth and rationality. As such, Foucault sees them as **relativistic**, that is, each discourse will have its own particular norms and there are no norms independent of discourses whereby such norms can be evaluated. Discourses are articulations of power and domination (for example, in one famous comment 'You don't speak the discourse, the discourse speaks you!'), but are not to be thought of as the deliberate attempt by a group to impose its will on another. They grow in historically particular circumstances and the power relations they legitimise may be part of the unintended consequences of the intentions of those engaged in the practice. Thus 'Take the example of philanthropy in the early nineteenth century: people appear who make it their business to involve themselves in other peoples' lives, health, nutrition, housing: then, out of this confused set of functions there emerge certain personages, institutions, forms of knowledge, public hygiene, inspectors, social workers, psychologists' (1978: 62). And , although such practices may give great power to professionals engaged in the practice, for example, doctors and social workers, they may also empower a previously unempowered group, for example, mothers.

Discourses bear relationship at the micro level to **ideologies**; however, Foucault wants to disclaim any attempt to relate the power relations entwined in particular discourses to any general power relationship that exists at the macro level of society, for example between bourgeois and working class. In this he posits a Weberian, rather than Marxist, view of society, where power is not the function of one relationship, the economic, but may flow from other sources such as status or charisma.

One of the major problems for Foucault's analysis is where it leaves the individual in society. In his earlier work he seemed to see the discourses as entirely deterministic but in his later work he seemed to think there was a possibility of the individual 'authentically' resisting the domination of the discourses. However, he died before articulating whether such resistance simply involves manipulating the discourses themselves and the alternative possibilities that different discourses offer (for instance, the medical picture of childbirth as disease gives a very different role to the mother than the picture, supported by many midwives, of childbirth as natural), or whether he thought that there was somehow intellectual space outside the discourses from where to mount resistance.

Given the influence of Foucault's thought elsewhere, for example, in sociology and philosophy, and given that the growth of the educational institutional establishment is part of his picture of the growth of the modern state, it is rather surprising to find so little on his work within philosophy of education. There is one book of collected essays (Ball 1990) and a few articles (Marshall 1990; Wain 1996). However, the continued interest by mainstream philosophers in his thought (see Hacking 1986; Taylor 1985), the increasing importance of European thought in Anglo Saxon philosophy and the fact that **schooling** should prove a fertile ground for Foucault-type analyses should all ensure that this lack of attention is soon remedied.

discovery learning   'Discovery learning' was, and is, part of the favoured methodology of **progressivism**. Letting children discover things for themselves was thought to cater to children's own interests and curiosity, to ensure that the lessons learned were well absorbed, and to free the children from the possibility of **indoctrination** – at the worst – and the offensive hectoring – at the best – that teacher instruction was supposed to bring in its wake.

As Dearden (1965) points out, such accounts of discovery and instruction often misunderstand and misdescribe the logic of these concepts. It is hardly possible to conceive of an education going on with no instruction at all and children just left to discover things. Even with what we deem is the appropriate equipment, they are hardly likely to do so if they lack the conceptual understanding which is necessary in order to make discoveries. Whilst discovery – in the proper sense which includes preparation in the matter in hand – may be a useful adjunct to some teaching, it is impossible for it to be the whole and its usefulness is likely to be compromised by the amount of time it consumes.

diversity   It is generally recognised that people differ in their abilities. There is less of a consensus on how these differences should be (a) conceptualised and (b) catered for. There are two answers to (a); the first is that people differ in the degree of **intelligence** that they possess; the second is that ability is diverse and not to be encapsulated in a unitary concept of intelligence. As regards (b), most proponents of the first view believe that education should be selective and that assessment of intelligence should determine the kind of education an individual should receive (e.g. Bantock 1971). For those who believe that ability is diverse, the position is not so clear.

Some maintain that the diverse range of abilities can all be catered for in the common school, with the provision of a sufficiently wide-ranging curriculum. They usually maintain that diversity and **equality** of treatment can be reconciled. Others maintain that the best way to fulfil potential is to develop it to its fullest extent in schools dedicated to the formation of particular abilities (e.g. Entwistle 1970). They argue for their position by maintaining that equal citizenship is constituted by recognition of equal worth rather than sameness, and recognition of equal worth can only be secured if everyone is able to fulfil their potential. Those in favour of the common school argue that differentiation inevitably leads to some kinds of schools having a lower status than others because some kinds of abilities are less valued than others.

E

education   The word 'education' may be derived from one of two Latin words or perhaps, from both. These are *educere*, which means 'to lead out' or 'to train' and *educare* which means 'to train' or 'to nourish'. Whilst the derivation of the word matters not at all for any modern substantive debate concerning education, it seems fitting that a concept that seems to lend itself to persuasive definitions, that is, definitions that smuggle in preferred meanings under the guise of objective analysis, should have an ambiguous and uncertain derivation.

In American philosophy of education there has actually been little work done on the meaning of this concept as compared to, say, **teaching**. However, in Britain educational discussion both within and without philosophy of education, was focused upon teasing out *the* meaning of education. This was because philosophy of education in Britain was dominated for twenty years – one is tempted to say created – by the work of one man, Richard Peters, and Peters's work was largely driven by his analysis of the concept of education. His first – and enormously influential – book on the subject, *Ethics and Education* (1966), spends its first third on this issue. Central to his analysis here were three complex criteria which he sees as enabling us to map the distinction between 'education' and other human pursuits.

The first criterion is that 'education' in its full sense, has a necessary implication that something valuable or worthwhile is going on. There may be secondary senses, for example, an anthropological sense where we refer to, say, 'Spartan education' or a sense where we wish to repudiate a certain set of practices, for example, 'she had a rotten education', where use of the term does not imply commendation, but in its primary sense it must; it would involve a contradiction to say that someone had been educated but that they had not changed for the better. But this value that Peters sees as necessarily involved in education must not be thought of as instrumentally connected to the practices of education. Education is not valuable as a means to a valuable end such as a good job, but rather because it involves those being educated being initiated into activities which are worthwhile in themselves, that is, are intrinsically valuable. In a momentous – but much misunderstood – distinction, Peters contrasts **training**, which carries with it the ideas of limited application and an external goal, that is, one is trained in something for some external purpose, with 'education' which implies neither of these things.

Second, 'education' involves the acquisition of a body of knowledge and understanding which surpasses mere skill, know-how or the collection of information. Such knowledge and understanding must involve the principles which underlie skills, procedural knowledge and information, and must transform the life of the person being educated both in terms of his general outlook and in terms of his becoming committed to the standards inherent in the areas of his education. To this body of knowledge and understanding must be added a 'cognitive perspective' whereby the development of any specialism, for example in science, is seen in the context of the place of this specialism in a coherent pattern of life.

Third, the processes of education involve at least some understanding of what is being learnt and what is required in the learning, for example, so we could not be 'brainwashed' or 'conditioned' into education, and some minimal voluntary participation in such processes.

The world into which those being educated are being initiated into is one with cognition at its heart – although Peters makes it clear here (pp. 48–9) and elsewhere (1973) that he sees cognition as having necessary links to other capacities of mind, for example, concerned with character development and emotions – but it is also a public world, for the structures of cognition are, by and large, those structures of thought and awareness which are contained within modes of thought such as science, history, mathematics, aesthetic awareness, which the initiate inherits from past ages.

And it is within this world that the question of worth-whileness which is raised by Peters's first criterion gets answered. There, Peters drew a distinction between activities that are extrinsically worthwhile, that is, valuable because they lead on to some other valuable end, and those that are intrin-sically worthwhile, that is, valuable in and for themselves, with education securely tied to the latter. But it also turns out, according to Peters, that such activities can be justified as 'educational' activities because it is only in the context of activities such as science, literary appreciation, history, philos-ophy, that the question of the justification of educational activities can be asked and answered. Thus Peters's ultimate argument for the content of education is a **transcendental deduction** from those pursuits and activities which, according to him, must be presupposed in asking and answering the question 'Why do this rather than that?' For example, those activities presupposed by the process of justification as such.

After the appearance of *Ethics and Education* Peters's approach to the concept of 'education' became, in different ways, a main focus of debate within the philosophy of education. Often those who turned their gaze on his analysis were critical of his approach. Sometimes this was upon methodological grounds, for example, he was accused of presenting prescrip-tions for education as if they were part of the description of the concept itself (or, at the very least, of accepting, in an uncritical manner, prescriptions built into a particular version of the concept) (Woods 1967; Dray 1967; Edel 1973; Frankena 1970); sometimes, he was accused of ignoring societal factors in his account and thereby offering an account of 'education' that was at best conservative and at worst reactionary (Adelstein

1972; K. Harris 1979). What was notable, however, was the way in which critical commentators, whether they were on the whole sympathetic or hostile to the Peters agenda (Woods and Barrow 1975; Kleinig 1982), tended to seem to be tinkering with the individual items of his analysis whilst accepting much of the structure.

Probably the central criticism of the analysis presented in *Ethics and Education* is that it tries to do far too much with far too few resources: it seems unlikely that it is possible to answer all the questions that Peters claims to answer with the machinery on offer. Peters seems to have reached this conclusion himself and in the years following the publication of *Ethics and Education* he conducted a fighting retreat from his initial position. In 'Education and the Educated Man' (1970b) he accepted that the notion of 'education' that he was defending was a historically located one and that it encapsulated values which simply could not be derived from conceptual analysis. He also corrected some of the misunderstandings that had resulted from his distinction between 'education' and 'training'. In the 'Justification of Education' he returned to the account of justification offered in his previous work (Peters 1973) but his attempt to recast this account simply succeeded in further revealing its weaknesses (Hirst 1986). In two later papers: 'Ambiguities in Liberal Education and the Problem of Its Content' (1977) and 'Democratic Values and Educational Aims' (1979) he seemed to abandon the formal purity of his earlier account in attempts to locate the practices of education solidly within some understanding – however general – of the social world. However, whilst this involves a welcome recognition that such a context may be necessary to avoid the charge that he is simply building into the concept those features that he happens to favour and thus begging the question against competing accounts, there is still an unwillingness to accept that 'education' may be an **essentially contested concept**, that is, one in which no neutral definition is possible, and therefore that the process of analysis is necessarily biased towards a certain set of values which need explicit defence. Peters does, in his later work, distinguish those parts of the conception of education which are purely analytic from those parts which are value laden and therefore contestable. But it is not all clear that this attempt at demarcation is successful because the analytic elements that he still insists upon, for example, that education involves some kind of learning and that it develops capacities for living, either are left empty of content and are incontestable because they say very little or, they get filled by particular value-laden contents and they again become contestable and in need of explicit defence.

Philosophers of education owe many debts to Peters's work. And one of these debts is an awareness of the types of argument to be avoided if at all possible. Peters's work has shown that an approach to education which simply relies upon analysis to solve substantive educational questions is unlikely to bear any real educational fruit. He has also shown that trying to answer too many questions at once runs the considerable risk of giving too many hostages to fortune.

Recent work within the field has taken these lessons to heart and is noteworthy for offering minimalist – and therefore minimally controversial – definitions of 'education'. White (1982: ch. 1) simply defines it as 'upbringing' whilst Winch (1996: ch. 2) offers something like 'a preparation for adult life'. In being so seemingly unambitious in the matter of definition both writers avoid some of the hazards which Peters encountered: first, they may engage in the substantive debates concerning education, for example, with regard to the content of the curriculum, without being accused of covertly smuggling in their own answers from the outset. Second, because the elements of their arguments do not depend upon one central – and disputed – move, they run less risk of the whole edifice falling if one element is found faulty.

If this seems a small heritage from twenty years of debate it should be remembered that philosophy of education as it is in Britain would not exist but for Peters's work and that his ideas led to profound changes in the British education system at every level.

effectiveness   The effectiveness of schools is sometimes distinguished from the performance of their students at the end-point
of an educational cycle. The idea is that the **achievement** of
students and hence of schools, is to be measured in terms of the
extent to which students have been educationally transformed.
A school may achieve high scores in exit examinations but (the
students having achieved high entry scores) may still not have
transformed them to any great extent. On the other hand, a
school with low entry scores may have transformed students
considerably but may still end up with low exit scores compared
with national norms. It has created more 'added value' than the
first school.

Furthermore, factors for which a school is not directly
responsible, like the social class, poverty or ethnic grouping of
the students, may have a decisive effect on the ability of a school
to transform them. Any attempt to assess the effectiveness of
schools, it is maintained, needs to take account of these factors
as well as the value added. Some also maintain that one needs
to assess the performance of a school against its potential for
achievement (Jesson and Mayston 1988). Agreement about the
need to measure effectiveness has not led either to agreement
as to *how* it should be done or even whether it *can* be done. The
most popular approach seems to be *multi-level* modelling
(Goldstein 1987) which assumes that the data can be fitted to
a linear model. However, the approach assumes that there is a
certain amount of statistical error in the data which can only be
interpreted within certain bands of probability (confidence
intervals). The practical upshot is that effectiveness measures for
most schools show an overlap for the great majority with a small
distinguishable number of high and low achieving schools (e.g.
Gray and Wilcox 1995). The possibility of measurement is
further compromised when students change schools during
the interval between the two measurement points. All these
considerations suggest that the statistical measurement of school
effectiveness is an inexact, controversial and inaccessible science
of little direct use to the public.

When researchers have tried to identify the factors underlying effectiveness (e.g. Mortimore *et al.* 1988) they have often

been accused of pointing to the obvious or **commonsensical** (White 1997a). School effectiveness needs to be distinguished from *school improvement*, which is an attempt to increase the effectiveness of schools. School improvement based on effectiveness research is also thought to be of limited value (Gray and Wilcox 1995). Nevertheless, the desire for **accountability** is likely to ensure that the search for means of assessing effectiveness will continue. One possibility is through the use of **inspection**, which is widely used in some countries, such as the UK, or through close analysis of educational practices. The focus then moves from outcomes to processes. One problem that all approaches face is that it makes no sense to assess the effectiveness of schools unless one is clear about what they are effective *for*. This means that they must be assessed against their effectiveness in achieving educational **aims** which must first be agreed upon.

elitism There are two senses of elitism which are pertinent to education. The first flows from the fact that given any educational enterprise, be it teaching dance, pottery or physics, and given the range of human interests, aptitudes and application, then it is likely to be the case that some students will do consistently better at the enterprise in hand than other students. They will form an elite with regard to this subject matter. (Of course a radical egalitarian who regards any inequality of outcome as unacceptable will take exception to this situation. But whether such a person really exists is an open question.) However, given a change in subject matter then it is likely that those who did well in the first subject will do badly in the new subject and vice versa. This situation reflects the truism that no one is good at everything and that performance will vary accordingly to context.

Given a wide enough **curriculum** in which a whole variety of intellectual pursuits are catered for and a real attempt is made to identify and foster the talents that students possess then this situation is not, or should not be, problematic. And such a situation does not imply that all pupils should not receive a good basic grounding in numeracy and literacy in order to properly function in their everyday lives.

However, given a curriculum that very narrowly defines what is to count as educational and which either ignores or gives low status to a large range of human excellences, then we do seem to have a situation that is unacceptable. It is unacceptable because it is failing to provide for the talents and interests that a large number of pupils have, which they might reasonably expect to be developed within a schooling system. Unfortunately, this seems to be the type of curriculum which is in place in many developed countries at the moment.

Such a curriculum can come into being by historical accident and this was probably the case in Britain where an upper-class curriculum whose major concerns were the classics and the humanities − and lately theoretical science − was applied unreflectingly to mass education. But it can be supported as the implication of rational choice for those that are ready to define 'ability', 'rationality', and 'intelligence' in certain ways. So, for instance, if you take a person's capability at the creation or appreciation of literature as the sole measure of their **intelligence** (See Barrow 1993) then a vast number of pupils in our schools become intellectually second-class citizens. Or if one believes that ability and rationality can be measured totally by IQ tests or by Bernstein's (1973) notion of elaborated and restrictive codes or by Piaget's (1953) distinction between the concrete operational and the formal operational stage (see Bantock 1971 and for criticism, C. Winch 1990) then the same thing happens. Such moves provide us with our second sense of 'elitism', a sense in which only a very narrow range of abilities are considered to be educationally worthy and are therefore specially catered for in our education system. Such moves are pernicious in theory simply because they do violence to our normal notions of intelligence, rationality and ability, for example: the Piagetian distinction with its emphasis on formal operations would mean that possession of GCE 'O' level mathematics made one more intelligent than a painter of the talent of Rembrandt who was non-numerate, and they attempt to rank human intellectual attributes in an unreasonable manner.

(Does it even make sense to ask if an intelligent cabinet-maker is more or less intelligent than an intelligent musician or poet?) They are practically pernicious because they ensure that an education system which should cater for all, in fact, only caters for some and that therefore large numbers of children do not get the first-class education that they deserve.

emotions Concern about the education of the emotions in this century begins against an unpromising philosophical background. The central modern tradition on the analysis of emotions originates with the work on morality of David Hume. Hume, famously, distinguished reason and emotion (passion), believed that reason in itself was unable to motivate us and therefore held that morality, with its motivational essence, must be based upon emotion. The emotions, according to Hume, are 'original existences', that is, states that a person comes to be in which have no reference to anything outside themselves. For example, Hume compares being angry with being 'more than five foot high' in that neither of these things has any reference to any other object; whereas reason, because it deals with either the relationship of ideas (for example, in mathematics) or the relationship of things (as in science), does have reference to things outside itself. And it is this reference that enables us to talk about truth and falsity with regard to reason (you refer to these things either correctly or incorrectly), but makes it totally inappropriate to believe that emotions can be true or false. But, if they cannot be such, then they cannot be reasonable or unreasonable because truth and falsity just is the province of reason; it makes sense to think that a proposition in mathematics is true or false and therefore reasonable or unreasonable, it makes no sense at all to think that a pain or a pleasure is true or false.

Hume's analysis overturned nearly two thousand years of philosophical speculation concerning morality. It was a direct attack on the Platonic and Christian idea of morality as a battle between (angelic) reason and (animal) passion where being good is a question of reason resisting the promptings of desire: whilst

Hume's analysis, if accepted, shows the fundamental importance of the emotions to morality. But it also seems to show that any talk of the education of the emotions is beside the point. If emotions just happen to us or not, if they by their very nature cannot be reasonable or unreasonable, then how could we possibly go about educating the emotions? (Hume 1958, 1962).

The assault on the Humean position was seriously begun by Bedford (1956–7) – although Bedford's paper was not directly aimed at Hume but rather at the faculty psychology theories that derived from a Humean picture – where it was pointed out that an account of emotions which focuses upon what we feel when we experience a particular emotion (i.e. upon the 'original existences') must be seriously inadequate given our rich vocabulary for emotional description and our lack of criteria for distinguishing feelings in terms of this vocabulary. So, for instance, shame and embarrassment are both emotions but to try to distinguish them in terms of either the feelings experienced when someone is ashamed or embarrassed or the behaviour exhibited seems impossible. Rather than looking at psychology – or behaviour – for the distinction, we need, instead, to look at the logical differences in the terms themselves. So, in this instance, shame has a necessary connection with being at fault for something that embarrassment does not. We can make the same point concerning terms such as envy and jealousy, anger and indignation, expectation and hope; that the latter of the pair in each case must include a judgement about the situation in hand which the former does not. For example, you may envy someone their girlfiend but you can only be jealous of them if, in some way, you believe the girl belongs to you. Emotion words 'form part of the vocabulary of appraisal and criticism, and a number of them belong to the more specific language of moral criticism' (Bedford 1956–7).

That is, they involve beliefs, and as such beliefs can be well- or ill-founded, perceptive or unperceptive, rational or irrational, true or false; we can, contra Hume, properly talk of the emotions associated with such appraisals as reasonable or unreasonable.

Bedford's paper seemed to open the door again to talking about educating the emotions. His points were taken up and further elucidated in Peters (1970a, 1971) Peters, like Bedford, insisted that emotions have cognitive content in that they involve appraisals of the world and holds that such appraisals can be the focus of educational endeavour, that is, we can try to ensure that we teach children to see the world clearly. But further, Peters also believed that there are other educational tasks associated with the emotions. He noted that we can suffer emotions passively or such emotions can become the motives for appropriate – or sometimes inappropriate – action and believed that it was attention to this area of our emotional life which merited work by educationalists. But he also believed that a psychology which was confined within the behaviouristic or physiological traditions and thus simple-minded concerning the range of emotions was singularly ill-equipped to contribute to this educational task.

The Bedford–Peters position is both interesting and important with regard to the education of the emotions. However, serious doubts still remain. It is not at all clear, for instance, that all emotions have the cognitive content which gives a grip to education. It may be the case that we cannot be jealous or indignant or proud without reason but the same does not seem to be true of cheerfulness or misery. The clarification of appraisals which Peters recommends also may have significant limits. It may be the case that, faced with the task of giving reasonable appraisals concerning our emotions we would have to stop talking – except in very particular cases – of being afraid of spiders (because fear of X involves the belief that X is dangerous and spiders are not usually dangerous). But the realisation that we have used the wrong word – or, perhaps made the wrong appraisal – is hardly likely to prevent our unease when spiders are about. Indeed, it may be the case that our talk of being afraid of spiders is an attempt to rationalise completely irrational feelings, that is, we talk this way because we are afraid, for no good reason, of spiders. This may be important in terms of moral education because it may give pause to an unreasonable optimism that, when we tackle the false beliefs in a statement like 'I hate black people because they take our jobs', the hostility expressed will vanish. Lastly, the talk of properly canalising the emotions into appropriate action both begs certain questions as to what is deemed appropriate and seems an unlikely target for direct attack. Whilst it does connect with certain approaches to moral education (see Ryle 1972 and D. Carr 1991) it is noteworthy that such approaches see the growth of morality as something to be learned rather than taught through **training**, exemplification and the use of vicarious examples (see **virtue theory**).

A recent addition to the literature of the education of the emotions is Scheffler (1991). Whilst sharing the Bedford–Peters line concerning the role of cognition in emotion, Scheffler concentrates upon those emotions which grow out of the educational enterprise itself. So, for instance, he follows Peters (1966) in seeing a crucial role in education for developing the intellectual/academic emotions such as a care for truth and justification. But he also insists that along with those 'calm emotions' – as David Hume might have described them – we also nurture emotions such as cognitive surprise and the joy of verification which may accompany academic endeavours.

A rather different approach to emotional education is found in Hepburn (1972). Whilst Hepburn is aware of the cognitivist drive in modern analyses of emotion, his concern is not with this aspect of their elucidation but, rather, with the way in which the arts, and especially literature, may be used to sharpen our perceptions of the emotions we feel and replace emotional clichés with a concern for the proper details of emotions in all their complexity. He is also concerned with the way in which the arts, in offering us different emotional reactions to situations, may increase our sense of emotional choice and therefore of emotional freedom. It is clear from the examples used in his analysis that Hepburn's argument depends upon an education drawing from 'high' **culture**. However, although this may be out of favour today this does nothing to undermine his position.

entitlement Nozick's (1974) account of justice is based on entitlement. If one has acquired goods justly, one is entitled to them irrespective of desert or need. What entitles someone to educational goods? Ability to pay would be one criterion, but could one allocate goods according to an entitlement criterion in a public education system in order to give different students different forms of schooling? The problem here concerns the criterion of entitlement. One might say that past performance constitutes an entitlement, since a student who has previously worked hard to meet the selection criteria deserves a place. On the other hand, the performance of another pupil might be less good in raw terms, but far better in value-added terms. Here, one could say that the latter student has a more deserving claim to a place.

Past performance may not be a sure guide to future performance and one might argue that desert is irrelevant as a selection criterion for educational goods. Alternatively, one could argue that either ability or future promise form the basis of the entitlement. Provided that there are just means of assessing these, entitlement could form the basis of a meritocratic selection system. If, however, the **aim** of the system were to produce the highest possible results for some students (e.g. Cooper 1980), future performance would be judged in one way. If the aim were to produce the highest aggregate performance, future performance could be judged in another way. Entitlement by itself cannot provide a selection criterion.

epistemology Epistemology or the theory of knowledge has often been thought to be at the heart of the philosophical enterprise. In Plato, it is also taken to be central to the practice of education. Thus, it underpins the 'teaching' of the slave-boy by Socractes in the *Meno* (Plato 1970a) (see **erotetics**) and it is supposed to support the banishment of the artists from the ideal republic (Plato 1970b). Whilst the particular conception of the search for knowledge which occurs in Plato has long been neglected, his conception of the conditions necessary for ascribing knowledge to anyone have lasted until the present time. Thus, he presents a definition of knowledge that has three elements. For someone to know a statement X, say that 'Socrates is bald', they (a) have to believe X; (b) X has to be true; and (c) they have to have good reasons for believing X.

This 'justified true belief' account of 'knowledge' has been and remains, the usual starting point for investigations into the nature of knowledge (but see Ryle 1949), despite the fact that, since Plato, it has been realised that the third condition is extremely problematic (if you have to *know* that you have good reasons for a belief before you claim knowledge then it seems that the definition is question-begging).

Most epistemologists, until the present day, in accepting some form of this definition, have also accepted that the process of justification has to stop somewhere. That is that, whilst most beliefs have to be justified by other beliefs there must be some basic, foundational beliefs which do not stand in need of justification. The great divide amongst philosophers, at least since the eighteenth century, has been with regard to the nature of these foundational beliefs, with rationalists, following Descartes and Leibniz, thinking that pure reason can provide such foundations, while empiricisits, following Locke and Hume, believing that it is only experience of the world that in some way can provide the foundational propositions. Modern epistemology, whilst continuing to tease out the problems with the third condition (see Everitt and Fisher 1996 with regard to Gettier problems) has taken a rather different turn, with the main battle being between those who want to deny that knowledge needs foundations and those, following Popper and Quine, who believe that it does.

Whilst it would be unrealistic to believe that **education** would follow the twists and turns of this debate − although it would be gratifying if it showed some awareness of it − it would also be surprising if it had no influence at all on such things as the curriculum. Thus, it seems likely, that the high status accorded to mathematics and science within schools, is partly a function of the fact that most epistemologists believe that *if* knowledge is to be found anywhere, it is to be found within these domains. However, the other side of this belief does not seem to have registered in the same way. Since at least the eighteenth century the cognitive status of statements within morality, artistic criticism and religion have been seriously in question. This should mean that if such areas are taught in school there should at least be some consideration of their cognitive status, and therefore some consideration of the type of support that can be given to statements within these areas. Whilst there is some work on some of these areas within philosophy of education (see Best 1992), it is not at all clear that such work has penetrated our schools (see **knowledge**).

Of late, different challenges have been raised against the epistemological enterprise. Philosophers influenced by **postmodernist** thought such as Rorty (1980, 1991) have questioned the very possibility of giving an account of knowledge which is universalistic and culture-free. Instead, they propose attention to the different accounts of knowledge found in different cultural contexts (see **relativism**). However, such a relativisation of knowledge is not widely accepted – although it seems more widely accepted in education than it is within epistemology and it has been cogently argued by philosophers such as Siegel (1997) that this approach assumes exactly the type of assumptions that it seeks to deny.

equality   Traditionally, arguments about equality have been closely concerned with questions about **justice**. Since **education** must be closely concerned with justice, the relationship between education and equality is important; however, since 'equality' means so very many different things, it is not easy to establish such a relationship. It is helpful to start with an account of the key distinctions.

Equality as procedural justice. In this sense, equality is the requirement that members of the same reference group receive the same consideration in relation to the allocation of scarce goods or desirable outcomes. Thus, all accused are entitled to a fair trial, all citizens in a democracy to a vote, students to proper assessment. This does not entail that they should all receive the same *treatment*. For example, procedural justice requires that all candidates for an examination receive fair assessment, it does not require that a candidate presents himself in an examination hall even when he is bedridden. Procedural justice does not answer the question as to what the relevant reference groups should be (for example, who is to count as a citizen). This question is one of *social justice*, that is, *which* groups should be treated equally?

Equality of treatment entails that all in the same reference group are treated in the same way. For example, all children follow the same syllabus and are taught together, irrespective of ability or motivation. Equality of treatment is often associated with comprehensive education and **mixed-ability** teaching, as well as with an absence of segregation on any grounds, including sex, race and disability. The aims of promoting equality of treatment in education are not always clear, since it does not seem to be a strict requirement of fairness (see above), but many proponents would see it as a means of promoting the esteem of relatively unfavoured groups as well as a potent means of promoting equality of outcome (see below).

Equality of outcome entails that the endpoint of a process (like education) is that all have the same allocation of desirable outcomes or scarce resources. For example, all receive the same exam grades or the same bursary. Although it is often thought that equality of treatment leads to equality of outcome this is likely to hold only when individuals in the reference group are the same in all relevant respects such as ability, motivation and interest. Where they are different in one or more of these respects, as it is likely that they will be, then they will not all take the same advantage of the treatment provided. This will inevitably lead to inequalities of outcome. The egalitarian appears to be in a dilemma. On the one hand she wishes to provide the same treatment, thus provoking different outcomes; on the other, in insisting on equal outcomes she is compelled to differentiate treatments through policies such as **affirmative action** and specialist **teaching**. The assumption of human **diversity** is enough to generate this dilemma.

Equality of opportunity. The usual liberal definition of this is as procedural justice, but it is common to hear more radical interpreters of the principle claim that, for it to be meaningful, resources must be equalised among individuals if there is to be a desirable outcome. So anyone accused of a criminal offence should receive the same quality of defence as anyone else accused, so as to equalise his chances of being found innocent. This claim has led some to maintain that equality of opportunity is not a coherent objective for an education system, since it is unrealistic to equalise resources relative to individuals (J. Wilson 1993). This might be a legitimate complaint against attempts to make equality of opportunity a form of equality of treatment, but not against the principle interpreted as a form of procedural justice; for all that the principle then entails is that no one is debarred from or discriminated against in seeking a desirable outcome such as accreditation. Others, more radical still, maintain that inequality of outcome constitutes a ground for presuming that opportunities have been unequal. On this interpretation of the principle, equal outcomes should be engineered through the provision of unequal treatments. However, it also appears to violate the weaker, permissive, principle of equal opportunity since, in order to secure the same outcome, it may often be necessary to deny provision to some favoured groups or individuals. This means in effect that the weakest and strongest forms of equality of opportunity are in conflict with each other and that one has to choose between them even if one is satisfied on practical grounds that the achievement of either is possible. The conflict is then between fairness and sameness as ethical ideals.

It might seem obvious that sameness cannot be such a powerful ethical value as fairness. Indeed this is the type of criticism of egalitarianism made by J. P. White (1994). It would be fallacious to conclude that inequalities of treatment and outcome are not, therefore, of any ethical significance. It has been argued at least since the time that Plato wrote the *Laws* (1970c), that too much inequality damages society's well-being and leads to resentment and social exclusion through the resulting unequal distribution of power and influence. It is quite possible for someone who rejects strong egalitarian arguments to hold nevertheless that there need to be strict limits on inequalities of distribution. Such a position would be at odds with the theory of distributive justice found both in the neo-liberal position of Nozick (1974) and the more conservative liberalism of Rawls (1971, 1993).

Educators have argued in favour of inequality on the grounds that it promotes excellence, which is an intrinsic good (e.g. Cooper 1980). It has also been argued that diversity is desirable in order to accommodate the range of human abilities and interests (Entwistle 1970; Winch 1990). Against this it is maintained that inequality (or excessive inequality) in education leads to social disaffection and power differences that lead eventually to injustice. Questions of equality cannot, therefore, be a matter of complete indifference to educators.

erotetic   Erotetic teaching relies on questioning as a central pedagogic technique. An early example can be found in Plato's dialogue *Meno*, where the slave is taught geometry through being reminded of what he already knows, under questioning by Socrates. Plato believed that people literally recollected what they had learned in a previous existence, but supporters of erotetics don't need to rely on these assumptions. Rousseau, for example, thought that erotetic teaching could activate recently acquired knowledge, as it does when Emile finds his way back to Montmorency after questioning by his tutor. More recently, erotetics has focused on the questions students ask. Macmillan and Garrison (1983) have asserted that 'to teach someone is to answer that person's questions about some subject matter'. When students ask appropriate questions, then erotetics can proceed unproblematically. When however they do not ask questions or do not ask appropriate ones, teachers ought to take into account the questions that students should ask and design their teaching accordingly.

Macmillan and Garrison's theory is a normative one. Teaching empowers students to answer the questions that they *should* ask. But one may wonder about what would happen if a student did not wish to ask a question that his teacher thought appropriate. Erotetics was proposed in order to counter student's lack of interest and alienation. Teachers are going to have to be very careful to formulate questions that bear some relationship to what students are interested in, if they, in turn, are not to risk their students' alienation from them.

essentially contested concepts   The idea of 'essentially contested concepts' was first introduced in the literature by Gallie (1955–6) and refers to those concepts which are in dispute but for which no neutral or agreed definition is accepted by the disputants. 'Political liberty' is such a concept where some theorists, following Berlin (1969), think that the only workable definition of the term emphasises its 'negative' characteristics, that is, we are free insofar as we are not interfered with by other people; whereas some theorists (Taylor 1979) believe that this is far too weak a definition and that 'real' freedom involves the power to determine oneself and the shape of one's life. Battles concerning such concepts, because they tend to involve an ideological dimension where the disputed concept occupies an important place in a complex and normative view of the world, tend to be fierce and protracted.

   It has been suggested that **'education'** is a contested concept (C. Winch 1996) in that those in favour of 'liberal' education have a view of the concept which emphasises the initiation of those being educated into intrinsically worthwhile activities, whilst those that oppose this view emphasise education's role in the preparation for life after education. It may be the case that the battle here has been partly hidden by the political and theoretical power of the theorists of 'liberal' education. However, it may be the case that what hides the dispute is that for a considerable amount of time the schooling system *seemed* to serve both the intrinsic and instrumental ends of both models. If so, then it is merely a contingent state of affairs which is at the mercy of matching the perspectives of school and society and it also, and importantly, ignores the fact that the intrinsic goals model may have frustrated the instrumental aims of a large number of children and parents.

excellence   An emphasis on excellence in education is usually contrasted with an egalitarian approach. However, because of the different notions of **equality** deployed in educational discussions, and the manifest difficulties of producing a coherent and acceptable egalitarian programme for education, discussions of excellence typically contain a few obvious – but necessary – points and then devote the majority of their time to revealing the inadequacies of the various egalitarian positions on offer. Thus Cooper (1980) in attacking egalitarian approaches to education says that a concern for excellence is a 'fundamental human concern in myriad areas of human practice' (p. 54) and that no one could count themselves as, say, a real lover of music or athletics without such a concern. It may be the case that 'The prime concern of the lover of music or athletics is not with a general, marginal improvement in the amateur playing of string quartets, or the times clocked by run-of-the-mill runners; but with seeing the higher standards of musicianship maintained or advanced, with seeing great athletes break new barriers' (p. 55). But it is not the case that 'Where there is a conflict, as there must be between attending to excellence and attending to an evenly spread, average improvement, there is rarely a serious question as to the preferred alternative' (p. 55).

We can see this if we take the wine industry as an example. Over the last fifteen years the industry has thrown up a great many ambitious winemakers. Such people could have aimed for positions with the great chateaux, such as Lafitte and Latour; instead they aimed first to produce excellent wine of their own, and then to increase the quality of wine produced in general. Both aims have been achieved. There is now more excellent wine in the world than ever before and the average quality of wine is far higher than it has ever been. Any serious wine lover must be overjoyed at their realisation of these aims. It may be the case, as Cooper argues for the educational context, that the stars of the system – or yesterday's stars – will now aim to outstrip their new competitors, but it is not clear that this is just an empirical question.

So, it is possible to aim sensibly for excellence and a concern for overall quality. In some contexts – for instance, medical provision within a welfare state – such concerns should go hand in hand. If, in such a case, there comes to be competition between these aims, it is not at all clear that one should aim for excellence rather than average improvement.

It may be the case, as Cooper argues it is, that this issue is best considered not as a competition between excellence and equality, but rather as a question of providing an acceptable minimum for all whilst maintaining a wish for excellence for some. Much here turns upon what is thought to be 'an acceptable minimum'. It may also be the case, as we suspect it was in the example of the wine industry, that the best way of ensuring more excellence – both 'distributionally' and 'ontologically' (in Cooper's terms) – is via a rise of overall **standards**.

existentialism Existentialism is a family of philosophies associated with thinkers such as Sartre, Marcel, Merleau-Ponty and influenced by the work of Nietzsche, Kierkegaard, Husserl, Heidegger and Jaspers. Although it embodies a distinctive epistemology which rejects Descartes, it is largely famous for its radical approach to moral philosophy.

According to this, people, unlike anything else in the world, are characterised by their freedom. Whereas the objects of the natural world (e.g. stones, trees) have an essence that comes into being with their existence, with people their existence precedes their essence and they are free to create themselves either through their choice of lives or through their choices in any particular situation. The freedom that characterises people means that there can be no rules, rational or otherwise, for choice (but see Taylor 1991). However, there are right and wrong ways of choosing. Choice can be authentic and in good faith or unauthentic and in bad faith.

It is the latter pair if it is determined by the views of others, for then such choice does not embody the radical freedom at the heart of this conception of ethics.

There are many serious problems facing an existentialist ethic. First, its simple emphasis on freedom from influence, seems, at the most, to offer a necessary but not sufficient description of moral choice; if I freely lift my arm is such an action necessarily moral? Second, it is not at all clear, especially in the light of the work of Bradley (1951: esp. ch. 4) and Foucault (1977, 1978) that the radical choice envisaged by the existentialists is possible. We live in a world in which the roles and actions possible for us are circumscribed by social reality; for example, no one in the modern world could choose to be a Teutonic Knight. Third, it seems perfectly possible, given some versions of the doctrine of freedom, for someone to make what many of us would take to be profoundly immoral choices for example, to authentically choose to be a concentration camp guard. Fourth, whilst unthinking conformity may be rather dull, it is not at all clear, in many cases, why it is wicked.

Existentialism, with its emphasis on authenticity, occasionally appears on the educational scene (see Greene 1988) but, for practical as well as theoretical reasons (what would an existentialist curriculum look like?), it has had little real influence in either educational theory or practice.

experience   'Experience' refers to our sensory commerce with the world. It is easy to overlook, however, the fact that this impact can be both veridical and nonveridical. Experience may take the form of hallucinations, for example. Only when our experience is not misleading about how things are, does it give us **knowledge**. **Learning** through experience cannot, therefore, guarantee knowledge, although it may be a precondition of it. Note also that the general definition above allows us to talk both of passive and of active experience. We may passively absorb sense data or have dreams or we may seek out experience through discovery and enquiry. Although it is sometimes thought that empiricism saw experience as passive, there is nothing in the accounts of Locke and others to suggest that sense data cannot result from self-directed activity.

Some writers, notably Dewey (1916), have regarded experience as our general engagement with the world. This more general use of the term includes inference and anticipation. This leads to a difficulty in expressing what is not experience. If everything that I do, as well as everything that happens to me, is experiential, then it is difficult to see how one could distinguish between how one acts on the world and how the world acts on one.

There are particular educational problems with the broad definition above. If one claims that children learn through experience, then it seems to follow that they will learn simply through having dealings with the world. To say that someone will learn through experience is, then, nearly tautologous since any dealing with the world will lead to learning. In a school where children did what they pleased there would be plenty of experience in this sense.

However, in a narrower sense, experience gives perceptions, sensations and beliefs and education can be organised so as to provide these. Some might say that this is still too broad a construal for educational purposes, since it fails to distinguish between veridical and non-veridical experience. Most educators still believe that the experiences that they give their students should be those that promote knowledge.

Even when we narrow valuable educational experience to the veridical there are still important questions to be answered. Dewey argued that experience, properly understood, was due to active rather than passive dealings with the world and this claim may survive even if the broader definition of experience is rejected. On this restricted view (which can be found in Rousseau 1911a), we gain experience through activity and most experience is of things rather than sensations. This suggests that learning takes place through activity of some kind. It is commonly assumed within the **progressive** tradition that it must involve self-directed bodily movement rather than, for example, recitation or memorising. But the assumption is only valid if experience is reinterpreted further so that valid educational experience arises only from self-directed activity. This is a point that **developmentalists**, following Rousseau and Piaget, have emphasised. But developmentalism is itself a controversial doctrine.

experts   Teachers, especially in primary schools, often worry about their expertise with regard to **curriculum** areas they teach (strangely enough, they seem hardly to worry at all about their status as experts with regard to manners and **moral education**). The curriculum worries are usually calmed by the thought that expertise, in itself, doesn't guarantee good **teaching** and that, at the least, they are more expert than the children they teach. Such relief may be bought too easily.

It is certainly true, that subject expertise is not a *sufficient* condition for good teaching but it seems obvious that it is a *necessary* condition. That is, if you don't understand the subject you are teaching you *cannot* teach it well. As far as being 'more expert than the children' is concerned, such a claim needs careful analysis. Expertise is a question of knowledge and understanding, it is not, and cannot be, simply a question of, for instance, reading a few books; because it is perfectly possible to read the wrong books or, even if you have read the right ones, to misunderstand them. (Such facts also undermine the claims made by some teachers, that if they don't know about a certain subject area they know how to show the children to find out about that area.) If this is so then it must cast doubt on any system of education, at whichever level, that does not insist that teachers have the relevant subject expertise. Until recently, the class-teacher system in British primary schools was exactly such a system. The imposition of a detailed National Curriculum, has partially exposed this system and has shown that it is simply not possible for one person to have the amount of expertise necessary to teach all its subjects. The present slimming down of that curriculum so that a far greater emphasis is given to English, maths and science, may solve the expertise problem. But it may also leave the children in our schools without any real teaching in the other curriculum areas (see Alexander 1984, 1992 for an attack on the class-teacher system).

Of course, other theories are going to run into similar problems. So, for instance, if you believe that some subjects are simply a question of subjective preference (see **objectivity**) or believe that knowledge is impossible (see **postmodernism**, **constructivism**) then the type of **authority** needed for teaching to take place in any meaningful sense must be lacking and therefore people who hold such intellectual positions should not be appointed as teachers.

expression (free)   The cult of free self-expression which has dominated art teaching in British primary schools for forty years, probably derives indirectly from two sources. The first is Freud with his ideas that art represents the product of the sublimation of the promptings of the unconcious mind (see Freud 1985). The second is the Romantic tradition, represented on the one hand by figures such as Wordsworth with his stress on the purity of vision of childhood and his notion that 'poetry is the spontaneous overflow of strong emotion' and on the other by aestheticians such as Tolstoy and Collingwood (see Tolstoy 1930, Collingwood 1965) with their distrust of technique and their emphasis upon the expression of emotion. The movement also received support from the success of art movements such as Abstract Expressionism which both seemed to encapsulate the main ideas of such figures mentioned above and to divorce art from its traditional ideas concerning art education. The fact that the vast majority of artists for the last two thousand years neither trained in such a way nor worked in contexts that promoted free self-expression did not deter theorists, such as Lytton (1971), from believing that free expression was the key to artistic creativity and that the rule-bound structure of **schooling** was unlikely to promote either.

Philosophers of education writing about **creativity** have shown that a notion of free self-expression as a sufficient condition of artistic creativity is not tenable. However, they seem content to leave it as one of the necessary conditions of creativity, so that creative people must be free to express themselves even if, at the same time, they have to, say, produce work of originality and quality. What has not been examined, as far as we are aware, is the concept of 'free self-expression' itself. And the question that needs asking here concerns the criteria which distinguish such self-expression from other forms of behaviour. It seems initially to be the case that, at the very least, acting under coercion must inhibit self-expression. However, even here care is needed, for students working in an exam room sometimes seem perfectly capable of expressing themselves *vis-à-vis* the topic in hand. And if we regard **discipline** in all its forms as coercive then the discipline needed, say, to play the piano is not inimical to expressing oneself musically but rather a necessary condition for doing so.

The idea that free self-expression must lead to personal unconventionality again seems not to survive a moment's scrutiny. Obedience to convention is important to all of us in endless different situations and why should it be assumed that everyone has an unconventional personality? Nor does coherence of behaviour seem to work. Certainly, if someone is habitually tidy one might say that a particular piece of tidy behaviour expresses their personality. However, the fact that someone is idle with regard to some things such as washing the car, and energetic with regard to others such as cooking, does not mean that either the idleness or the energy must alone be the key to their personality. Most of us exist most of the time comfortable with the fact that we exhibit different character traits in different situations.

If free self-expression is thought to be a necessary quality for creativity then it appears that the meaning of the concept needs further teasing out. Such a task would be better served by concentrating upon the notion of style rather than becoming bogged down in psychologising about how people do, as a matter of fact, express themselves.

F

feminism Feminism has a much higher profile in philosophy of education in America than it does in Britain. This has to do partly with the length – and fierceness – of feminist debate in each country, partly with the level of radicalism inherent in the different approaches, and partly with the fact that no really prominent feminist philosophers of education like Jane Roland Martin and Nel Noddings have, as yet, appeared on the British scene.

However, whether in America or Britain, it is true to say that feminist challenges to the prevailing philosophical or educational orthodoxy have varied in both their scope and content. Some have been simple arguments for justice either with regard to the **curriculum** and its areas (Martin 1985) or with regard to social life as such (Richards 1980) demanding that the inequalities of attention, opportunity and treatment that women suffer in our societies be properly addressed in an educational context. Other, more radical, voices issue challenges to many of the basic assumptions which seem to underpin the educational enterprise. So, for instance, the so-called 'standpoint' epistemologists (Scheman 1993; Collins 1990) question the whole thrust for **objectivity** which has characterised the western approach to knowledge for the last two thousand years. Such radical critiques tend to emphasise the special claims of particular groups and insist on privileged knowledge for particular social groups with regard to particular issues. Thus, women have access to privileged knowledge with regard to gender, the poor with respect to poverty, ethnic minorities with regard to ethnic issues. Such claims are often radically ambiguous. They might mean that in approaching such issues it is only fair if a proper voice is given to women, the poor, ethnic minorities, *et al*. Such a request seems difficult to deny. However, they might mean only women, the poor, ethnic minorities have the right to speak on such issues and that what they say must be taken as truth.

Apart from the enormously important fact that none of these groups speak with one voice, such extreme claims run into the traditional problems of **relativism**. First, if it is claimed that the truth of any statement or position is relative to membership of a particular social group then what becomes of the truth of this statement in itself, i.e. is it only true for particular social groups or is it true universally? If the former, then our particular social group may disregard it; if the latter, then it has to be explained why this statement is different to all other statements. Second, if true statements cannot be made across the boundaries of social groups then it becomes impossible for, say, feminists to say *anything* about social groups to which they do not belong (e.g. men, the poor, ethnic minorities), and any attempt at understanding or dialogue *must* fail. Even the claim by social group X (e.g. women) that social group Y (e.g. men) do not understand them seems to claim more than the theory will allow; i.e. if one group really has *no* understanding of the other group then they can have no understanding of what that group does or does not understand.

Noddings has attempted to apply feminine insights into ethics (see Noddings 1984, 1992, 1995). She wants to replace the traditional account of morality based upon principle and calculation, for example, as exemplified in Kant and certain forms of utilitarianism, with an account that emphasises the type of spontaneous response to the plight of another which she calls 'natural' caring.

Noddings gives a comprehensive account of care and the phenomenology of caring relationships and details the implications of these for moral education. However, she seems at times to be trading upon an ambiguity in the concept of 'care'. So, in one sense, to be told to care for another is simply to be told to take them fully into account. Such a sense is recognisable in Kant's injunction to treat everyone as ends in themselves and not merely as means, or in the utilitarian notion that in any moral calculation one person is to count as one person and not more than one person. In another sense 'caring' characterises the special relationship between friends or members of a family, the relationship that has been characterised by the term 'self-referential altruism'. Now, if Noddings is simply drawing upon the first sense of 'care' then it seems that all she is offering is a slightly enriched version of traditional moral philosophy. However, if she is, as she seems to be, suggesting that what we need is the second sense of care *applied to everyone*, i.e. that we treat everyone as a friend or member of our family, then such a proposal seems to empty that notion of 'care' of determinate sense. The point of special relationships is that they are special and if everyone is special then no one is. One could make the point in a slightly different way by asking, if we follow Noddings's proposal and, say, treat everyone as a friend, how are we supposed to treat our friends?

genre 'Genre' refers to type of cultural artefact, for example, landscape, portrait or still-life in painting. Each of these has its own conventions of production and recognition. Genre pedagogic theorists maintain that children best learn to work within a genre through introduction to and practice of its conventions (Reid 1987). Genre theorists have been particularly influential in the field of writing (e.g. Cope and Kalantzis 1993); they advocate a pedagogy that is, on balance, more instructional than facilitative. Those opposed to genre theories of pedagogy do not deny the existence of genres, but maintain that genre-oriented pedagogies stifle the **creativity** of pupils (e.g. Dixon 1987). The dispute between genre theorists and their opponents is part of a wider-ranging debate between **progressivism** and traditionalism in pedagogy.

Genre theorists maintain that worthwhile cultural products are only identifiable within a genre framework and that students will not pick up genre conventions without guidance, or that they will do so less easily without guidance. Personal creativity, it is maintained, depends on a mastery of these conventions (Best 1992). Opponents tend to place less importance on genre as an indicator of product creativity and stress the subjective response of the recipient as a surer sign of the value of what is produced. They also point out that the most striking work is often that which transcends any clear genre classifications. Alternatively, they argue that students can best attain mastery of genre conventions through unconstrained experimentation rather than through instruction and drill.

giftedness   There are four important questions about giftedness. First, what are the origins of exceptional abilities? To say that someone is gifted is to describe their disposition to produce outstanding performances. When one asks why they do this, the explanation is often that they are gifted. The expressions 'giftedness' or 'outstanding ability' are, therefore, descriptive and do not explain the origins of the capacity to produce such performances. Psychologists have suggested three sorts of explanation which are similar to those put forward for the origins of intelligence, namely: heredity, environment and the interaction between them. Since these are discussed in relation to **intelligence** they will not be reviewed here.

Second, how are we to characterise exceptional ability? One of the problems is that the terms used are not just descriptive but evaluative. This is so with the adjective 'gifted' and the noun 'genius'. People who are gifted are praised and admired because we value what they are capable of doing. This makes it difficult to look at exceptional abilities with a dispassionate eye. Furthermore, someone may be called 'gifted' but this does not tell us *what* they are gifted at. One view is that someone who is gifted has the potential to produce outstanding performances in pretty well any area of human accomplishment for which they have the physical capacity. This is the idea that giftedness is really nothing more than very high intelligence in the psychometric sense. The opposing view is that to be gifted is to be capable of outstanding achievement in one or more specific *activities*. On this view, there is no underlying entity within the individual such as 'global giftedness'. Holders of this view might, however, believe that there are specific biological causes for particular kinds of giftedness, like musical ability. Alternatively, one might believe that 'giftedness' is nothing more than the disposition to produce exceptional performances. Which of these three views one takes is likely to be determined by one's view of the origins of such traits.

Third, under what circumstances do we attribute qualities of high excellence to achievements? It is possible that luck and changing fashion play a role. For example, the compositions of J. S. Bach were not regarded as exceptional in his lifetime.

Fourth, can we be sure that we have not missed gifted people? Some exceptional abilities may only develop under the right individual circumstances; others may be recognised as exceptional at one time and quite ordinary at another (for example, the ability to read).

'Giftedness' is, then, in part, an evaluative expression whose application depends to a degree on the extent to which circumstances provide opportunities to individuals and the extent to which particular abilities are valued by society.

good practice   Appeals to 'good practice' are legion within British educational literature especially that which relates to primary schooling. Such appeals are usually high on assertion and low on justification. In some cases the assertions are extremely counter-intuitive. So, for instance, it was a wide-spread fashion, for a time, to believe that if you are talking to a child you should maintain eye contact at all times. (The disconcerting nature of this is easily demonstrated in everyday life.) In at least one county of England, it was deemed 'good practice' for teachers *not* to have desks. (The problems here are self-evident to anyone who does any amount of paper work.) Even when the appeals to 'good practice' were couched in less dubious recommendations they were often either so vague as to be useless or truistic to the point of tautalogy, e.g. in a good lesson there should be good management of class time (OFSTED 1994).

The reaction to such talk came from Alexander (1992), who had argued in the past for a positive role for philosophy within education (Alexander 1984). He identified four interpretations of the notion of good practice:

1 As a statement of *value* or *belief*, i.e. this is a practice which I like, and which accords with my personal philosophy of education.

2 As a *pragmatic* statement, i.e. this is a practice which works for me, and which I feel most comfortable with.

3 As an *empirical* statement, i.e. this is a practice which I can prove is effective in enabling children to learn.

4 As a *political* statement, i.e. this is a practice which I (or others) expect to see, and it should therefore be adopted.

Whilst he made little explicit criticism of these various alternatives it was clear that he regarded the first and the last as questionable and the second and third as the basis for any reasonable notion of 'good practice' and saw questions of good practice as addressing conceptual, normative, pragmatic, empirical and political issues. Above all he emphasised that good practice was a question of judgement (Alexander 1992: 179–91). (See **advice**.)

Alexander was accused by D. Carr (1994) of having a technical vision of education which subordinated the values implicit within any education in a manner akin to scientific methodology. However, such an attack seems difficult to sustain given Alexander's explicit reference to and discussion of educational values. And, although values are crucial to education, empirical matters may also be crucial. Thus if we have three, morally equivalent, approaches to teaching reading it might be a matter of great concern if one of them is found to be less effective than the other two.

health education Health education first appeared on the curriculum under the name 'Hygiene' in the 1890s (Laura and Heaney 1990). Since then it has changed both its name and its scope. There are three main areas of philosophical interest in health education. The first concerns the concept of health and its relationship to other concepts. Possible definitions range from absence of biological dysfunction to generalised well-being (WHO 1946). The nature and scope of health education will depend on which conception of health is adopted. Second, the relationship between health education and the wider promotion of health is a matter of uncertainty. Health can be promoted in a variety of ways, including mass vaccination, for example. It can also be promoted through **training** in various procedures such as food preparation and domestic hygiene. Where the border lies between this kind of activity and health education properly so called is not always clear and may be drawn in slightly different places according to different purposes. Finally, there is the related question of what the **aims** of health education should be. Answers to this will, in turn, depend on answers to questions about the nature of health and the scope of health education within health promotion.

One answer to the question about aims is to subsume them under more general educational aims. If one adopts **autonomy** and, in particular, strong autonomy as an educational aim, then health education becomes directed towards the enablement of individual choice. The individual must then be free to make choices about the ends of life, some of which may be disapproved of by society. For example, children may be educated about the consequences of either smoking or not smoking or engaging in promiscuous sexual behaviour, but the choice of whether or not they did so would be left to them. Such views have been criticised because they appear to accord too high a priority to individual self-gratification rather than improvement (M. Phillips 1996). More serious, perhaps, is the strong health autonomist's reluctance to recognise the social consequences of individual action. Someone may be entitled to risk lung cancer by smoking; it is quite another question as to whether they should be entitled to jeopardise someone else's health through involuntary passive smoking. Similar points could be made about sexual behaviour. The problems here are very much problems of strong autonomy as an aim.

In relation to the conceptualisation of health, most health educators would agree that a narrow biomedical model of health is unsatisfactory and that any definition should encompass some idea of well-being. It is also claimed that health status is affected, not just by physical causes but by the total environment in which an individual operates (Laura and Heaney 1990). Both these considerations will broaden the scope of health education well beyond training in procedures to eliminate biological dysfunction. But, to the extent that they are broadened, it becomes increasingly difficult to mark out a distinct sphere of health education as opposed to education as such.

higher education   According to some critics (MacIntyre 1990, Bloom 1987), Higher Education is in crisis and this crisis concerns not the usual issues of funding and access but deeper and more important questions of identity. Whereas once, the story goes, Higher Education and particularly the universities had a clear idea of their place and function in the world and therefore a clear idea of what was and was not a proper part of university or college **education**, this clarity of vision has now been lost in the fragmentation of culture and the responses of this sector of education to external pressures. The remedies suggested by such critics vary. For Bloom it is a return to Higher Education seeing itself as the guardian of traditions, as for instance, embodied in the 'Great Books' tradition of American universities. For MacIntyre, whose scepticism outstrips that of Bloom, the only way forward is to establish different institutions committed to different forms of rational enquiry but each committed to a particular moral or world outlook. A commentator on this position, Mendus (1992), has noted the subscription to 'the Myth of the Fall' in both positions, that is, that there was in the past some fully integrated and harmoniously functioning society which we have fallen away from, and she shows that the conflicts between different traditions of thought may help to play a part in fully rational discussion within a university rather than simply confuse such discussion.

A rather less apocalyptic vision of the problems of Higher Education is put forward by Barnett (1988, 1990) but his thesis is equally controversial. He thinks that we have reached a position where 'truth', 'objective knowledge' and 'rationality' cannot be understood in their traditional senses and therefore cannot be pursued by students or teachers in universities in these senses. Instead, he believes, following Habermas's critical approach to knowledge, we need to reform such notions and see the search for objective knowledge in terms of social interaction, personal commitment, the development of mind, value implication, and, above all, openness to criticism. We need to reveal to students that 'all is ideology' and by dedicating Higher Education to reflective learning and teaching – rather than research activities – and emphasising student freedom and open learning methods, we can emancipate students.

There are large problems with this project. In his earlier paper (1988) Barnett makes much of the 'fact' that the aims of education in Higher Education have to be largely realised by the learners rather than the teachers. What he fails to realise is that this is true of education as such and therefore if this is a key to seeking emancipation then it is an emancipation that has to be aimed for in the whole system not just in the universities. Second, much of Barnett's concern seems predicated upon something that has not happened. It is simply not the case that the traditional notions of 'truth', 'rationality' and 'objective knowledge' have been swept away in the last few years – as a glance at the *Companion to Epistemology* will show (Dancy and Sosa 1992). It is true that, since Hume at least, philosophers have been wrestling with the problems inherent in scientific knowledge and that some progress seems to have been made on this problem this century. But, if we accept, for instance, that 'realist' conceptions of science are more important and influential than relativistic approaches, then the traditional searches for truth and objective knowledge in the spirit of rational enquiry are alive and well (see Newton-Smith 1981). Such searches, of course, are fallible but fallibility does not equate with *relativity*. Nor is it true that a focus on teaching, freedom and openness will, in Barnett's terms, emancipate students. If all is ideology then it is, but then Barnett's thesis is equally ideological, as are the philosophical, sociological and interdisciplinary studies which are the 'means' of emancipation.

Barnett wants Higher Education to place emancipation alongside research and its service function (to outside interests). The truth is that universities have always done this with varying degrees of success, but the notion that this should be their only aim – when students just want to study medicine or economics, and academics want to get on with research, often funded from outside – sounds dangerously like Rousseau's notion of forcing people to be free.

homosexuality   The key text here is Stafford (1988) who, very much in the spirit of liberal **education**, argues that lessons concerning homosexual preferences and practices should find a place in, say, the part of the curriculum dealing with sex education because, if they do not, we are guilty of condoning ignorance of an important fact regarding a significant portion of the population at large and the school population in particular. Homosexuality, according to Stafford, should be treated in such lessons not as a perversion, a disease or a species of moral wickedness but as a morally neutral variation in human preferences. There is little reason to believe, if we accept Stafford's arguments, that such lessons will influence anyone actually to become a homosexual – although, if Stafford is right concerning his characterisation of homosexuality, it is not clear why we should worry whether they should or not – and homosexual preferences should be explored in the 'emotional and moral context of caring relationships' (p. 47).

Two recent articles concerning this issue try to show that the situation is not quite as clear-cut as Stafford seems to think. Britzman (1995) argues that the notion of toleration that Stafford appeals to is, with its implication of moral judgement, part of the problem for homosexuality rather than part of the solution. Rooke (1993) in a very interesting article, tries to show that Stafford assumes that lesbianism and male homosexuality can be treated in the same way despite significant differences. So, for example, lesbianism suffers under the double burden of homophobia and patriarchy. And, if we think that lesbianism is, even in part, a 'political' reaction to the latter, then lessons dealing with this issue may be thought to offer pupils alternatives in a way that Stafford deemed impossible and therefore seem to be threatening to some in ways that Stafford's original proposals were not.

human nature   One of the differences between philosophy of education in the United States and in Britain is the way in which, in the former, but not in the latter, the subject is contextualised within wider concerns. Largely this has to do with the influence of Dewey within the American tradition. Because he located concerns about **education** squarely within his ideas about politics and human nature, these two areas of enquiry have always been on the agenda of politicians working within this tradition. In Britain, because of the dominance of the idea that education is self-justifying it is rare to come across any attempt to relate it to these vitally important adjuncts. It is only very recently that the political dimension of education has been discussed (see **markets**) and the part that human nature might play in education has either been taken for granted or left to the attention of educational psychologists. There are signs that this neglect is coming to an end. O'Hear (1981) tries to relate education to ideas concerning both society and human nature and, more recently, Winch (1998) tries to reclaim some of the ground that was given up to psychology.

idealism Idealism is the doctrine that reality is ultimately mental rather than physical; it is an ontological position. Absolute idealism is the doctrine that this reality unfolds in an objective manner according to the nature of the concepts which characterise it. It follows that the most progressive societies and states are those which represent the evolution of reality to an advanced degree. One of the key characteristics of this evolution is a growing self-realisation of the world-spirit, which is instantiated in the minds of individuals. Education was important for absolute idealists because they believed it brought about a greater degree of individual self-realisation. Hegel and other idealists such as Fichte were active in promoting mass education in Germany, while their followers in the UK later in the century, such as T. H. Green, were also enthusiastic promoters of educational reform, seeking to extend educational opportunities to those previously denied them (White and Gordon 1979).

Objective idealism, the doctrine that, although the mental is the ultimate reality, it has an *objective* rather than a *subjective* existence, seems to be entailed by absolute idealism. As a philosophical position it has enjoyed an independent existence predating absolute idealism through the work of Berkeley (1929) and, in the US, through Jonathan Edwards, who later influenced the **pragmatist** philosophers Peirce and James in the US (Mounce 1996). Peirce was committed to objective

truth while James developed a distinctive pragmatist doctrine. Later pragmatists, such as Dewey, and particularly Quine and Rorty, shed the earlier pragmatist idealism and adopted instead a position of ontological materialism.

ideology   It is generally accepted that an ideology is an outlook on the world. However, it is disputed as to whether or not 'ideology' is a generic term applied to *any* world-view, or whether it is of more specific application. Marx and his followers were the first systematic users of a concept of ideology, although a harbinger of the concept can be found in Vico's (1968) work, particularly on the origin of mythology. Central to the concept of Vico and Marx is the claim that humans generate systems of ideas about the nature of the world that arise out of class struggle. In Marx's writings ideologies are world-views that largely misrepresent the world as it is (Marx and Engels 1970). They arise so as to justify the interests of the dominant economic group in society. On this account, an ideology is not a *science*, which is an enterprise (like Marxism), which seeks to represent the world as it is. The contrast between science and ideology is particularly strong in the writings of Althusser (1968), one of the modern champions of scientific Marxism.

Writers who are more ambivalent about the concept of absolute, or even objective, truth tend not to make so much of the contrast between ideology and science. Gramsci (1971), for example, emphasises the persuasiveness rather than the truth of systems of ideas as a reason for their adoption. Wittgenstein (1980), although he does not use the term ideology, sees scientific research programmes like Darwinism, arise as a result of a switch in perspective on the world rather than as a result of rational and deliberate decision.

In the broad sense of the word, all educators have an 'ideology' since they conduct their activities against the background of a view of the world in general and of education in particular. In the latter case, they may subscribe to a particular view of the **aims** of **education** which then constitutes an educational ideology. This ideology may not be formally articulated in a teacher's mind but express itself as a 'commonsense' view of the world (see W. Carr 1995). An example of such an educational ideology is **progressivism**, although it should be pointed out that writers like Rousseau would have insisted that their educational prescriptions were based on a true account of human psychology. In addition there are theories relevant to education which claim to have a scientific basis (e.g. Murray and Herrnstein 1994), which is disputed by some. Finally, there are philosophically articulated normative theories of education which are justified on an *a priori* rather than an empirical basis (e.g. Egan 1986).

It is hard to avoid the conclusion that education involves ideology in one of these senses, but exactly which remains debatable. It is a matter of dispute as to whether or not education is a science or can be based on science, for example. However, debate about the nature and purpose of education, insofar as it involves the articulation of a view of the world, is bound to be not only ideological but, in a broad sense, political as well.

imagination Since Plato banished the artists from his ideal Republic on the grounds that their works tended to distort reality and teach children to feel rather than think, the cultivation of the imagination has not occupied a high place among the aims of education. Partly this has to do with its connection, Gradgrind style, with mere fancy. Partly, because **assessing** the products of the imagination is considerably more difficult than assessing the search for truth. Certainly whilst philosophy of education is replete with discussions of **knowledge** and its implications for the **curriculum** there is very little discussion of imagination and the part it might play in education.

Despite this dearth of encouragement for the education of the imagination there still occur attacks on its place in education. Meager (1981), for example, in very Platonic mode, argues that an emphasis upon the imagination will detract from the search for knowledge which is at the heart of schooling. In reply, Elliot (1981) has very little trouble showing that imagination in all its aspects must be crucial for schooling. Another defence of the place of imagination within education is to be found in Warnock (1977) where she claims that its development should be one of the key aims of education.

Both Elliot and Warnock stress the variety of forms that imagination can take. It informs our perception of the world; it is the faculty that provides meaning and value for our lives at every level; its use underpins our curiosity and wonder; it is essential not only if we want to create works of art but if we want to appreciate them. The teaching of most school subjects would be seriously impoverished if deprived of their imaginative aspects (even as 'cold' a subject as philosophy would lose immeasurably if philosophers were forbidden to 'suppose that . . .' or 'imagine how . . .'). Without the imagination, our emotional lives as well as our rationality and care for truth, would cease to function.

Given that this is so, then it is time that philosophy in general, and philosophy of education in particular paid proper attention to the scope and limits of the imagination. In the latter case this means thinking about how, given the growth of the imagination as one of the central **aims** of education, we can construct the curriculum to reflect that aim and encourage ways of assessment that, imaginatively, enable us to measure such growth.

individuality 'Individuality', which refers to the distinctness of each individual human, should be distinguished from 'individualism' which is a doctrine that prioritises the rights of individuals over social rights. The two are logically independent of each other. One can imagine a society where each individual is accorded a great many rights, yet each has no distinct personality. Likewise, one can imagine a society which exercises significant rights over individuals, each with unique personalities. An education that has, as primary aim, the cultivation of individuality, will seek to identify and develop individual abilities and interests to the maximum, without prescribing a particular form of **pedagogy**. A society based on individualism will run the education system so that individual rights are always respected as a first priority.

The protection of individual rights does not, however, guarantee the growth of individuality since social pressure may shape people's preferences, attitudes, interests and abilities so that these develop in very similar ways (but see Mill 1974). Since the rigorous protection of rights will entail **autonomy**, it is possible that individuals will all choose much the same ends in life and much the same ways of achieving them. An education that seeks to develop individuality may wish to prevent premature exposure to social pressures (e.g. peer pressure, consumerism), that lead to the inability to make meaningful choices at a more mature stage of life. While an individualist education will entail **progressive** pedagogies, an education concerned with individuality might well choose more traditional methods, at least during the early stages of education.

indoctrination The concept of indoctrination is one of the most well visited in the area of philosophy of education. This is partly because the notion of indoctrination is used either implicitly or explicitly to contrast with education and the proper processes of **teaching** and **learning**, and partly, we suspect, because the concept was a useful one during the period of the Cold War to contrast schooling in the West, concerned with education, with schooling in the Soviet Bloc, concerned with indoctrination.

All commentators on indoctrination identify it as a species of teaching and take it that the term has pejorative overtones. However, when it comes to precisely identifying the set of necessary and sufficient conditions which function as criteria for the use of the term there are major differences of opinion.

The first major contributors in the field (J. Wilson 1964; Flew 1966; Peters 1966), whilst acknowledging the role that the intention or aim of the teacher might play in characterising indoctrination and realising the importance of the method of teaching, argued that the crucial criterion was the content of what was taught. Indoctrination, according to these theorists, essentially consisted of the passing on of doctrines. Whilst there seemed to be no difficulty in indicating examples of doctrines: Communism and Roman Catholicism were favourite examples; there was difficulty (Gregory and Woods 1970; Gribble 1969) in providing a definition of doctrine which would enable us to pinpoint all and only the material thought to be offensive. So, for instance the notions that doctrines are 'not known to be true or false' (Gregory and Woods 1970) or rest upon assumptions that are either 'false, or which cannot publicly be shown to be true' (Gribble 1969) seems to include within the doctrinal completely inoffensive material to do with everyday beliefs or the foundational beliefs of some subjects such as science.

These difficulties and the fact that there are obviously non-indoctrinatory ways of passing on information about doctrines and practices which seemed, at the very least, similar to indoctrination without involving doctrines (J. P. White 1967) led to the next movement in the field. This argued that it was not content or method that was crucial but the intention or aim of the teacher. Again, there was argument as to how precisely to characterise the key intention with probably the best characterisation being offered by Snook: 'A person indoctrinates P (a proposition or set of propositions) if he teaches with the intention that the pupil or pupils believe P regardless of the evidence' (Snook 1972b).

The rather comfortable idea that if one did not have this intention it was impossible to indoctrinate was rejected by some theorists (Kleinig, Beehler) who pointed out that, in some circumstances it seems perfectly possible to talk about unintentional indoctrination and that one may have the key intention and yet fail to indoctrinate. Rather than aim or intention these writers wished to emphasise the outcome of indoctrination, such as the fact that indoctrinated people exhibited a 'closed' mind with regard to the material in question.

While the arguments that the outcome theorists mounted against taking intention as the key to indoctrination were often persuasive, and whilst they pertinently drew attention to the underlying and often unexamined beliefs that seem to underpin liberal education in the western world; they did not seem to face explicitly earlier criticisms that have been made (Snook 1972b) concerning the identification of indoctrination in terms of outcome. These are that whilst 'closed' minds may be a result of indoctrination there are other things (e.g. lack of intelligence, emotional incapacity) which may also result in having a 'closed' mind. Also, given that indoctrination is a process, it surely must be possible for someone to go through the process but to resist the outcome and to end up with an open mind. If these points are correct then an identification of indoctrination solely in terms of outcome must be insufficient.

While theorists in the analytic tradition have concentrated upon content, intention and outcome as criteria for indoctrination, sometimes taken in isolation but sometimes take together (Woods and Barrow 1975), in America there has been much emphasis on the method of teaching as a criterion. This is due partly to the continuing influence of Dewey's philosophy, partly to a wish to write into the concept of teaching some restriction upon the methods used (Scheffler 1973, Martin 1967). The method criterion has been roundly criticised by analytic philosophers, first, because methods of teaching cannot be separated from the content of what is taught. Second, because the notion of isolating the particular method in use in a classroom over any period of time seems fraught with difficulties. Third, because if the methods involved are to be non-rational in some way, then we cannot avoid using them with very young children. Such objections are supposed (Snook 1972b) to indicate that method is not a sufficient criterion of indoctrination. That they are not a necessary criterion is shown by the fact any competent indoctrinator must, at least some of the time, make use of the type of methods such as the use of argument and discussion, used by any good teacher (ibid.). Whether such arguments are really destructive of the method criterion or whether they simply call for added care in any future work is, we think, an open question.

inspection   Inspection should be distinguished from **advising** which, as Hobbes pointed out (1968), involves the giving of counsel which may be ignored. Inspection involves making a normative judgement on the worthwhileness of a school or an educational activity by someone in a position of **authority** (C. Winch 1996). It is an important instrument of **accountability**. Inspectors, then, mainly assess the quality of **pedagogy** and whether the practice in the school is good. The question arises as to what norms these judgements are derived from. Ideally, they should be related to whether or not an inspected educational practice serves the **aims** of the education system. There is a danger that inspectorial judgements will be subjective if the norms are personally held values of inspectors, only loosely related to the aims of the system. The problem does not disappear if the intersubjective agreement of a group of inspectors fails to relate to aims.

A solution adopted in the UK is to train inspectors to use a governmentally designed normative instrument (OFSTED 1994). Close inspection of this instrument suggests that, in the central area of pedagogy, the norms give way to subjective inspectorial agreements as to the quality of educational processes (Maw 1995), so that the underlying problem is not addressed. There is, in any case, a tension between an accountability system that emphasises *outcomes* as a criterion of effectiveness and one which emphasises *processes*. If a process is worthwhile to the extent that it leads to desirable outcomes, then it is hard to see what is gained by judging the process rather than the outcome. One could see a role for the identification of faulty processes and subsequent advice on how to rectify them, but this would not be inspection.

instrumentalism   Instrumentally-oriented **education** sees it as a means to an extrinsic **aim**. Many liberal educators see the aim of education as intrinsic, that is, its pursuit is a self-fulfilling aim, valuable in its own right (Peters 1966). Instrumentalism should not be confused with **vocationalism**, which is a particular form, concerned with education as preparation for work. Other instrumental aims include preparation for citizenship or parenthood, or the maintenance of a cultural tradition (Bantock 1965). It should be evident from this list that, although instrumentalism is, in pure form, quite different to liberal approaches, it is not incompatible with them.

For example, those attitudes, virtues, values and items of knowledge that might be thought necessary for a good citizen may well have a lot in common with what a liberal educator would wish for. There is, therefore, no philosophical problem about formally reconciling the two. There is a problem about reconciling them in practice, since there are real questions about the relative weighting of instrumental and practical aspects of education. For example, an educator more concerned with developing parenting skills than with developing the virtues of patience, caring, etc. *in general*, may well wish to place different emphases in the curriculum to a liberal educator. There are then, real points of difference about the implementation of instrumental aims within a broadly liberal context which may be difficult to resolve (C. Winch 1996). The resolution of such difficulties through toleration and the ability to compromise is, however a proper part of democratic educational practice.

intelligence   There are two problems of educational and philosophical interest with regard to intelligence: (1) Are human abilities unitary or diverse? (2) Are they determined by heredity, environment or a mixture of both?

The idea that they are largely unitary and fixed at birth can be traced back, with some modifications, to Plato who thought that there were three qualities of the soul, which were largely determined at birth. The highest of these was rationality, which only a few possessed to any great degree. Proper endowment at birth was a necessary condition of achieving its full flowering which could occur, however, only after long and arduous study.

Modern preoccupations with intelligence can be found in the work of Galton and others in the nineteenth century which followed the ideas of Plato quite closely. Galton believed that intelligence was inherited, unevenly distributed and unitary, a kind of mental analogy with physical strength. Galton's ideas were developed into the science of intelligence testing, pioneered by Binet, Spearman, Terman and Burt. Many intelligence testers assume that there is unitary quality of intelligence (*g*), others, like Burt saw intelligence as a hierarchical concept with *g* at the top of the hierarchy. Others again, like Thurstone, thought that intelligence was multifactorial, composed of several different key attributes not organised hierarchically. The idea of 'multiple intelligences' has been championed in the 1980s and 1990s by Gardner (1993), although in a very different form from that proposed by Thurstone (1957). The ideas of Spearman and his followers were developed mathematically through a technique known as 'factor analysis' which, according to different interpretations, indicated one of the three alternatives outlined above. The crucial move was, however, to assume that, behind the correlational techniques of factor analysis lay real mental entities. By correlating mental test results with genetically related and diverse subjects and by testing at different ages, it was claimed that intelligence as a real entity was (a) largely genetically determined, (b) varied little with age and (c) was differentially distributed in different class and ethnic groups.

The hereditarian thesis of innate, invariant and hierarchical or unitary intelligence has been highly influential in the UK (where it contributed to the methodology of the 11+ examination for academic selection) and in the US (where it contributed to theories of racial differences in intellectual ability, notably through the work of Jensen, Murray and Herrnstein). Intelligence theory has been criticised from both empirical and philosophical points of view. Its proponents have variously been accused of data suppression, manipulation, biased interpretation of factor analysis and illegitimate extrapolation from factor data to the existence of a real mental entity of general intelligence. A good summary of the criticisms can be found in Gould (1981).

The philosophical critique of the general intelligence thesis is supplementary to the empirical criticisms mustered by

Gould and others, but takes a different path. Writers like White (1974) and Ryle (1974) have objected that the way in which we talk about human ability is not as a general factor, but as an enormous range of diverse abilities which are related to each other in various complicated ways. It is a grammatical feature of the use of such expressions as '*A* is able at . . .' that they need to be completed by some activity, such as 'calculating', 'debating', 'writing poetry' or 'swimming'. It is, therefore, nonsense to describe someone as 'able' or 'intelligent' without specifying at *what* they are able or intelligent. Insofar as the terms are used intransitively it is as an ellipsis. Given this diversity, it is a distortion to describe ability or intelligence either as a general factor or small group of factors or as having a real existence in the human nervous system. All that we know of human abilities is contained within that diversity. In order to find out what people are good at we should not test their intelligence through a test (which only tells us how good they are at intelligence tests) but through an examination of their progress at different activities.

Philosophical objections have also been raised to the claim that intelligence is determined and invariant. It might be thought that if the concept of general intelligence is incoherent this might be unnecessary since something that *could* not exist would *a fortiori* be incapable of possessing any attributes. It is thought, nevertheless that there are important conceptual connections between the concepts of *ability*, *curiosity*, **motivation**, *effort*, *encouragement* and *interest* which it is important to emphasise if we wish to understand the conceptual geography of our talk about human ability. One who has done this is Howe (1990) who, although his main concern has been with exceptional ability or **giftedness**, has drawn attention to the relationship of these concepts and to the real interaction of the factors expressed by these concepts in the genesis and development of ability. Howe has also drawn attention to the fact that some abilities are highly valued at some times and places more than at others, and that these culturally determined variations are also important to our assessment of the worth of an individual's activity. According to this approach, not only should we use the concepts mentioned above as ways of making inferences about the development of abilities but that we should regard these concepts as the main or even only access that we have to understanding the genesis and development of abilities. The problem, on this view, is that we fail to see what is in front of us while pursuing a reification which seems plausible almost through a quirk of language (C. Winch 1990).

Disputes between the various schools of thought concerning ability continue, but increasing attention is being paid to non-experimental work which attempts to explore the relationships between cultural attitude, motivation and achievement in order to see whether ability is as invariant as the proponents of intelligence theory allege. It is quite plausible to suggest that cross-cultural comparisons and the need to compete with emerging powerful economies may bring about a re-evaluation of the influential western notion that nature has endowed us with our abilities at birth and that there is little that we can do to change them.

J

judgement Judgement is a mental act and one may wonder how such an ability may be taught, given its apparent 'inner' quality. Geach's (1957) account of mental acts may help. This suggests that they are *analogical extensions* of verbal acts. They get their sense from the prior public practice of asserting, questioning, commanding and so on. Geach's account has a lot in common with Vygotsky's (1962) description of the genesis of inner thought. According to Geach's account, an act of judgement is an analogical extension of the verbal act of assertion.

Geach offers an account of concepts as abilities exercised in acts of assertion (and other linguistic acts) and, by extension, in acts of judgement (and other mental acts) which are themselves construed as abilities to follow the rules governing the use of concept-words in concrete practical situations. Geach's account of **concept formation** is thus one of learning, through practice and different forms of social encounter, the application of concept-words, at first in public and later in non-discursive acts of judgement and so on. This account of the social genesis of judgement is somewhat at odds with other influential theories such as that of Piaget, which suppose that the inner mental life is prior to discursive mental acts. **Cognitivist** thinkers such as Chomsky also suppose that some form of judgement, albeit of a non-conscious variety, underpins our ability to make ordinary judgements.

On the socially-based accounts of Geach and Vygotsky, an account of **learning** can take shape, which takes seriously the social nature of human beings.

justice   Questions concerning the nature of justice are among the most important and fiercely contested raised in moral and political philosophy since its inception. They have lately come to the fore again because of the work of philosophers such as Rawls (1971, 1993) and Nozick (1974). Unfortunately, different conceptions of justice seem to be at work in different social contexts so, for instance, someone might be happy with an outcome or end-state conception, for example, a utilitarian, when it comes to the distribution of property, but profoundly unhappy with this conception if it was used to allocate jobs or legal penalties. Justice as impartial treatment seems to work well in some parts of the legal process, say, trials, but seems to need supplementing by justice as desert, when it comes to **punishment**.

In **education** the same problems arise. The areas of education where questions of justice are relevant are many and various and, as in social life generally, one conception does not seem to fit all areas. Justice, for instance, is relevant in **assessment** but awarding marks in terms of some favoured end-state, say, that everybody passes, would seem to most people manifestly unjust. Children have a right to be treated impartially by our education system but they also have a right to their just deserts. It may be the case in education – again as in life generally – that we cannot distil one notion of justice to fit every possible context and that we need different notions to do different jobs (see Winch 1996: esp. ch. 10).

justification   Justifying something is providing sufficient grounds (see **definition**) for its truth, rightness or appropriateness. As far as **education** is concerned, such justification can work on several levels. One may attempt to justify statements within a discipline, or pursuit of the discipline itself; or one may try to justify a particular curriculum or the manner and matter of schooling. It is important to see that justification goes beyond the simple giving of reasons. It is concerned with the provision of compelling reasons. (Too often, for instance, people who give a reason for, say, the study of a particular subject think they have provided a justification. But this, typically, involves not merely a consideration of this subject but an examination of it in the context of all the subjects that might be on offer and the constraints that effect curriculum choice.) It is also important to realise that justification, at least as it is concerned with practical matters, is always justification for someone. That is, that it assumes both a context and a person working within that context that has certain characteristics (e.g. *interests* (in both senses), capacities, purposes). All that this means is that one cannot, say, justify the study of art history for the blind or the study of tracking for the modern urban dweller.

Given **education**'s role in our lives one would expect its justification to loom large in the literature and for this to be examined at every level. In fact, this is far from the case. Until very recently, for instance, the political aspects of education such as, 'Why should a democratic state provide a schooling system of the sort that is provided and compel children to take part in it?', have been all but ignored. Such questions are simply not addressed in pointing out, say, that *education* involves the initiation into intrinsically worthwhile activities; for this may be true but provide no reason for state expenditure or compulsion.

In the tradition of liberal education most attempts at justification have been curiously bloodless affairs, which might persuade an Oxford Don that his choice of career was worthwhile but would do little to reassure a cynical civil servant or the concerned parent of an average ability child (see Peters 1973 and Elliot 1977).

Indeed, apart from some **utilitarians**, who at least appeal to something that seems to be self-justifying such as happiness (see Barrow 1976) and at the same time connects education to life after education, there are few attempts to connect education to what most people would consider as everyday life.

Given that a public education system is likely to have several functions: the transmission of the major values in a society and its cultural heritage; the transformation of children into individuals who can function with a large degree of efficiency and contentment within the particular society; the under-pinning and servicing of the economic functions of society; it is likely that education will be over-justified. However, this does not mean that a consideration still does not have to be given to particular justifications. But it does mean that we have to have some justification for relative priority and some ways of ensuring that particular interest groups with partial perspectives do not hijack the discussion and implementation of educational **aims**.

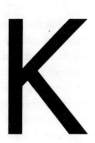

knowledge For most people, the idea that pupils being educated should end up being expected to know more at the end of the process than they did at the beginning, would be a non-negotiable demand. If this is so, then the delineation of the scope and limits of knowledge must be central concerns for any theory of education. Since Plato in the *Republic* argued for a conception of education which takes knowledge and coming to know as its central themes, these have been prime concerns for philosophy of education. Such a focus upon knowledge and the place it might play in the curriculum, need not exclude other criteria for educational choice (Frankena 1970) nor need it turn aside questions concerning the worthwhileness of the pursuit of knowledge for its own sake (Illich 1971, Kleinig 1982 and Martin 1993).

In the western philosophical tradition the most influential account of knowledge derives from the classical Greek philosophers. In this account, for something to be an item of knowledge it must satisfy three conditions. First, it must be believed. Second, there must be a good reason for the belief – to distinguish a real knowledge claim from a mere lucky guess. Third, whatever is claimed as knowledge must, in fact, be true. This traditional account of knowledge – and especially its second condition – has recently come under heavy attack (see Everitt and Fisher 1996: ch. 2). However, philosophers concerned with the theory of knowledge usually wish to somehow rescue the account rather than repudiate it. Coming to have knowledge, on this account, is a process of acquiring rationally justified true beliefs and it is this model which has dominated educational concern in Great Britain. In America, the situation is rather different. Dewey repudiated many of the dichotomies taken for granted in the western philosophical tradition such as reason and emotion, fact and value; and one of the dichotomies dispensed with was that between a theoretical account of knowledge based on the Greek model and knowledge as displayed in practical performances. However, whilst Dewey has always been influential within American education, such influence did not spread, until recently, into the work of mainstream philosophers who retained their belief in the Greek model.

In Britain an emphasis on practice was part of the focus of Ryle's (1949) work. Whilst Ryle accepted that much knowledge is propositional (that is, knowledge of true propositions), he questioned whether an account which emphasised the classical model really dealt with much that we classify as knowledge. As well as knowledge of facts (knowing that something is the case), he argued that there was also procedural knowledge or knowing how to do something, and that such knowledge, whilst extremely important, is both not reducible to factual knowledge and is essentially a matter of practice rather than theory. Thus, someone may know how to ride a bicycle or how to swim and such knowledge cannot be reduced to any set of facts that they know about the activity in question (e.g. that the pedals drive the back wheel), and such knowledge is properly demonstrated – and tested – not by any theoretical exercise like a written exam on swimming, but within the practice of the activity in question. In his later work on **intelligence**, Ryle extended this emphasis on the practical, pointing out that theorising was itself a practice that could be done intelligently or unintelligently and that knowledge in academic subjects such as history was not a question of the store of facts that a student acquired but also, and perhaps more importantly, the student's display of know-how in the organisation of such facts.

The focus on practice emphasised by Dewey and Ryle has been influential within disciplines, so for instance, National Curriculum documents in England insist that students develop skills (know-how) as well as learning facts. However, the extent of the radical challenge that these two thinkers pose for **curriculum** planning has not yet been fully appreciated. If we repudiate, as both did, the importance of the theoretical and acknowledge that procedural knowledge has at least as great an epistemological status as knowledge of truths, then a curriculum based upon the acquisition of knowledge suddenly has an enormous scope; everything from bedmaking through to astrophysics, and the distinction between the academic and the practical which has traditionally provided the narrow focus of the curriculum has to be abandoned.

Such an opening up of curriculum debate has only recently happened (e.g. Pring 1995; C. Winch 1996). Instead, in Britain the most influential account of education based upon a philosophical position concerning the nature of knowledge has been that developed over thirty years, associated with the work of Hirst. In the paper in which he first introduced this account (Hirst 1965a) – he begins with an examination of Greek thought about knowledge and education. Although obviously sympathetic, Hirst rejects it for its unacceptable metaphysical implications. However, his own theory retains the close conceptual relationship that the Greeks discerned between the development of the rational mind and the nature of knowledge. For Hirst, to think rationally at all, is to think in ways determined by sets of conceptual schemata that have been progressively developed over the centuries. Such schemata not only incorporated criteria for the correct use of terms within the schemata but they also throw up ways in which forms of expression within the schemata such as statements, can be tested against experience to determine whether they are true or false. The schemata thereby delineate the different 'forms of knowledge'. In this first paper Hirst identified the forms of knowledge as 'mathematics, physical sciences, human sciences, history, religion, literature and the fine arts, philosophy, morals' (Hirst 1965a). He subsequently amended this list (see below). The criteria for determining that these are *the* forms of knowledge are that: (a) each of these has central concepts that are peculiar to the form (for example, gravity and acceleration in science, God and sin in religion, good and wrong in moral knowledge); (b) each has a distinctive logical structure, that is, forms of argument and verification; (c) each has expressions that are, in some way, testable against experience; and (d) each has its own methodology. (This last criterion was soon merged with (c).) Although, according to Hirst, the eight forms of knowledge are *the* bases of rational thought and therefore the basis of any education which aims to develop the rational mind, it does not follow that they necessarily have to present themselves on a **curriculum** in this pure form; for instance, they may be organised in terms of 'fields of knowledge' which incorporate two or more forms, for example, geography with its roots in both the physical and human sciences.

The forms of knowledge thesis not only seems to provide a neat basis for an *academic* curriculum – Hirst has never insisted that these are the only things that should go on in schools – but, because of its genesis, a justification for the study of such a curriculum. For, if Hirst is correct, given that the forms of knowledge are the articulation of what it is to have a rational mind, then any attempt at rational justification for a curriculum must simply presuppose the forms. Thus, the study of the forms is justified by a **transcendental argument**.

The 'forms of knowledge' thesis immediately attracted attention. Some seemed concerned with the details of the thesis (e.g. Brent 1978). Some reactions were more robustly critical. A particular focus was the presence within the eight original forms of areas which have long been battlegrounds in terms of cognitive status. Thus, for two hundred years, the claims of morality and religion to provide us with knowledge have been seriously disputed (e.g. Mackie 1977, 1982). Ironically, Hirst himself, in a paper published the same year as he introduced the forms of knowledge thesis (Hirst 1965b) – questioned whether religion met the testability and truth criterion for a form of knowledge (and in an appendix added later, doubted whether it met the meaning criterion). But the most potent criticism was addressed to the notion that literature and the fine arts constitute a form of knowledge, especially as it became clear with Hirst's further writings (Hirst 1973a) that it was not the statements of artistic criticism, for example '*Macbeth* is a more unified play than *King Lear*', which were thought to be the bearers of truth, but, in fact, works of art themselves so that paintings, concertos, sculptures, poems, could be true or false and known to be so. Some critics reacted to this claim with simple incredulity (Barrow 1976) others, whilst equally critical of the notion, showed a more measured approach (Gingell 1985).

What often was not noticed in many of the critical commentaries upon Hirst's thesis were certain ideas of Hirst concerning meaning and truth which both explain and necessitate the 'forms of knowledge' thesis. According to Hirst the meaning of terms is established by the agreement among people to use a certain mark or sound in a certain context – for example, to use 'cat' to refer to small, furry, feline creatures. But such an agreement on the meaning of a term must bring with it an agreement as to when the term is properly applied or not. The meaning of 'This is a cat' can only be established by agreement when the term is truly applied to a cat. Thus agreement brings meaning and meaning brings truth (Hirst 1973a). If this is so then any system of conventionally agreed signs must generate both meaning and truth and thus must establish the grounds for knowledge. And it is certainly the case that literature and the fine arts, religion, morality, as well as science and mathematics are such systems.

However, if this overall theory is to be shown to be sound, at least two things have to be done. First, the counter-intuitive notion that artefacts such as paintings and concertos are really the bearers of propositional content has to be established in the face of considerable and substantial criticism (Beardsley 1958). Because, if a general theory leads to an absurd conclusion then it must be the case that the theory is absurd. Second, it has to be shown that the type of agreements envisaged by Hirst cannot generate systematically misleading realms of discourse in which there is the *appearance* or truths but, in fact, no truth. Because, if such realms of discourse are possible then any of the individual forms may be such a realm and it would have to be established, form by form, that what we have is the real thing and not a forgery. Again, there is substantial literature within philosophy which claims that certain of the putative forms, for example, morality and religion, are exactly such forgeries (Mackie 1977; Nielson 1971). However it is not the case that the individual forms have been defended against such attacks.

Hirst's theory of knowledge, whilst novel in some ways, accepts certain of the presuppositions which have characterised the treatment of this concept over the centuries. The most important of these is that knowledge has a necessary connection to truth and, because of this, achieving knowledge is, essentially, a theoretical activity, that is, it is a question of acquiring more and more truths independently of doing anything with the truths acquired. However, Hirst, without acknowledging the work of Ryle, has cast doubt on his earlier position and the neat answers it provided for curriculum choice, and instead put forward an account which emphasises know-how and cultural transmission (Hirst 1993). Thus schools should be in the business of passing on the valued knowledge – theoretical *and* practical – of the cultures they inhabit. The cultural transmission condition is important because it provides some limit for choice within the myriad forms of know-how, which could possibly be developed. Certainly, such a suggestion is to be welcomed if we are to move away from the theoretical bias which has bedevilled our education system and provide education which serves the talents and interests of *all* our children. But developing curricula along these lines has yet to be done. The work involves arguments, yet to come, which enable us to identify such valued knowledge and plot the process of such cultural transmission.

L

leadership Whether education needs leadership is disputed. Weber's typology of traditional, charismatic and rational–legal forms of authority is a useful place to start. Modern public education necessarily takes place within bureaucratic, rather than traditional structures and it is undeniable that, at some level, there have to be such structures accountable, at some levels, to democratic authorities. The interesting question for schools and universities is whether or not authority for educational leadership should be collective or individual and whether it can allow any room for charismatic leadership. It is relatively easy to see how a form of charismatic personal leadership could exist within the constraints of bureaucratic accountability. Admittedly, such a leader would not have the scope that the founders of innovative educational movements had for radical innovation in **pedagogy** and **curriculum**, but there is much that a leader can do in raising expectations and morale amongst students and staff through a moral rhetoric of idealism and improvement.

Collegiate leadership is not so common in public school systems. Where colleagues regard themselves as equals, it might be difficult for an individual leader to emerge. It might be argued that school leadership requires someone who embodies a certain amount of charisma and that collegiate governance is ill-suited to the emergence of such a person. To the extent that charisma is needed for effective school leadership and to the extent that collegiality works against it, there is a challenge for the advocates of democratic worker democracy in school governance (Mortimore *et al.* 1988; White and Barber 1997).

learning Learning is fundamental to education. Much thinking about it has, in recent years, come from a psychological perspective. Philosophical reflection about learning has, to a large extent, marched in step with one of the most influential accounts of the human mind, **cognitivism**, but there have been exceptions, the most noteworthy of these being Hamlyn (1978) and, more recently, C. Winch (1998).

Following Ryle (1949), one can distinguish between two senses of a concept like *learning*. The first is the *task* sense; when I say that I am learning German, I mean that I do not yet grasp the language, but the grasping of German is what I am undertaking. When, on the other hand, I say that I have learned German, I am speaking in the *achievement* sense; I have succeeded in learning German. Usually context and the use of tense, present for task and past for achievement, mark the difference between these two senses. Educators are interested in learning in both these senses, they want to know what makes a successful process and they want to know when an outcome is achieved.

There is a conceptual connection between learning and **teaching** in the sense that if I have successfully taught something (achievement), then someone has been learning something (task). It does not follow that if I have taught in the task sense then someone has learned either in the task or the achievement sense. It is, for example, possible for a vigorous and successful teacher to have an incorrigible daydreamer in her class. Learning can also take place without any teaching. Those who are self-taught, for example, have not needed any other person than themselves to enable them to learn. This may, however, be too simple. So far it has been taken for granted that teaching is an intentional process. While this is mostly true, one can also teach unintentionally by, for example, writing a book and accidentally leaving it open for someone to read. More broadly, even the self-taught have to make use of materials provided by others in order to acquire the skills and knowledge they seek. Even if these materials were provided intentionally, the provider, if he is deceased could not intentionally be teaching that person, although there is a sense in which he *is* teaching. These points should make us cautious about the idea that learning can be completely divorced from teaching and that it can take place outside the medium of society, even when it is self-directed.

If learning has taken place in the achievement sense, then something has been learned. But how does one establish this? The most common approach is through a form of **assessment** in which the learner is asked to demonstrate her skill or knowledge. Given that, it seems to follow from the fact that X has learned (achievement) that p, that X can in some way demonstrate the knowledge that p. If there are no conceivable circumstances in which this could be shown, then one has no way of assessing the truth of the claim. It seems, therefore, that just as teaching and learning are closely related concepts, so are learning and assessment.

If one could establish general principles as to how people learned then it should be possible to generate pedagogical approaches which would facilitate successful learning. The twentieth century has seen a flowering of such theories ranging from **behaviourism** to **cognitivism**. While some of these are partially complementary, they are very often incompatible, even before the truth of any of them has been established. In other words, it is quite likely that most learning theories are contraries, they may be jointly false but not jointly true. This poses a large dilemma for educators, including self-educators. On the one hand they may adopt a learning theory as a basis for pedagogy and take the risk that it is partially or wholly false, or they may dispense with theory altogether and take the risk that any gains that might be achieved by a systematic approach will be lost. It is no wonder that learning theories have enjoyed such popularity, because, whatever the risks, their purveyors have always been clear and often eloquent about their truth. Their popularity has also been due to the prestige of scientific explanations, particularly those that aim for a high degree of generality. It is at least conceivable, however, that the search for a high degree of generality in the explanation of how humans learn is misplaced (C. Winch 1998). One criticism of the scientific approach is that it systematically undervalues social and affective aspects of learning (Alexander 1984). Despite their popularity and the influence which they have given to psychology, it may be that the claims of learning theories are due for a radical reassessment.

The dilemma mentioned above may be a false one. While comprehensive theories about learning may be of dubious value, it does not follow that more modest theories, that take into account particular circumstances, and which are cautious about generalising, are of no value. If our knowledge about human learning is necessarily bound by human circumstance and history, then accounts of how people learn will have to follow those contours. But educators are bound by human circumstance and history and they have to work within particular situations. If they can be reliably informed about approaches that are likely to be successful in their historical and social contexts, then they will be much better off than remaining either in ignorance or in error.

Beyond this, can any general points be made about human learning? Those who argue that it is social, affective and dependent on circumstance are themselves making a kind of generalisation. But even they, it could be argued, might be missing something easily missed in the scientific temper of our times, namely the possibility that there is an element that is utterly mysterious about our ability to learn, something that is hinted at in our everyday understanding of the power of love to transform both the lover and the object that is loved. If we fail to grasp this, it might be argued, we fail to understand how learning is also concerned with the pursuit of excellence or perfection. One needs to go back to Plato for such an insight.

leisure   The notion that education should be a preparation for a life of leisure seems suited to the children of the wealthy or the aristocracy; it hardly seems to be relevant to the needs of students in public school systems. However, J. P. White (1990, 1997b) has argued that education should prepare students for a life in which paid employment will be relatively unimportant and leisure relatively important. The lack of paid employment does not necessarily imply the availability of leisure, as domestic workers will testify. Furthermore, there are great difficulties in specifying what leisure, as opposed to the absence of paid employment, is. These difficulties parallel those faced in defining **play**. White's attempt to define leisure activities in terms of their lack of outcome seems open to the same objections to the definition of play in such terms by Dearden (1968). Put briefly, there are many activities, such as hobbies, normally considered to be part of leisure, which involve an outcome.

It is more helpful to make a map of human activity and to identify those areas which are inadequately catered for in current education. Many of these activities will involve effort and the striving for excellence. Others will involve a response to social pressure to do well in the pursuit of common projects. In many ways the skills and qualities required will overlap with those required by paid employment. Education for leisure may not be as different from education for work as might be supposed at first glance.

liberation   The idea that education leads to freedom from **oppression** is a popular one. Education for liberation can be contrasted with **indoctrination**. It can take various forms, the most significant of which concern personal liberation on the one hand and social or political liberation on the other. The former, particularly attractive to **feminism** and other theories of personal oppression, seeks to develop education in the direction of strong **autonomy**.

Social and political liberationists place the emphasis some-what differently. Following the work of Freire (1972) they emphasise the importance of education in responding to the needs of communities and to the need for communities to win autonomy for themselves. As such, they are as concerned with adult as with child education, since it is only through the education and radicalisation of adults that the liberation project becomes possible. Radical liberationists often see themselves working in a **Marxist** tradition, but their main emphasis is usually on quite radical forms of egalitarianism. **Equality** is seen as the only sure way of eliminating oppression. The more conservative type of liberation theory, perhaps best represented in the work of Gramsci (1971) (also Marxist in inspiration), suggests that the existing culture has first to be appropriated before it can be overcome and that, perhaps, a conservative pedagogy and curriculum may be the best way of achieving this. Liberation ideas have had an influence on adult theories of learning such as **open learning** and andragogy.

literacy 'Literacy' is the term for the ability to read and write. It is thought by many to be, together with numeracy, a foundation for a modern civilisation. As such, it is thought to be a fundamental duty for schools to make students literate (Letwin 1988). In one sense, the claim that our civilisation rests on literacy is self-evident; we all have to use it to conduct our daily lives. But the claim is also made that the advent of literacy changes the nature of civilisation itself (e.g. Goody and Watt 1972). The permanence of writing, it is argued, allows a collective memory to be built up, which in turn permits the development of history, science and literature. Even logic and hence **rationality**, is said to be dependent on writing, since it is only in writing that arguments can be set down in an explicit form. Implicit reasoning of the kind used in spoken argument and conversation is not properly reasoning as it is not fully articulated (Olson 1977, 1994). These claims have been challenged. It has been argued that the experimental method predates literacy by thousands of years (Levi-Strauss 1966), that literature exists in non-literate societies (Finnegan 1973) and that implicit reasoning is still reasoning (C. Winch 1983). Even if the claims of writers like Olson are rejected it still does not follow that literacy is of no importance because it can be argued that *our* civilisation is literacy-dependent, even if it doesn't embody a superior rationality to non-literate cultures.

In recent years some critics of contemporary schooling in the US and the UK have accused schools of failing to accomplish their basic duties of imparting literacy. Psycholinguistic methods of teaching literacy associated with, among others F. Smith (1985), stress student autonomy and interpret accuracy in a fashion influenced by **pragmatist** accounts of **truth**. It is argued that the adoption of these methods leads to illiteracy and the growth of dyslexia (M. Phillips 1996). Some commentators have called for an increasing emphasis on sound–symbol correspondence and an exploitation of the alphabetic nature of our script as a way of ensuring that standards are maintained (Bryant and Bradley 1985).

Others have argued that we are entering an age of post-literacy, where electronic media will render the need to communicate through speech and writing unnecessary (Postman 1970). This argument largely ignores the tendency of users of electronic media to continue to employ literacy, albeit in combination with graphics. In many ways, electronic media exploit tendencies that are not fully available in paper-based literacy for example, through the development of hypertext. Nevertheless, a continuing emphasis on student autonomy together with scepticism about the efficacy of methods of teaching that rely on instruction and **training** (as most phonological approaches do) will continue to mean that many teachers and students are likely to remain resistant to the attractions of literacy, if not in the elementary school then in later years when the availability of communicative media other than literacy becomes greater. Literacy will continue to be contested as the touchstone of success for public schooling systems.

markets Education can be regarded as either a private or a
public good or, possibly, a combination of both. Some of
those who think that **education** primarily benefits individuals
rather than society take the view that it is best supplied
through a market mechanism. Markets consist of buyers and
sellers of commodities and in an educational market the
suppliers of education will sell it as a commodity which
provides benefits to individuals. The *public* benefits of education are, on this view, a by-product of the successful provision
of education to individuals. Parents and students will see that
education is in their or their children's interests and will act
accordingly. Furthermore, education provided by markets
allows more choice and also the right of exit if a consumer
is dissatisfied with what is offered by a producer. A further
advantage of market-provided education is that the risk that
public providers will do so at their own convenience rather
than at that of the consumer, is thereby avoided (see A. Smith
1981). Advocates of this approach include Chubb and Moe
(1990) and Tooley (1995).

Opponents of markets in education tend to argue (a) that
education is more of a public than a private good (e.g. Grace
1989), (b) that education is not a commodity and (c) that
attempts to provide education through a market mechanism
result in failure (e.g. Jonathan 1990). It is difficult to provide
public goods through markets because their benefits are

138

distributed to the public rather than to individual purchasers. The fact that the benefits of education are widely distributed leads to a related problem, namely that people may withhold purchasing education in the knowledge that they will be able to enjoy the purchases made by others. Since everyone will reach the same conclusion, nobody will be inclined to purchase and no one will be educated. This is an example of the free rider problem in game theory. For those who hold that education is a pure private or positional good and is desirable, this does not pose a problem. For those who do not find it desirable, either for themselves or their children, there is no inclination to purchase education. But if this is so, then some will go uneducated. This is a problem for those who hold that the market can do just as good a job as the state in providing universal education. Consideration of education as both a private and a public good leads anti-marketeers to say that the universal provision of education needs both an element of compulsion and a degree of central provision in order to correct the tendencies of markets to ignore non-purchasers or those who are ignorant or short-sighted.

However, it does not follow that, if one rejects the *central* role of markets in educational provision that they do not have some role to play. It may be, for example, that post-compulsory education is best provided for by a market mechanism, or that certain kinds of services like advice or catering are best provided in this way. Another approach advocated by some who are sympathetic to the role of markets is to create a *quasi-market*, in which the State provides funding but obliges suppliers to compete with each other on quality and price. At a certain point in practical policy-making, the arguments shift from ideology to detail.

Marxism   The Marxist educational heritage is complex. On the one hand, some Marxists see education as a potential means of proletarian emancipation. Others see it as a means of maintaining capitalism and hence of actual **oppression**. This is the substance of many Marxist critiques of education

(Bowles and Gintis 1976; but see also K. Harris 1979; Kleinig 1982). The picture of education under capitalism given by such writers is largely negative. It is only through subversion of the existing system that emancipation of the proletariat can take place.

However, the important Italian Marxist Gramsci's (1971) work on education suggests that it provides skills necessary for adult independence and the intellectual tools with which to develop alternative forms of proletarian **common sense**. Gramsci was suspicious of **progressivism** because he feared that it would deprive workers' children of such preparation and, through excessive concentration on **practical activity**, would develop a narrow vocational outlook. Gramsci advocated the polytechnical view of education that later came to prevail in many of the communist states. Polytechnicism advocates a broad preparation for work and citizenship, combining a broad curriculum for all with a strong sense of the future role of the citizen in the world of work.

Marxist practice has been broadly true to the polytechnical ideal with one important qualification. The public education systems of the Soviet Union and her satellites were strongly **elitist**, using selection to promote the talented in diverse fields in specialist schools. Education was seen as an important means of developing human resources for competition in the worldwide struggle against capitalism.

means and ends It used to be said that whereas traditional education was good on ends it was weak on means. Progressive education, on the other hand, was good on means but weak on ends. Taken at face value only one of these descriptions can be true. Whereas it is perfectly possible to have a clear end or goal in view but have either no idea how to realise it or ineffective ideas (for example, to want to go to Peru but either to have no idea how to get there or to think that you can go the whole way by sea), it is not possible to be clear and competent about means whilst being unclear about ends. The reason for this is that something is never a means in itself

but only a means to a certain end; we can only identify something as a means if we have an idea of the end it is a means
to; and being good at the selection of means has to be understood in terms of the selection of things or activities that are
likely to be efficient in producing the desired ends.

So what was the point of this rather misleading comparison? Such point that it has is nicely teased out by Cohen
(1982). She contrasts **instrumental** approaches to education
involving such things as conditioning, sleep teaching and hyp-
nosis, in which all that counts is that the subject reaches a
desired end, for example, the mastery of French irregular verbs,
with learner-centred methods which emphasise individual discovery, self-direction, self-expression and autonomy. Her
discussion shows that pure instrumentalism is (a) likely to work
when the end in view is relatively simple, (b) that even in such
cases it is unclear whether the subject has actually learned anything, and (c) that such approaches tend to – or must – neglect
the subject's individuality, imagination and rationality.

However, extreme learner-centred approaches, whilst they
pay proper attention to individuality, imagination and rationality, may be extremely ineffective in promoting learning,
even self-chosen learning, and may, by their lack of intellectual structure actually impede such learning.

Cohen's solution is the compromise that she sees in liberal
education with its emphasis on individualism and humanism
and its equal emphasis on cultural initiation. Whilst this
compromise is attractive we doubt whether it settles the argument. Whilst Cohen is good on the educational significance
of **training** and the part it can play in education, we suspect
that even her final position might not appeal to extreme
learner-centred theorists. This is because she, like others, may
have missed the point of their theories. And the point is that
such theories do not care at all about some end divorced
from the processes implied by the theories; rather engagement
in such processes is the end of education. That, for instance,
it does not matter whether children actually discover some
new – for them – scientific truth by using discovery methods
but that they engage – in some way – in the process of trying

to discover it. That is, it does not matter if they get where *we* want them to go by choosing educational activities for themselves but what does matter is that *they* so choose.

Such a position completely subverts the usual means/ends dichotomy and, whilst it is unlikely to appeal to anyone who thinks that education must have to do with the mastery of some determinate subject matter, it is a distinctive and radical educational theory.

memory   Memory is fundamental to **learning**. If something is learned and subsequently forgotten then its value is lost. While all educators agree that learning not retained is of no value, the role that *memorisation* plays in learning is disputed. There are different kinds of memory. First there is *practical memory*, whereby a skill such as swimming is acquired and retained. Second, there is the ability to retain factual information, such as that Albany is the capital of New York State. Finally, there is the ability to recall personal experience. Philosophers have tended to pay a great deal of attention to the last, because of its alleged importance for a person's sense of identity, but educators are more concerned with the first two. Abilities are usually acquired through practice and **training**, interpreted broadly. Disputes about the role of memorisation in practical learning tend, then, to be disputes about the efficacy of training as a method of **teaching**.

What is the role of memorisation in learning facts? One school of thought, originating with Plato but also advocated by Chomsky (1988) and Fodor (1975), is that learning is a form of recall of information already present at birth. Teaching is then either unnecessary or just a technique for drawing innate knowledge out of the student, perhaps by **erotetic** methods. Others, following St Augustine, have seen memory as a kind of storehouse containing items acquired in **experience**. The act of memory is then a retrieving of an item from this storehouse. In the work of the British empiricists, however, experience was seen as the imprinting of data on a largely passive mind, which then stored it for future use. Memorisation was seen as a largely automatic and impersonal process, requiring neither effort nor any affective engagement. It is not surprising that Locke, for example, disparages the role of memorisation in education (Locke 1964). If data is automatically stored in memory then no amount of effort will assist the process.

However, many, including those who have thought of memory as a storehouse, have maintained that memorisation requires effort and even training (Yates 1984). Memory teachers from Antiquity to the Renaissance have paid attention to technique and affective engagement in promoting it. For example, one can learn a speech by imagining different sections of it in different parts of one's house and then mentally go round the rooms in the appropriate order, or one can, by using the memory theatre of Giulio Camillo, attempt to give an encyclopaedic account of human knowledge, using the planets and the emotions associated with them as an organising principle for knowledge that can be obtained in the theatre (Yates 1984: 144). Contemporary educators, however, tend to disparage memorisation for a variety of reasons: the availability of artificial forms of storage such as print and computer hardware; an aversion to training and a belief that a memory is a physical trace left in the brain by an event which is automatically there irrespective of memorisation. However, the trace theory has grave problems in making intelligible the idea of a representational trace within the brain (Malcolm 1977) and thus shares the more general problems of **cognitivist** accounts of **learning**.

metanarrratives   According to some **postmodernist** thinkers, influenced by Foucault and Lyotard, we are caught in **narratives** which enable us to give sense to our lives but which are entirely socially constructed from various social practices and completely immune from rational criticism in any objective sense of this term. Because such narratives are themselves the places in which notions such as 'rational' and 'criticism' come to have meaning, there is no place outside of particular narratives from where they may be judged.

Thus, such a picture denies the possibility of metanarratives, such as universal reason, which can be used to assess the many and various narrative structures. However, this dismissal of overarching structures which may sit in judgement of particulars runs into serious problems. First, because a type of thought originates in a particular social context does not mean that it only applies to that context. For instance, the fact that the beginnings of mathematics and logic arose in the world of classical Greece does not mean that such things are not universally valid. Second, any attempt to state the impossibility of metanarratives looks very much like a metanarrative in itself, because it claims that it is universally true that there can be no universal truths. Third, the fact that those thinkers who want to banish thought of metanarratives use arguments to undercut the position they are trying to establish; in that there is something paradoxical in using reason to deny the relevance of reason. (For a discussion of these issues see Nagel 1997, and for such a discussion in an educational context see Siegel 1997.)

metaphysics Traditionally, metaphysics has been subdivided into three branches: *cosmology* which deals with the nature and origins of the universe; *ontology* which is concerned with different kinds of being; and *theology* which is concerned with the nature and properties of God and divine creatures. To the extent that metaphysical ideas underpin knowledge which we take to be valuable and useful, metaphysics has at least an *implicit* role in determining **curriculum** content. This is particularly easy to see in the case of theology, where doctrines concerning divine reality inform **Religious Education**.

The example, however, illustrates the difficulty for metaphysics in education. The controversiality of many metaphysical doctrines leads to disputes over curricular choices that rely on such underpinnings. One possibility is to present metaphysical doctrines as meaningful alternatives, one of which may be selected at maturity. There are, however, particular problems with theology, as religious education is, typically, affectively charged and does not normally present its doctrines as mere alternatives (see religious education).

Haldane (1989) has argued that metaphysics can provide a justification for the **aims** of education. The Aristotelian/ Thomist teleological view of man as pursuant of those things that constitute human flourishing should ground education, whose job it is to act as midwife to the kind of flourishing proper to humans. Haldane sees this metaphysical view opposed to the physicalism of, for example, Evers (1990) whose educational prescriptions ignore the kinds of ethical and meta-ethical issues that he sees as central to education.

mixed ability   There is often passionate debate about the pros and cons of the practice of mixed ability grouping (MAG). One of the arguments in favour is egalitarian. Mixed ability teaching implies **equality** of treatment for diverse individuals, often on the grounds that equality of treatment will be more likely to lead to equality of outcome, which is thought to be an intrinsic good. It can be argued however, as does Cooper (1980), that human diversity will guarantee that equality of treatment will lead to inequality of outcome, thus undermining the rationale for anti-selective practices. Bailey and Bridges (1983) argue in favour of MAG, maintaining that the value of *fraternity* is best served by it. This raises two issues. The first is the extent to which fraternity, or **social cohesion** is an important educational *aim*; the second is the extent to which, given that it is, MAG is an effective way of promoting it. On this latter point the evidence is not particularly strong. The society which elevated fraternity into a cardinal civic value (postrevolutionary France) does not hold any particular brief for mixed ability teaching in its own public schooling system.

It has been argued by Strike (1983) that the practice of grouping by ability is justified if it is used to promote Rawls's (1971) principle of equal liberty. Where it is used to disadvantage any individual, it is unjustifiable. Ability grouping can only be justified if it is decoupled from future meritocratic choice. Since the difference principle is compatible with fair competition for economic benefits, Strike would presumably disallow the difference principle, that distributions are only just when they favour the least well-off, as a justification for MAG. One could, however, use it as a ground for MAG if one believed that alleviation of the economic position of the least well-off was a desirable educational aim. Even if one were to accept this, the contention that MAG is the best arrangement to underpin the difference principle is one that has to be empirically justified. There are no *a priori* grounds for thinking that it is more likely than any other method to do so. Bailey and Bridges however, argue that the difference principle can be used to support MAG if it can be shown that without it, the least well-off would be *educationally* disadvantaged. Since Rawls holds that **self-respect** is an essential primary good and if educational disadvantage could lead to a lack of self-worth, the difference principle could be used to justify it.

Cooper (1980) rejects the principle as a valid one for the distribution of educational resources, arguing that high absolute **standards** are the principal intrinsic educational good and that they can only be obtained through ability grouping. Cooper's own model assumes that non-selection implies lower standards or performance but it is not obvious that this need be so at every level of schooling. It is quite possible to support MAG at one phase and to withdraw support at a later phase.

moral education   Given the time that children are at school in the developed world, the demand that schools are morally educative institutions is perfectly understandable. Sometimes this demand involves little more than that schools reinforce the agreed moral norms of the particular society, for example, that they have enforced rules concerning stealing and bullying. However, many commentators want schools to have a much more positive role than this. For some modern writers (D. Carr 1991) moral education is *the* essential role of the school and therefore the focus of institutional policy. For others (Straughan 1982) although moral education has to coexist with the other main aims of schooling, it is an area in which schools can make a distinctive contribution.

The literature of moral education is vast. There is, for instance, one whole journal devoted largely to *one* approach to moral education (despite the fact that this particular approach has been the subject of a devastating critique see D. Locke 1979, 1980). As well as the theoretical material dealing with this area there is an abundance of practical material for use in schools (see for instance the Schools Council Project in Moral Education, McPhail *et al.* 1972). This vast literature is not necessarily reassuring. Given the number of commentators and programmes and given the fact that there are enormous differences between the approaches championed it may indicate not simply the importance assigned to moral education but rather that this is an area where there is no consensus as to what is to be done. The situation is further complicated by the fact that the field of moral education seems, rather more than other educational fields, to be subject to changes of fashion. So, for instance, when the work of Hare was popular (Hare 1956, 1963), it gave rise to numerous works on moral education based upon Hare's view of morality (See J. Wilson, Williams, and Sugarman 1967; J. Wilson 1973). After MacIntyre (1981) revitalised the Aristotelian tradition, this was followed by works on moral education based upon this tradition (D. Carr 1991; see **virtue theory**). Whereas some may be comfortable with the notion of educational ideas that respond to fashion, none, we think, should be comfortable with the notion of a 'fashionable' morality.

In fact, the greatest gulf which separates the commentators in this area may not be one between particular positive approaches but rather one between those who believe that we can have lessons in schools concerned with moral education and those, such as Ryle and Phillips, for whom the whole idea of such lessons is anathema (Ryle 1972; D. Z. Phillips 1979).

147

For Ryle, for instance, lessons in morality face several insurmountable challenges. Firstly, the idea of teaching anything involves the passing on of expertise. However, any notion of moral expertise seems deeply dubious. If such expertise did exist we would expect, as Ryle says, for it to be institutionalised and for there to exist lecturers in honesty and professors in courage. A related point concerns assessment. If education must involve **assessment** then so must moral education. It is certainly the case that teachers in their everyday interaction with pupils do morally assess them and think this one honest and brave and that one sly and cowardly. However, there is a vast difference between such informal assessments based upon children's actions in morally challenging situations, and the idea that we can actually have lessons set aside for such assessments. There is evidence, both in England and America, that children exposed to a moral education programme learn to respond in moral education classes in ways that their teachers deem appropriate (McPhail *et al.* 1972). However, there is also evidence that such responses are, at least partly, hypocritical (see Hartshorne, May and Shuttleworth 1930) and that therefore the moral education programme is encouraging at least one vice. There seems something perverse in the idea of tests or exams for moral character.

Second, Ryle points out that morality seems unlike the other things we expect schools to pass on through formal lessons. **Knowledge**, for instance, can be passed on but can also be forgotten, whereas it seems odd to talk of someone forgetting to be kind or forgetting to be honest. We may be taught skills in school (e.g. how to read, write and mix chemicals) but any skill can be used for morally good or morally ill ends whereas the learning of morality cannot be so used.

For Ryle morality is caught not taught and it is caught via the emulation of these people we see as exemplifying the type of moral character we wish to possess and by the practice of those moral characteristics we wish to cultivate. Other theorists of this essentially sceptical position point out that teachers, simply by being good teachers, must exemplify virtues such as fairness and honesty which we wish our children to acquire. (See D. Carr 1991; D. Z. Phillips 1979.)

An instructive contrast is between Ryle's doubts and the approach advocated by Straughan (1982). Straughan conducts a critical survey of approaches to morality and the forms of moral education that such approaches engender. His conclusion is that neither approaches based upon the form of moral reasoning nor approaches based upon the content of morality can be accepted without very serious reservations. Then in his final chapter Straughan gives his own suggestions for a positive approach to moral education. He admits that no precise boundaries may be found either to the form of moral reasoning or to the content of morality. Nevertheless he argues we can base our teaching on the typical features we find in morality. It might be thought that this notion of the 'typical' begs certain important questions, for example, surely what counts as typical will vary according to one's moral point of view. However, exercising generosity here, Straughan may be given his point. His suggestions for moral education are then explained in terms of three areas: 'teaching that . . .', 'teaching how . . .', and 'teaching to . . .'.

> 'Teaching that . . .' will consist in teaching children the relevant facts for situations in which they might be called upon to make a moral choice. 'Teaching how . . .' will involve teaching how to think for themselves as autonomous moral agents and 'teaching to . . .' will involve teaching children to want to be moral.

Straughan admits that this list and its implementation is fraught with difficulties. However, it might be thought that even his worries underestimate the difficulties. For instance, as Straughan seems to admit, any fact may be relevant given a particular context and a particular moral point of view. But schools cannot teach every fact because the number of such facts is infinite. So they must select those that seem most important. But surely, this is exactly what curriculum choice is supposed to do *completely independently of any kind of aim concerning moral education*. The same type of point can be made concerning 'teaching how . . .': of course we want children to think for themselves, but surely this is an **aim** of education

149

as such and not a particular aim of moral education. As far as 'teaching to . . .' is concerned Straughan correctly identifies the key role that motivation must play in morality but his positive suggestion comes down to little more than the notion that if you want children to want to be moral you have to act morally toward them.

But this last point concerning **motivation** *must be* the crucial point. Let us imagine the first two suggestions successfully completed without the success of the motivational task. So we could have people emerging from education who were capable of realising which facts were morally relevant and of thinking for themselves. Would such people be necessarily be morally good? The answer must be no. The notion of the well-informed, logical and autonomous moral monster is, unfortunately, all too coherent. Doing a school equivalent to moral philosophy does nothing to guarantee moral goodness. The same point applies to all approaches to moral education which simply stress the clarification of values (Chazan and Soltis 1975; Kohlberg 1984). But if this is so then all the weight must be on 'teaching to . . .' and here Straughan seems simply to be repeating the role of exemplification insisted upon by Ryle, Phillips, and Carr.

motivation   Motivation is thought to be one of the most powerful influences on **learning**. If someone has the motivation to learn, they are likely to succeed in doing so. If not, they are much less likely to do so. Motivation is sometimes thought to come from innate biological drives such as sex or hunger (Hull 1966) but also from an innate biological drive to learn (Rousseau 1911a). If there is an innate drive to learn, then education can be designed around the developing emergence of this drive (see **development**). Since such motivation does not have to be supplied by outside influences, it can be based on the current interests and developing readiness of the child. This doctrine forms much of the intellectual basis of **progressivism**.

Motivation can also, however, be extrinsic. If one does not have a biological drive to learn and one is not currently interested in the subject matter, then it may be possible to provide motivation through the prospect of future benefits or through fear of **punishment**. Traditional education tends to take extrinsic motivation more seriously than does progressivism. The two types of motivation are not incompatible with each other and all educationists would agree that intrinsic motivation makes learning more pleasant and effective than extrinsic motivation. If however, the quasi-biological theories are false and, in a non-ideal world, students are not always intrinsically motivated, then extrinsic motivation may be an unavoidable necessity.

multiculturalism   Questions concerning multiculturalism are among the most important and pressing that some modern polities face. Such questions are therefore fundamental for the education systems within such polities.

The notion of liberal democracy, deriving initially from the work of John Locke (1924a, b) is of a system of government which does not embody any conception of what counts as a good life. Rather, it consists of a set of procedural principles which enable it to neutrally adjudicate between the various conceptions of a good life which are held by its citizens. Such conceptions typically – perhaps, essentially – derive from the different cultures that such citizens inhabit. For such a state not to recognise such a conception of the good life – or even worse, to recognise but disdain such a conception – is for it to offend against the notion of **equality** which underpins liberal democracy and therefore to be guilty of a grave injustice with regard to the citizens in question. In doing so it offends against the notion of identity and authenticity which such citizens have of themselves and thus strikes a grievous blow against their dignity as citizens. Such a liberal state has a duty to give equal recognition – in a very full sense – to the cultures of all of its citizens. If it moves away from its role of neutral arbiter, say, because as in the Canadian province of Quebec, the state feels that it needs to protect the survival of certain cultural forms such as a francophone culture in an anglophone country, then such a state may both be offensive to the members of that society who do not share the 'protected' cultures and, at the same time, curtail their freedoms in ways which they morally resent.

The above scenarios and their problems – and some of the language they are described in – will be familiar to anyone who knows Charles Taylor's influential and important paper 'The Politics of Recognition' (see Taylor 1994). However, despite the depth and lucidity of his treatment of these issues, it may be the case that Taylor underestimates some of the problems. In the second part of his paper, for instance, Taylor rather too quickly dismisses those for whom the procedural losses of the liberal state such as freedom of speech and freedom of religion, are, in themselves, offensive. There may be a paradox in a situation where people use their freedom of speech to complain about the freedom of speech of others, but the Rushdie affair has shown that it is a paradox that needs to be addressed and argued for. Even if we place this in the context of English laws concerning blasphemy which seem to be openly discriminatory because they only protect one religion, the remedies for such discrimination seem equally problematic. If, for instance, you remove such laws totally people may complain that a vital part of their life is left vulnerable to gratuitous attack. If, on the other hand, you try to frame such laws to encompass all religions you are likely to end up with a liberal fudge which satisfies no one who is serious about religion, for example, because for the religiously serious it is precisely other religions, or other variants of their own religion, which constitute blasphemy.

But the main failure of the Taylor paper lies in the fact that it does not take educational issues seriously enough. As one of the commentators on the paper observes (see Waltzer 1994), all societies – and not merely special societies like Quebec – tend to try to reproduce a version of themselves and they do this, largely, through their education systems. But such systems cannot, we think, possibly adhere to the type of neutrality which characterises the original liberal model. Education has to be carried out in a language but the choice of such a language immediately sends cultural signals which may be odious to – and may seriously disadvantage – some participants in the culture. However, to refuse to make such a choice, for example, to leave the language of instruction to be chosen by local cultural groups, is to threaten to undermine one of the strongest supports of the polity as such (as Waltzer says 'carrying out a Quebec, as it were, or a number of Quebecs, on its own soil, where none exist', p. 101). And if some subjects on the curriculum such as mathematics, can claim cultural neutrality, such subjects are in the minority. The study of literature, the arts, history and even science all involve making significant cultural choices. (By such choices we do not mean, for instance, studying the British Empire from a particular point of view – the ethics of scholarship *should* prevent *that* – but rather the choice of studying British history at all. The days when all francophone children in French schools throughout the world, for example, in Senegal, recited at some time in their schooling 'Nos Ancêtres, les Gaulois' are long gone but the choice which this practice highlighted and made absurd still remains.)

The situation is made worse by the widespread injunction, both in Britain and America, that since every culture is of equal value our educational systems should play their part in the celebration of cultural diversity. Such a notion of celebration goes far beyond the recognition – even in a full sense – which is explicit in Taylor's paper. And it implies a notion of substantive a priori evaluation that Taylor quite explicitly rejects. Whilst it is true in some sense that all persisting cultures are equal (e.g. in that they equally provide an identity for those within the culture), it is certainly not true that they are equal in every sense and that a common education system should – or could – pretend that this is so. When, for instance, an eminent historian remarked that Africa had no history – a remark taken as racially offensive by some people of Afro-Caribbean background in England – he did not mean that it had no past. Rather he meant that the reliable primary sources such as written documents, upon which the academic study of History depends simply do not exist in large parts of Africa. (This *may* engender new and equally legitimate ways of studying the African past but such a possibility has not been realised as yet.) So, for the moment the notion of celebrating African history is simply empty of content. The same is true of other facets of culture. There are languages in which, at the moment, it is impossible to study science because the technical vocabulary does not at present exist (English, like the patois spoken in Freetown, Sierra Leone, is a creole language but it is a creole language that benefits from a thousand-year history) and there are cultures where certain cultural forms, for example, written literature, simply do not exist. Again the notion of giving such culture parity of esteem with, say, English or French in regard to science or, say, the novel does not make sense (which is not to say that the history of science taught in our schools is not disgracefully Eurocentric nor that such cultures do not have rich oral traditions which repay study).

Even where the parity of esteem which celebration calls for is possible it cannot be given prior to an examination of the cultural artefacts which are claimed, by some, to be of equal worth with the plays of Shakespeare or the novels of Tolstoy. For, as Taylor argues, this a priori estimation of worth would deprive estimation in itself of any significant content and therefore of any value.

There are other equally serious problems for liberals who counsel estimation given wholesale. As has been pointed out (see Flew 1976) to hold all cultures as equal is to hold sexist and racist cultures as equal to those that are non-sexist and non-racist. And it has been argued (see J. Harris 1982) that a paradox appears if we accord equal worth to cultures who deny such worth to their own inhabitants, for example, caste society in India or the Taliban in Afghanistan; for our granting of cultural equality serves to endorse and, perhaps, promote profound and disturbing inequalities within these particular cultures. There are few western liberals, we suspect, who are prepared to celebrate or recognise the worth of female genital mutilation even if it is thought to play an important part by many of those – including women – in whose culture it occurs.

Cultural diversity and the educational questions it raises have different impacts in different parts of the world. The United States of America which is now, to a very large extent, a society made up of immigrants – albeit with large cultural groups whose immigration was far from voluntary – faces a different, and perhaps more extreme, set of problems that somewhere like England and/or France where at least some argument can be made that any immigrants are voluntarily joining a host culture and therefore can be expected to play their part within that culture. The position, frustrations and demands of Afro-Americans who are the descendants of slaves and who have inhabited the country at least as long as any other immigrant group may be very different, both in quality and quantity, to such things applied to an Afro-Briton or a French Algerian whose recent forebears came to the host country for economic reasons. In places in the world where cultural choice is a necessity rather than a privilege, such as parts of West Africa, it may be fraught with enormous difficulties. So, for instance, one of the educational battles which has occupied people in the British West Indies in recent years has been between those who see West Indian culture – regretfully perhaps – as a tributary of British culture and those who favour a more particularistic version of culture which emphasises the differences between the West Indies and Britain but also the differences between island and island. Some particularists would like to see the official languages of the particular islands – and therefore the language of instruction in schools – as a reflection of the linguistic history of the island in question. So, it has been suggested, that St Lucia, for instance, moves from English as the mode of instruction to a French-based creole which was, at one time, widely spoken in the St Lucian countryside. Such a move, if adopted, would at a stroke cut St Lucian children off from easy access to British culture and the cultures of the other islands and, at the same time, deny them access to the work of the St Lucian, Nobel prize-winning, poet Derek Walcott who uses English as his favoured medium.

narrative 'Narrative' refers to the telling of a story. Narratives are structured and, as such, they are an important component of **genres** such as the short story or novel. Such genres form part of the literary and cultural traditions of particular societies, and as such, part of the educational experience in those societies. Some moral theorists, notably MacIntyre (1981) have argued that human lives have a narrative structure and that it is the realisation of this and the equipping of people to shape the narrative of their own lives that form important components of **moral education** (also **virtue theory**). This structuring is provided by the life-cycle of human beings, consisting of key events such as: birth, childhood, courtship, the raising of a family, grandparenthood and old age.

Kazmi (1990) argues that it is traditions which provide the material for a self-construction of an individual life-narrative through narrative archetypes and an institutional context in which the narrative may take place. It seems to follow that inculcation into cultural tradition is an important feature of education and that transplantation into a culture with different traditions will constitute a massive disruption of the individual's ability to construct a life-narrative. However, one should not assume that, even in a different culture there is no possibility of borrowing and adaptation. Indeed the experience of multi-cultural societies such as the US and the UK suggests that this is how people adapt to alien cultural traditions in which they find themselves.

nationalism Nationalism has long had rather a bad press in liberal western democracies because of its links with unthinking jingoism, superpatriotism and nationalistic claims of superiority over other nations. In education the issue of nationalism usually only surfaces when there are debates concerning the content of the history or literature syllabus (debates which are strangely inconclusive; in that, even if the history syllabus in British schools has to deal largely with British history this does not mean that the anti-nationalistic history teachers cannot spend a great deal of their time teaching about the 'evils' of the British Empire) whilst the contribution of such subjects towards a national consciousness is obvious, it is to a large extent uncontroversial as long as this consciousness is not its direct aim and there is no evidence that it is being made to serve some notion of superiority.

Recently, perhaps in the wake of multiculturalist theories, there have appeared works which attempt to show the benign face of nationalism and its relevance to education (see Miller 1993; J. P. White 1996).

nature/nurture Arguments concerning whether certain human characteristics are inherited or given by nature, or are produced by the environment that the child grows in, have figured large in the educational literature this century and therefore it is unsurprising that such arguments should find a place within the philosophy of education literature. The most obvious dispute concerns **intelligence** with the believers in IQ theory and psychometric testing on one side (Burt 1973; Jensen 1973a, b; Eysenck 1973) and philosophers on the other side disputing the basic presuppositions of both the theory and the tests (Ryle 1974; Kleinig 1982; C. Winch 1990). But there have been other areas of dispute. So, for instance, it is difficult not to see the arguments concerning **creativity** as, at least in part, a dispute about whether creative

157

people are born or made. The same is true of moral character. Whereas most communicators assume that morality comes from upbringing some educationalists seen to believe with Neill (1965) that the child 'is innately wise and realistic' (p. 20) and that 'the child has been born good . . . (and) will inevitably turn out to be a good human being if he is not crippled and thwarted in his natural development by interference' (p. 224). The father of **progressive** or *child-centred* education, Rousseau (1911a) sometimes writes in this vein – usually like Neill when he is concerned to combat the doctrine of innate wickedness – but his more considered view is that children are born as a moral blank slate. (However, like Neill, he did believe that much of what goes on in the name of education is more likely to corrupt children than teach them to be good.)

A more interesting debate, because less finished, concerns gender identities and their relevance for education. It is a commonplace of sociology concerned with gender that whereas the sex of a child is a given, the gender is a social construct. This has obvious relevance to questions concerning **sex or gender** specific areas of the curriculum, for example, Women's Studies, but it also has ramifications for questions concerning **co-education**. The above are given fuller treatment under their respective headings.

needs One of the central concepts associated with **progressivism** both in England and America is one whose use went far beyond the work of the explicit supporters of this educational movement. So, for instance, over a period of twenty years (1960–80) it was rare, in both informal contexts such as Primary School staffrooms, and formal contexts such as Government and Local Authority documents concerned with education, not to be confronted with the idea that education should derive from the 'needs' of the child. The notion of basing education upon children's 'needs' *seemed* to solve several educational problems in one neat move. It provided a solution to the problem of the **aims** of education which was particularly pressing for a movement often considered to be weak when it came to such aims; the aim was to meet the needs of the particular child. In solving the problem in this way this move ensured that – following the *Plowden Report* (1967) – the child was central to education. But it also seemed to mesh education in the empirical work of the psychological theorists such as Piaget and Maslow admired by progressivists, and thus bypassed what was taken to be a sterile argument concerning educational values and the way in which these could be located within a curriculum. It also seemed, to some, to solve the problem of motivation in a particularly forceful way in that pointing out to someone that they need something both *seems* to provide a motive for getting that something and – because it *seems* to imply a lack – a sense of urgency for the people concerned to satisfy the need. And last, but by no means least, it provided a nice *ad hominem* argument against the critics of progressivism who seemed to be forced into a position of denying children's needs.

However, as critics (Dearden 1968; Barrow and Woods 1975) were quick to point out, such solutions were illusions based upon a lack of analysis of the central concept. If needs statements are purely empirical, that is, concerned with matters of fact; then they cannot, in themselves, solve the problem of educational aims for such aims must involve values: things we *ought* to bring about; and statements of value cannot be derived directly from a simple statement of fact. The work of the admired psychologists either illegitimately smuggles in values disguised as facts (Barrow 1984; Egan 1983) or, equally illegitimately, simply assumes that if someone has a need then it ought to be met. As has been pointed out (Woods and Barrow 1975) would-be murderers need a weapon and an opportunity but this does not mean they ought to be given either. The question of motivation cannot be solved by statements of need because people may have needs of which they are completely unaware, such as for a blood transfusion when they are unconscious, and therefore they are not motivated to seek to satisfy these needs. Also awareness of needs and therefore desire to satisfy them, for example medical needs, depends upon a level

159

of sophisticated knowledge which many people, especially children, simply do not possess. It is certainly not the case that people always want what they need, like painful dental surgery, or need what they want, for example, a large, expensive car (ibid.; but see also Rousseau (1911a) who is clear that wants and needs in education are distinct). Nor do needs statements imply a present lack; I need air to breathe but I have never lacked it. As far as the centrality of children's needs is concerned – and therefore the force of the *ad hominem* argument – any educationalist, including the most anti-progressive traditionalist, may agree that we ought to meet children's educational needs; however there will be vast disagreement as to what constitutes such needs. In this sense every curriculum, however different, is a 'needs' curriculum (Komisar 1961) and thus statements of putative 'needs' will not solve any significant educational questions.

Whilst the critical points made above do a good job in containing some of the wilder progressivist claims, there often seems to be a lack of clarity or sharpness in the analyses in which they are found. So, for instance, it often seems to be implied (Dearden 1968; Woods and Barrow 1975) that 'needs' statements are essentially evaluative despite the fact that there are plenty of commonplace examples such as that my car needs petrol to work, which do not seem to involve values at all. Likewise, it sometimes seems to be suggested (Dearden) that needs statements imply normative considerations, where again there seem to be plenty of counter examples to such a claim, for example, if you wish to go from Northampton to Bath by train you need to change trains in either London or Birmingham. Part of the problem here is that 'needs' statements are often elliptical, that is, radically incomplete in a way that precludes a decision about truth content. So, for instance, on being told that Carol needs a new dress we cannot tell whether this is true or false unless we are told what she needs the dress *for*. And given there may be many different objectives for which the dress might or might not be needed: so as not to offend public decency; to please her boyfriend; to match her new shoes; to go to the ball; it is likely that given some of these objectives it is true that she needs the dress but given others it is false. For example, it is true that she needs one to match her shoes but false that she needs one so as not to offend public decency (Brandon 1981). If a fully determinate needs statement must specify an objective (ibid.; Woods and Barrow 1975; Dearden 1968) then perhaps the best analysis of 'needs' is in terms of them being necessary or essential requirements for the realisation of the given objective. As such their truth, or falsehood, will be purely a matter of fact; either it is true that X is necessary for Y or it is false. However, the factual nature of the needs claim should not obscure the fact that choice of objectives is a matter of values – and thus often makes reference to norms – and that therefore whether we think that such a necessary requirement should be met or not will depend upon whether, or how much, we value the objective in question.

It may be the case that, following Brandon, we should eschew any talk of 'needs' in education. However, given the disagreements which continue concerning educational value and the lack of reliable information concerning educational processes and their effects, we suspect that such statements will continue to proliferate and to cause confusion.

neutrality The idea that the teacher should be neutral with regard to the presentation of, at least, some subject matter in schools derives partly from child-centred notions of **education** with their faith in discovery learning and their fear that any direct instruction is liable to be, or to become, **indoctrination**, and partly from a liberal concern that pupils be allowed to make up their own minds at least with regard to controversial matters. The latter position, but not the full blown version of the former, avoids the absurdity of a teacher being neutral as far as the sum of $2 + 2$ is concerned and the impossible demand that teachers impart no information to their pupils. But even the demand for partial neutrality with regard only to controversial issues encounters enormous problems.

First, there is the problem of deciding when a neutral presentation is appropriate and when not. In making such a decision it has to be the case that, at the very least, one is non-neutral about taking up a neutral position. And, given the range of issues that might be designated as controversial: the goods and ills of industrialisation; the role of women within certain religions; the existence or extent of the Holocaust; evolution versus creation; we suspect that often a decision is taken here not with regard to some intellectual principle, such as what counts as History or Science, but rather with regard to whether or not there exists within the community a powerful constituency which may condemn the taking of sides. (Watching respectable 'liberal' academics try to maintain 'neutrality' in the Rushdie affair has been an education in the shallowness of much modern liberalism.)

Second, the profession of neutrality with regard to controversial issues seems to offend against one of the purposes of decent education and also, against the logic of moral discourse. If education must be more than a question of giving students *the* facts – and it must be because facts need selecting in terms of evidential credibility – then a teacher who refuses to take a stand with regard to any particular position is refusing to show her students how to rationally order facts so that conclusions derive from evidence. It is not helpful for a teacher simply to go through a variety of positions on the matter in hand with no attempt to separate sense from nonsense, the rational from the irrational, or the supported from the unsupported.

As far as the logic of morality is concerned, it is simply impossible to take any moral stand (and care for **truth** and **rationality** *are* moral stands) and, at the same time, profess neutrality with regard to those who differ from you, that is, I think X is wrong but I will be neutral if others disagree. It is, of course, possible to believe something right or wrong and pretend to neutrality when the subject is discussed but such a pretence, in itself, sends worrying moral messages, for example, that the matter in hand is one where a certain degree of hypocrisy is allowable.

Lastly, the nature of much subject matter within education, for example, in History, Literature and the Social Sciences, and the social and institutional nature of the processes of education, seem to force teachers to take up a position *vis-à-vis* a wide range of issues. That is, there simply may not be a neutral way of discussing, say, the Holocaust and no neutral way of organising such a discussion. (For all the above see Warnock, Norman and Montefiore in Brown 1975.)

An interesting paper by W. D. Hudson (1977) deals with some of the above issues in its claim that such issues are not, necessarily, matters for individual teachers but, rather, matters for school policy. He claims that if we really want to avoid indoctrination and provide students with a balanced – if not neutral – educational diet then we have to ensure that such students are taught by a variety of teachers who come to their subject matter from different perspectives. For example, if there is a vacancy in the History department and the present staff all represent a particular position with regard to history (they are all Whig historians), then there is a strong argument for hiring someone with a different perspective like a Marxist historian. Of course, such a policy still needs to pay attention to the limits of intellectual and moral tolerance.

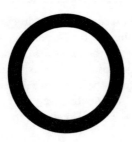

objectivity It should be one of the principles of non-indoctrinatory education that students should not be given biased or subjective opinions and information. It may seem that it is obvious whether or not bias and subjectivity are exhibited; where, for example, only one side of a case is presented or where facts are omitted when it is obvious that there are two reasonable sides, or where the omitted facts are generally agreed to be of the first importance. There are difficulties however, where a teacher thinks that what she is teaching is not subject to doubt, even though there is no consensus on the matter. A sincerely committed creationist may believe that she is being objective about matters when presenting creationism as a true doctrine and natural selection as a false one, for she may take creationism to be completely uncontroversial (but see Woods and Barrow 1975).

The problem is not confined to religion. Most British citizens would find it outrageous if any history teacher questioned the idea that Churchill was a great leader of the UK. Such a person would probably be accused of spreading subjective, biased and controversial views to her students. If she were to protest that there was substantial scholarship available to support an alternative view (e.g. Charmley 1993) that would probably not be enough to justify her, as few would take the alternative scholarship seriously. The problem of objectivity is, then, that it is difficult, in many cases, for a society to be objective about what really is an objective approach.

open learning   Open learning is an approach favoured in adult education and some forms of **training**. It is adopted by such institutions as the UK Open University. Saying exactly what it consists of is less easy. It can be distinguished from *distance learning*, where the student is not in direct contact with the teacher, and from *flexible learning*, where the student is able to make choices about when and where to learn, although many open learning programmes incorporate these elements. Open learning systems are said to be distinguished by giving the student an element of choice in how to learn and even what to learn (Boot 1987). It is in relation to these latter two claims that open learning, as a distinctive form of adult learning, becomes more difficult to carry out.

Choice of the means of learning is often constrained by the resources and technology available. An Open University course, for example, will provide the student with prescribed study materials. Choice of what to learn may be available in institutions like the Open University, but is constrained by the range of courses available. On the other hand, businesses who wish to train their employees may be unhappy about the idea that the trainees should choose what or how they should learn. It seems that choice is always constrained either by resource limitations or by the requirements of others and that the advocate of open learning, while championing learner **autonomy**, has got to accept practical constraints on what can be achieved.

oppression   *The Oxford Paperback Dictionary* (1988) defines 'oppress' as 'to govern harshly, to treat with continual cruelty or injustice'. Someone who is oppressed is, then, in a *subordinate* position in relation to their oppressor, that is, the oppressor has power or **authority** over them. It does not follow that, in all cases, to be subordinate to someone is to be oppressed by them. It cannot therefore follow from the simple fact that there are relationships of authority and hierarchy in an institution, that these are in themselves oppressive. It is a tempting rhetorical trick by those who dislike any educational authority and hierarchy to describe it as oppressive, but it is less easy to show that the authority is actually being oppressive in the sense above.

There is a similar problem in identifying oppressed groups who should be represented on the curriculum. It is easy to see how slaves and mistreated workers and peasants fall into the category of the oppressed (see Freire 1972), but less easy to see how *all* women, although they have undoubtedly enjoyed a subordinate status for much of history, should, by this fact alone, achieve the status of an oppressed group. Educators need to take a step back from the rhetorical claims of would-be curricular innovators and to ask whether or not the use of such terms as 'oppression' in relation to subordinate groups is always justified. If they are not, then the case to be made for the inclusion of the putative 'oppressed group' is correspondingly weakened.

P

paradigm case arguments The citation of what are taken to be uncontroversial examples to deny sceptical theses goes back at least to Plato, so that when someone claims that we do not know what a particular word means we produce one or more examples of the word in use where it seems that the meaning is clear. This technique gained prominence in the 'ordinary language' philosophy associated with the work of G. E. Moore in England earlier this century and some versions of it became known as paradigm case arguments. Thus, when Moore was faced with claims like 'There are no material things', or 'Time is unreal', he would reply by using a standard and everyday example of the thing in question, such as 'Here is one hand, here is another, so there are at least two material things' and 'After lunch I went for a walk' so events do succeed one another, so time is not unreal in this sense (see Malcolm 1968); such arguments became widely used although their exact status was sometimes not clear. Were such examples supposed to provide a complete refutation of the sceptical position or simply a timely reminder of the type of thing that the sceptic must explain away?

The use of such arguments has been discerned within the philosophy of education (see Beattie 1981), though whether or not such arguments have been consciously used and to what effect remains an open question (see Flew 1982). However, it is certainly the case, that faced with a claim not to understand a particular concept such as 'creativity', one of the ways of moving the argument forward – at least – is to provide examples of what is taken to be an everyday use of the word, e.g. 'Well, Shakespeare was a creative playwright and Beethoven a creative composer', and ask the sceptic to deal with them.

parental   The relationship between parents and children has been evolving since the times of the Old Testament. There we are told that paternal (rather than parental) authority is absolute and includes the power of life and death (see e.g. Genesis 22). Vico (1968) makes the same point in relation to the history of the Gentiles in Antiquity. The Christian tradition took over the notion of absolute paternal authority but modified it through the constraints imposed on parents through natural law. God limited parents' rights to act unjustly and God's word was accessible to all Christians.

However, the tradition of absolute paternalism continued into the seventeenth century in, for example, the work of Filmer, who applied the biblical account to the relationship between sovereign and subject to his contemporary situation. This account was rejected by John Locke in the *First Treatise* (1961b), but Locke was still left with the problem of explaining *parental* authority in the context of a political system that was accountable to its citizens. His solution, proposed in the *Second Treatise* (1961c) is to make parents the interpreters of their children's interests, because the limited rationality of young children does not allow them to determine those interests for themselves. Parental authority is derived from children's **rights** to a proper upbringing, which is in turn derived from their interest in one. It is thus conditional and temporary authority and is circumscribed by the requirement that the interests of children are at all times attended to (ibid., ch. 6).

The Lockean account thus uncouples the contractarian theory of the state (which assumes citizens to be fully rational beings) from the account of the child in the family (which assumes that the child is imperfectly rational), thus providing a defence of the legitimacy of the private life of the family in the context of an accountable state. Since the time of Locke, the parent–child relationship has come to be interpreted in a more contractarian fashion. In part, this is because of a decline in the religious belief that sanctioned parents, in the context of the family, as the custodians of a child's best interests. Since religious belief underpinned the customary acceptance of parental authority by both child and the broader society, with the decline in religious belief, customary adherence to parental authority has also declined.

Children's rights have come to be interpreted as if children themselves are the best judges of what those rights are (see Archard 1993) and parental authority has itself become subject to various forms of legal contestation mainly relating to the relative weighting, on the one hand, of children's perceptions of their interests as opposed to those of their parents and, on the other, of society's as opposed to parents' interpretations. Of particular educational importance is the extent to which parental interpretation of what is in a child's best interests predominates in institutions like schools and libraries. A further, and related, question is the extent to which different parental interpretations of their children's interests (in, for example, areas like morality and religion) undermine the possibility of common schooling. The weak point in the Lockean account is the importance that it places on the interpretation of rights by parents. For if interpretation is allowed unlimited latitude there is no intelligible sense in which there is a connection between conceptions of the **common good** and parental rights.

paternalism   Paternalism is having a bad press recently. So much so that one rarely comes across a defence of paternalistic activity even in areas where it could be thought the concept has a proper and non-contentious use; that is, when it concerns the benevolent direction of children by a father – or, better, a parent – perhaps against their wishes, but certainly for their own good. Insofar as schools act *in loco parentis* they will also be fulfilling a paternal role.

The notion of paternalism has obvious connections to notions of childhood and children's **rights**. It is clearly the case that with these connections comes the possibility of argument concerning the rights, duties and interests of children *vis-à-vis* the rights, duties and interests of parents (or their representatives). In such cases it is clear that either parties' perceptions of such things may be either partial or completely wrongheaded. (Hence, something like the Children Act in England which gave the Courts powers to intervene on behalf of children and against parents.) But it is also the case that the *locus parentis* position of schools can be fraught with difficulty. So, for instance, schools may disagree with parents about a child's well-being, say, with regard to **punishment**, **Religious Education** or **censorship**. Some of these issues are explored by Kleinig (1982) but it is probably, fair to say that we have not as yet a fully worked out conception of childhood and the rights and duties that attach to it (but see Archard 1993).

pedagogy 'Pedagogy' means the 'method of teaching' interpreted in the widest sense. The variety of pedagogical techniques can broadly be classified as follows: conditioning (the use of stimulus–response techniques); **training**; instruction (direct conveyance of information); supervision (learning overseen and regulated); facilitation (providing opportunities and resources for learning), modelling (providing an example for the student to follow); and **erotetics** (the use of questioning). These methods can usually be used in combination with each other to varying degrees. The question of which to employ is partly, but not wholly, a technical one about which is the most effective, given certain aims. Questions of pedagogy are rarely, however, purely technical questions because teaching is itself a morally significant activity. Furthermore, the issue of which method to adopt is also contingent on one's position concerning the epistemology of learning. Two examples will illustrate each of these points. First, the tutor's decision in Rousseau's *Emile* never overtly to impose his own will on the child was based on the belief that Emile's **self-respect** or *'amour propre'* would be fundamentally compromised if he did so. Second, Socrates's decision to teach the slave-boy in *Meno* erotetically was based on the belief that the boy already knew what Socrates wanted him to learn and that the task of the teacher was to enable him to *recollect* what he already knew (Plato 1970a).

Choice of teaching method can, then, be both controversial and highly contested. As Alexander (1992) has pointed out in his discussion of **good practice** (which incorporates pedagogy) there are various ways in which such decisions can be made, and these depend, to a considerable extent, on power relationships within an education system. It is probably true to say that there is a rough alignment of pedagogical approaches with educational **ideologies**. So for example, **progressivists** tend to favour apparently non-directive pedagogical methods like facilitation and erotetics, traditionalists tend to favour training and instruction, while **behaviourists** tend to favour conditioning. Nor can the issues between them simply be settled by determining the efficiency of each in promoting learning. For a progressive, the aim of education may be **autonomy** in the strong sense and he may resist any form of teaching, like training or instruction, that he thinks will compromise this aim. Likewise, a traditionalist who values the acquisition of propositional knowledge above all else, might have no qualms about dispensing with any form of autonomous learning provided that the goal of knowledge acquisition was best served (see **means and ends**). It will, therefore not be automatic that of two morally acceptable teaching methods A and B of which one, A, is more efficient at teaching material M than B, that A will be chosen by all rational people. Although both A and B may both be morally acceptable to the wider public, some teachers may only consider one of these to be morally acceptable. Alternatively, they may consider, for example, B to be more morally acceptable than A and favour it, although A is demonstrably more efficient than B in inculcating a certain subject matter. Pedagogical decisions are, therefore, often particularly bitterly contested.

171

philosophy   This volume takes for granted the notion that *philosophy* in general and *philosophy of education* are important activities. That the search to explicate, understand and criticise the foundational ideas which underpin particular *disciplines* and our everyday life is a task worthy of pursuit at the highest intellectual level. It is also the case that philosophical ideas throughout the ages have permeated society in general and therefore we cannot have an understanding of previous ages or how we have arrived at our age without an understanding of such ideas. Given that these two things are true, does this not constitute a case for teaching philosophy in schools?

It may well do, but a recent discussion (Ross 1988; Jonathan and Blake 1988) shows some of the scope of the problems. Philosophy is notoriously difficult and this must lead to the question of whether schoolchildren of whatever age are intellectually developed enough to cope with its difficulties. If it is thought that some of them are then this leads to questions of how to approach the teaching of the subject. Should it appear as a watered down form of a university syllabus? Should it be via a study of the history of ideas? Should it be embedded in courses on 'thinking skills' or informal – and, perhaps – formal logic? Given a content, should it be taught as a discrete subject by specialists or should it be an add-on to other subjects? Once such questions are answered, further ones appear: how are we to assess this new subject within schools? (It may be the case, for instance, that taught as an add-on it would disturb the type of certainty that public examiners seem to demand in schoolchildren and thus cause children to do 'less well' in the parent subject.) Given the interest in this area at the moment, continued experimentation is likely to go on. It is only to be hoped that such experimentation will address the above questions.

physical education   It used to be the case that children in British schools routinely engaged in physical **training** and **competitive** games. The reasons for such engagements were broadly utilitarian. Given that health is a good thing and regular exercise contributes to such health, mass education helps to create health habits for later life. Games are important in that they give focus to the exercises and because they are a potent source of pleasure for both participant and spectator (see Barrow 1981: ch. 2).

However, both training and competition have passed out of fashion in our school system and, under the influence of liberal educationalists (see **education**), anything not directly concerned with **knowledge** and understanding looks dubious on a school curriculum. Therefore, one is just as likely today to come across children studying theories of fitness or the aesthetics of sport (see Best 1985) as to come across children getting fit or playing sports.

play The concept of 'play' is one that shows that philosophy of education does not always take its 'under labourer' task seriously enough. The concept is important in the history of education (Plato 1970b; Rousseau 1911a; Neill 1965) and has become extremely important in theories of early years education where there is much **progressivist** emphasis on the importance of play in the junior school (Moyles 1989). The level of conceptual confusion and theoretical opaqueness is extremely high in a lot of this work (see Moyles, especially the first chapter, where unsupported empirical generalisations, tautologies and definitions are all confused). However, there has been only one serious attempt at analysis within the analytic tradition. This occurs within Dearden (1968) where he analyses play in terms of three ideas: (a) that it is by its nature *non-serious* in that it is devoid of real ethical and cultural value; (b) that it is *self-contained*, being set apart from the 'duties, deliberations and developing projects which make up the serious web of purposes of ordinary life' (p. 100); that it is *immediate in its attractiveness*. It seems likely, given the different uses of 'play' (at games, playfully, with instruments, as concerned with drama), and given the claims that have been made concerning the worth of play (for example, that play at games both inculcates certain moral virtues and thus prepares children for life) that the necessary and sufficient conditions type of analysis used by Dearden is likely to run into difficulties. Probably a more fruitful approach would make use of the insights with regard to games made by Wittgenstein (see **definition**).

pluralism   Pluralism is the political doctrine that different values should be allowed to coexist within the same society. It raises the question as to what should be the minimum values to which all should conform if pluralism is to be viable. Some would say that a child should be brought up in a public culture of respect for secular institutions and different value outlooks if pluralism is to work. They might claim that forms of child-rearing that do not satisfy these requirements should not be allowed. Such communities as the Amish might then find that their preferred form of child-rearing has to be modified. More positively, other liberals might claim that a sense of justice and certain civic virtues need to be actively promoted both within the family and within schools, if pluralism is to work. Others, such as Gray (1995) claim only that diverse value groupings should be prepared to tolerate and compromise with each other and to come to a *modus vivendi*.

Should pluralists allow non-secular values to be taught in publicly-funded schools? Those who think that pluralism implies a secular public life would say 'no' (see Macedo 1996). On the other hand, it might be argued that if such schools subscribe to a common curriculum which incorporates a consensual outlook and if they also inculcate tolerance towards out-groups then the answer should be 'yes' (see Callan 1997). A particular problem arises for systems which embrace **autonomy** as an aim whether or not to fund schools for communities for which it is inimical.

political economy   Political economy is the study of economics in its political context. Its relevance to education is apparent when one considers the financing of public education systems and the determination of their **aims**. Broadly speaking, there are three different kinds of political economy relevant to the contemporary world: laissez-faire capitalism, social capitalism and socialism. Each of these models has a different approach to **vocationalism**. Laissez-faire economies, following Adam Smith (1981), tend to downplay the role of the state in preparing students directly for the labour market (Shackleton 1976; Tooley 1995). Some countries, like the United States, believe in the creation of a large graduate-level managerial class, with a more limited subdegree labour force and a large and flexible army of semi- and unskilled workers. This seems to be the pattern that the laissez-faire economies of the UK and the US are following in the late twentieth century.

By contrast, those capitalist economies which rely on a higher degree of **social cohesion** and state intervention, tend to emphasise the development of the craft and skilled worker (Streeck 1992). In doing this they are following the prescription of the nineteenth-century political economist Friedrich List (1991) in building up productive power through the development of social and mental capital at all levels. The socialist societies tended to emphasise the polytechnical tradition, which involved a generalised preparation for work through a broad curriculum at the secondary level and more specialised institutions of professional formation at the tertiary level. Different conceptions of political economy exert a powerful influence over vocational education.

postmodernism 'Postmodernism' is a term given to a set of related attitudes to contemporary civilisation. The context is the decline of 'modernism'. Modernism is said to consist of two principal elements: the functional separation of different spheres of life and the rise of secular universalism, or what is sometimes known as the Enlightenment project (cf. Gray 1995). According to some commentators, the postmodern era is characterised by three features that distinguish it from the modern era: the failure of the Enlightenment project, the growth of intracommunal ethnic diversity and the ever-growing pace of social, economic and technological change. In addition

(Bauman 1997), the modern era had an understandable rationale for functional separation, specifically the belief that science and the economy needed to be freed from traditional and religious interference in order to progress. When, however, unconditional belief in the value of scientific progress and economic growth declines, as it appears to have done in contemporary times, functional specialisation appears to be nothing more than an anomic fragmentation of the unity of human life. This rationale-free fragmentation brings in its train an increase in the loss of belief in the idea of a common good. Admittedly a scepticism about the common good has been around at least since the time of Mill (1974) but the trends characteristic of postmodernity can be said to have accentuated it.

Postmodern socio-economic trends are as follows. (1) Post-Taylorist postmodern economies rely to a decreasing degree on mass production (what there is, is being carried out automatically to an increasing extent) and to a growing degree on the provision of various kinds of services, relatively small-scale specialist production and the growing importance of knowledge and intellectual property as economic assets. (2) The break-up of class politics. This is a consequence of post-Taylorism but has far-reaching social consequences. Taylorism (division of labour in the context of a continuous production line) brought in its train a working class with a relatively strong sense of its own identity which was expressed, particularly in western Europe, through trade unions and communist and socialist parties. These in their turn provided a normative structure for the conduct of life within and outside the workplace. The decline of class-based political agitation has loosened the normative bonds holding together working-class communities. (3) Psychic discipline. As a consequence of the decline of external normative constraints due to the changes mentioned in (1) and (2) above, there is an increase in the need for individuals to discipline themselves through internal mechanisms and a corresponding search for ways in which they can be made to do so.

There are two issues that need to be dealt with. First, is the contemporary state of affairs correctly described as 'postmodern'?; second, what should our reaction be if the answer to the first question is 'yes'? It is not, perhaps, so obvious on closer inspection that our era has enough distinctive features to be described as 'postmodern'. It is at least arguable that there is or was no such thing as an Enlightenment project. Intracommunal ethnic diversity and the problem of how to deal with it is nothing new; one only has to look at Hobbes's *Leviathan* (1968) to appreciate this. It is only the third feature of the postmodern condition, namely rapid and continual change, that seems to be an unequivocally characteristic feature of contemporary times. On the issue of our response to alleged postmodernity there appear to be three identifiable reactions. A recommendation for increase in personal autonomy to cope with uncertainty is one (e.g. Bauman 1997; Carlson 1995). A second is a continuing faith in universal liberal values not buttressed by absolutely true principles discoverable by reason, but by a pragmatic concern to maintain and develop what has been found to be the most congenial form of polity for humankind (see Rorty 1989, 1991). Rejection of the Enlightenment project, including the advocacy of universal liberalism is yet another, associated with Gray (1995). Gray proposes that multivalent pluralism is the essence of the post-modern era and that particular forms of liberalism, shorn of universalising pretensions, are one possible response. In some ways, liberal responses to alleged postmodernism owe a lot to more traditional liberalism. There is a Millian scepticism about the common good and an associated emphasis on strong **autonomy** as an educational aim. The downgrading of absolute conceptions of truth and a strong belief in **pragmatism** is another. The growth of a belief in relativism and a non-judgemental attitude is also popular.

What are the general educational implications of postmodernism? In a general sense they seem to suggest an increase in influence of already influential liberal ideas about education, particularly those that arise from both the American and European **progressivist** traditions (e.g. English and Hill 1994). More particularly, they herald a **vocationalism** that stresses preparation for a post-Taylorist economy; an emphasis on non-judgemental **multiculturalism** in education; and finally, a growing interest in individual self-supervision and coun-selling to achieve this. In the area of moral education the situa-tion is less clear. Some, like Rorty, break with the Deweyan tradition by emphasising the split between public and private personae (cf. Wain 1996). Gray (1995) stresses communal moral plurality possibly associated with communal schooling, but underpinned by a minimal conception of the common good, while MacIntyre (1981) recommends a return to an Aristotelian conception of morality, although without much hope of its being realised.

The question of whether we do live in a postmodern era is debatable. If the answer is affirmative, then there are various possible educational responses. It is interesting, however, that many educational liberals and progressives believe that the postmodern condition strengthens the case for many of their favoured policies while conservatives believe that it may undermine theirs. The question of whether we live in a post-modern era may not, therefore, be a matter of entirely disinterested debate among educational policymakers, but may instead provide a new backdrop to old debates.

practical education   Practical educators advocate some form of direct engagement with materials, usually through manual activity, as a means of developing desirable attitudes, skills and cognitive dispositions. They are to be distinguished from **vocationalists**, who also advocate practical activity, by not explicitly adopting future employability as an educational **aim**. The major **progressivist** thinkers, Rousseau and Dewey, were both practical educators in this sense but Rousseau was quite explicitly a vocationalist in his advocacy of practical education (Darling 1993). **Developmentalism** in the form advocated by Piaget also encourages practical engagement with appro-priate materials as a way of coming to understand the cognitive properties of the materials that children are dealing with.

Practical educators strongly disagree amongst themselves about the extent to which the material for practical education should be prepared beforehand. Montessori thought that they should be (Darling 1994), while Dewey disagreed. They also disagree about whether children, in their practical activity, should be introduced to adult **genres**, or whether they should create their own (see Reid 1987; Cope and Kalantzis 1993).

Fundamentally, these are disputes about the degree of child-centredness appropriate for different stages of education, and as such, disputes within progressivism. There is no reason, however, to suppose that practical engagement is only a progressive concern. Those forms of traditionalism, both vocational and liberal, which value a degree of practical engagement, through for example **apprenticeship** or working with a master in the discipline, as in forms of musical and art education, also prescribe a strong degree of practice, albeit in a structured environment.

pragmatism   The philosophical movement known as Pragmatism is primarily American in origin and development. Its founder was C. S. Peirce who, in the late nineteenth century developed themes found in the work of the American philosopher, Jonathan Edwards. Peirce's version of pragmatism stressed the importance of human activity and purpose in gaining understanding and knowledge. He opposed the idea, inherited from the empiricists, that knowledge was gained passively. Nor did he believe, like the rationalists, that much of our knowledge is already present at birth. Peirce emphasised the directedness of our perceptions. He maintained that our inquiries are related to our concerns, both practical and theoretical. Peirce acknowledged that our knowledge is fallible and subject to revision, but denied that all our beliefs could be simultaneously up for revision. Our modes of inquiry are shaped by these interests and truth is determined according to criteria appropriate to a mode of inquiry. It is important to realise that, for Peirce, there is such a thing as objective **truth**, irrespective of whether there are any knowers of such truths. Peirce's theory of meaning has affinities with that of the later Wittgenstein, as he held that the meaning of terms was to be found in their use. Peirce believed that **education**

had more than instrumental purposes and that by pursuing education for its own sake, one would serve instrumental purposes, almost as a byproduct. He also believed in the value of logic as an integrative study, a view which, arguably has greatly influenced the **critical thinking** movement.

William James applied a Peircean approach to the study of the mind and to religion. Like Peirce, he stressed the active and holistic nature of perception. However, unlike Peirce, he was sceptical about the possibility of objective truth and tended to see truth as a function of the success of propositions in furthering human purposes. The characterisation of truth as viability in relation to human purposes has come to be widely accepted in the modern pragmatist tradition and is to be found in its most influential form in modern **constructivism**. John Dewey is the pragmatist thinker most closely associated with the philosophy of education. Dewey's pragmatism continued James's line of thinking concerning truth and his epistemological doctrines had a considerable impact on his educational writings. His main innovation within the pragmatist tradition was to complete the alignment of pragmatism with science and to elevate science as the primary mode of knowledge in the modern world. Moreover, unlike Peirce, Dewey's conception of science was of a primarily instrumental activity carried out to serve human purposes. Dewey's emphasis on **experience** led to tensions with his espousal of science, since much scientific knowledge does not directly depend on experience, but on abstraction from it. In fact, he starts from a very wide conception of experience which includes what we ordinarily think of as knowledge. Our knowledge of the past and future depends on our experiences of the present, which include all our interactions with the environment. Furthermore, our experience of the present is future oriented; it is structured so as to anticipate and overcome future obstacles. So for example, the study of history is undertaken so as to solve problems for us that have arisen or are likely to arise.

These views in their turn had an impact on Dewey's educational theory. Although not the founder of **progressivism** in America, he aligned himself closely with the progressive movement, which saw education as a means of solving society's problems and for moving society forward so that it would be suffused with the critical or scientific spirit. Dewey, to some extent, subscribed to these views, but at the same time denied that education was merely instrumental. It had, he held, goals which were purely educational. Dewey's educational views have been criticised on the grounds that they seem to be inconsistent. It is quite possible to maintain that education has various **aims** including liberal, as well as vocational, ones. It is much more difficult to maintain that it has aims that are intrinsic to it as well as aims that are extrinsic if one wishes, at the same time, to hold that both the intrinsic and the extrinsic aims are primary. But this seems to be the position at which Dewey arrived at, and it is, as Mounce (1996) has noted, untenable for one person to believe both. The migration of logical positivists to the US in the 1930s initially led to a decline in the influence of pragmatism, but in the work of W. V. O. Quine, the two traditions came together.

Quine's work, although enormously influential in mainstream philosophy, has had little obvious impact on education or the philosophy of education. Dewey's scientism is extended in Quine's work and also developed in the work of Rorty. Rorty's work continues themes that were first developed by James and Dewey and, in particular, he shares Dewey's concern for the development of democracy in America. One of his principal themes is the development of a non-foundational form of liberalism and the public institutions necessary to sustain it. Like his predecessors, he is also sceptical about the possibility of objective truth as his well-known comments about Orwell's *1984* illustrate (Rorty 1989). Whether this project can be sustained, given the foundational claims of American liberalism is, as Gray (1995) remarks, problematic. The educational implications of Rorty's project appear to imply enculturation and socialisation, rather than justification. Whether this is compatible with other aspects of liberalism is, again, questionable. Another area where pragmatism has been influential is in the development of **constructivist** accounts of learning, which in turn, build on the pragmatist account of truth developed by William James.

prefiguration In order to read and write properly, one must first engage in reading- and writing-like activities. Some theorists of **literacy** education have maintained that this entails that children learn to read by **reading** (the so-called **apprenticeship** approach; Waterland 1988), or through the practice of emergent **writing** (Hall 1988). In this sense, prefiguration is a common pedagogical practice. But prefiguration is used in a stronger sense; some maintain that in order for a person, society or practice to embody certain values, those values must be practised from the outset. Thus, Emile is educated in such a way that his **self-respect** is not damaged in any way, in order that he will live his life as an adult with a healthy self-respect (Rousseau 1911a). More generally, if children are to grow up with certain moral and psychological attributes, such as **autonomy**, it will be necessary for autonomy to be practised as much as possible from the outset. This however, is a fallacy. It does not necessarily follow from the fact that, in order to do X properly one must practise doing X, that one must do X *to the fullest possible extent* from the outset.

However, prefiguration in **moral** and **religious education** also poses difficulty. If doing X successfully involves practising X, then becoming a successful religious believer involves practising religious belief and, furthermore, to the maximum degree of participation. But this could be held to violate the prefigurative requirement of autonomy. The same holds good of moral education conducted according to **virtue theory**. It is thus maintained that, in these areas, students be confronted with alternatives rather than established practices (e.g. Sealey 1985). Whether the prefigurative theorist is being consistent here is unclear.

process In British educational circles it became popular, for a while, to talk about the 'processes' of education and contrast these, with the 'products' of education to the detriment of the latter (see Blenkin and Kelly 1987: esp. ch. 4). Thus teachers were advised to cease concentrating on things produced in an educational context by children and concentrate instead upon the vital educational processes that children were going through, whether such processes produced a – successful – product or not. However, such talk, although it might form a useful reminder to look at *how* children are learning as well as *what* they are learning, seems conceptually flawed. It contains no clear definition of either 'process' or 'product' and therefore no clear distinction between the two. It is an obvious, but important, point that to identify processes as processes of a certain type, for instance, rational, imaginative or artistic is to identify them in their products, that is in the giving of reasons or the production of artworks. But if this is so then the process/product distinction collapses (D. Carr 1992). Whereas, if what is meant by 'process' is conceptually divorced from the type of product, say, whether the children are happy doing the task or not, then this may not be an educational concern and may be beyond the teacher's power to ensure (ibid.).

progressivism Progressivism is a cluster of doctrines concerning **pedagogy**, **aims** and the **curriculum**. It is characterised by a distrust of **authority** in education and by an emphasis on the individual child as the centre of pedagogic concern. The two key figures in progressivist thinking are Rousseau and Dewey; others are Pestalozzi, Froebel and Montessori. Although Dewey appears to have been influenced by Rousseau, they have distinctive approaches to education and while Rousseau and his followers have been influential in Europe, particularly in the UK, Dewey remains the dominant progressive thinker in the United States.

Rousseau's major educational text, *Emile or Education* (1911a) is best understood as a prolegomenon in moral psychology for the emancipatory political project outlined in *The Discourses on Inequality* (1911b) and *The Social Contract* (1913). Only in a society freed from the harmful influence of inflamed *amour propre* (see **self-respect**) would it be possible for humans to associate as free and equal beings capable of binding together for the common good. In society as it existed in Rousseau's time, patterns of domination and submission led, on the one hand, to people who enjoyed dominating others for the sake of it and, on the other hand, to people inflamed with paranoid resentment against those who wielded power over them. Rousseau does not distinguish between power and authority in existing societies and assumes any kind of social relationship that involves asymmetrical power relations, which is not consciously entered into by free and equal rational beings, even when it expresses legitimate authority, to be harmful.

For this reason he proposed to educate Emile away from society under the tutelage of an adult who would guide him to a state of independence free from any trace of inflamed *amour propre*. The tutor (Rousseau himself) is then the archetypal progressivist pedagogue, whose relationship to his charge is ambiguous. For the tutor could not have an *overt* position of power *vis-à-vis* his pupil for fear of bringing about the result that he had been put in place to avoid, namely, the engendering of paranoid resentment. This means that he could not engage in *overt* **teaching**, but had to rely on manipulation on the one hand and the spontaneous growth of curiosity in Emile on the other. This latter was dependent on his developing *amour propre* which was, in turn, dependent on the beneficial interaction of biological maturation and social intercourse. Rousseau thus introduced the ideas of **development** and growth into educational thought and these in turn influenced Pestalozzi (who emphasised the importance of readiness for learning) and Froebel (who emphasised the importance of **play**).

The upshot of Rousseau-inspired progressivism is that children should be enabled to learn what they wish to learn when they are ready to do so and the preferred pedagogical method should be play enriched with the covert guidance of the teacher/facilitator. These ideas entered mainstream psychology through the work of Piaget and, more recently have influenced **psycholinguistics** through the work of Chomsky. Rousseau presents an individualistic account of education which is difficult to apply in an unadulterated form to public education systems. Dewey criticised Rousseau on the grounds that he wished nature to do all the work of teaching and he also believed that Rousseau was mistaken in thinking that children should be taken out of the environment; rather they should be placed in an environment suitable to learning. As Darling (1994) has argued, both of these criticisms are misplaced. Rousseau assigned a very definite role to the tutor as arch-manipulator of the educational setting, exerting a covert but near-absolute power over the pupil. This in itself poses the danger that the child's discovery that he is being manipulated may lead to the very kind of paranoid resentment that Emile's education was designed to avoid (see **self-respect**). At the same time, Rousseau was very sensitive to the kind of environment that children were supposed to grow up in, rejecting sophisticated contemporary society for a much simpler social environment which could be controlled for the benefit of the child's education. However, these criticisms illustrate the differences of emphasis between the two thinkers.

American progressivism thus differs in important respects from the European movement, whose most important influence is Rousseau. The clearest difference lies in the former's very strong relationship with **pragmatism**, especially with the work of Dewey. Pragmatists insist that philosophy needs to put human beings, with their purposes and problems, at the centre of philosophical inquiry. In Dewey's philosophy of education, this means that the primary recipients of education, children, become central to education. Students' purposes and problems, as they are conceived of by students are the starting point for educational activity. Like European progressivists, the Americans stress the importance of growth in the educational process. The aim of education is to promote growth, since it is only through growth that people will be able to adopt a wider range of purposes, means of achieving those purposes and thus go on to promote further growth. Growth and democracy are intertwined since, according to Dewey, democracy involves the making of further connections among individuals in order to promote mutual growth in a social context in which no one is allocated undeserved privileges. Unlike Rousseau and his followers, however, Dewey stressed the importance of a social context in which this growth took place. In American progressivism, the public schooling system is an appropriate vehicle for education, precisely because it can serve as a breeding ground for democratic values through the promotion of connections between individuals that can further serve their purposes.

Of themselves, these views need not lead to the practice of child-centred forms of education, but Dewey (1916) insisted that the purposes and contextual features of schooling should be determined by the students themselves and their own perception of their interests, rather than be determined by adult perceptions. While Rousseau was concerned that a child's activity was not overtly other-directed, he retained the view that the tutor worked with the long-term interests of the pupil in mind, to promote a healthy form of *amour propre*. It is not clear whether Dewey should be called a liberal or an instrumentalist in educational aims. On the one hand, he believed that education had intrinsic aims, which were essentially defined in educational terms. On the other, he also believed that education should enable students to engage fully in the world and find a place there through the pursuit of their own projects which would, in most cases, involve gaining employment. There is definitely an emphasis on practical activity in the classroom, which Dewey saw as a necessary means of learning. Learning takes place through encountering difficulties, trying out responses to them and, when those responses are successful in furthering inquiry, adopting them as knowledge.

There are distinctive features of the pedagogy of American progressivism. First, the role of teachers is largely to further the collectively determined purposes of students. There is, therefore, a strong emphasis on social activity in the school. Second, the learning of material which is not immediately relevant to the purposes of students is to be discouraged.

Third, forms of learning that detract from student **autonomy**, such as rote learning, are also to be discouraged. Fourth, it was important for Dewey that students learn about the properties of materials through experimentation with them; he disliked pre-prepared materials which did not allow the students first-hand acquaintance with their properties. There is a further implication for the curriculum which follows from the first two points, namely that the field of inquiry should not be constrained by predetermined adult categorisations of the subject matter of human inquiry. There is, therefore, a strong emphasis on subject integration.

This educational programme has numerous critics, both on major issues and in detail. First, Dewey has been criticised for the vagueness and ambiguity of his stance on the nature of education. It is quite legitimate to refuse to draw a hard-and-fast distinction between liberal and instrumental conceptions, but it is less defensible to refuse to prioritise them and still less defensible to say that there can be two, mutually exclusive, conceptions, one liberal, the other **instrumental**. At one point, he says of the teacher that he is 'engaged not simply in the training of individuals, but in the formation of the proper social life' (Dewey 1929). At another, he maintains that 'the educational process has no end beyond itself; it is its own end' (1916: 59). Second, he has been accused of ambiguity as to whether education is to promote new values in society or to encourage students to improve on the old. Third, the adoption of growth as an aim has been thought to be unsatisfactory. Growth can occur in socially harmful, as well as beneficial, directions and it cannot be acceptable that schools promote the latter. Growing to be a criminal, for example, cannot be a legitimate educational aim in most people's eyes. Progressivists will reply that criminality doesn't promote further growth and so cannot be a legitimate educational aim. The existence of successful and unpunished criminals does not lend strong support for this view.

Just as in the UK, there are mixed views about the impact of progressivism on education and society in the US. It is at least arguable that the **vocationalist** and social tendencies within progressivism in the US are both an expression of perceived American values and a legitimate extension of them. On the other hand, many in the US are disturbed about the alleged lack of direction in the public schooling system and a consequent decline in educational performance. Dewey (1938) himself expressed reservations about some of the practices that were carried out in the name of progressivism. As the US has a decentralised education system, the impact of progressivism has, at the same time, been both more limited than in the UK but also, because it cannot be reversed by governmental *fiat*, it has, as a practice and a philosophy, possibly securer roots.

There is thus a tension within progressivism between individualistic and social conceptions of **learning**. The Rousseau variant emphasises the importance of the individual in constructing his own cognitive world, while the Dewey variant stresses the role of the group in doing so. The former strand appeals to the work of Piaget while the latter appeals to the social **constructivism** that is (questionably) associated with the work of the psychologist Vygotsky (1962). These tensions have a practical effect on pedagogic strategies. While Rousseauian progressives emphasise individual learning at a pace chosen by the learner, Deweyans stress group and project work. Both reject the teacher as authority figure and hence reject a social model that places the teacher at the centre of the classroom. In practice, group work tends to be more complex to operate than individual work and so much progressive education tends, in practice, to be individual work conducted at the child's own chosen pace.

In assessing the impact of progressivism on public education systems one must distinguish between influence in schools and influence amongst the educational elite of teacher educators, inspectors and educational academics. Dewey's work had a significant although limited impact on public education in America. Among the elite however, Dewey's and Rousseau's ideas have enduring appeal and constantly resurface in reworked form such as in the **apprenticeship** approach to reading advocated by F. Smith, or in the proposals for neo-Deweyan schools to be found for example in English and

Hill (1994). In continental western Europe the influence of both Dewey and Rousseau has been very limited. In other parts of the world such as the West Indies, progressivism has been stoutly resisted. In Britain however, the influence has been much more significant, particularly in primary schools. Significant landmarks include the publication in 1911 of *What is and What Might Be* by Edmond Holmes; an ex-inspector, the Hadow Report in 1931, which explicitly and unfavourably contrasted passive with active learning and finally, the Plowden Report of 1967. Progressivism was established in teacher training colleges preparing primary school teachers and was supported in varying degrees by inspectors and educational academics. As such it gained widespread influence throughout the 1970s and 1980s. It came under criticism from within philosophy of education, notably through the work of the analytical school, who defended traditional forms of liberal **education**, represented by, for example, R.S. Peters and R.F. Dearden. The substance of their critique was that progressive thinking was muddled and ambiguous and could not support the extravagant claims that it made. However, Peters is a far more generous critic of Rousseau than is the conservative writer G. H. Bantock (1965) who draws particular attention to what he sees as Rousseau's baleful influence on British education, identifying Rousseau's rejection of authority as a key feature of progressivism's harmful influence.

Although these critiques had little impact in the years immediately following their publication, political and public opinion was beginning to turn against progressivism. Academic critics of progressivism gained in confidence and mounted more unqualified attacks. Notable among these are Woods and Barrow (1975), Alexander (1984, 1992) and, more obliquely, Cooper (1980). Contemporary progressivism has no advocates of the intellectual and literary brilliance of a Rousseau or even the persuasiveness of a Dewey and its ability to defend itself from analytically minded critics is open to serious doubt. Since, however, educational change is not wholly a rational process, this may not materially affect the medium-term prospects of progressivism as an influence on public education.

psycholinguistics   Psycholinguistics is the study of the alleged psychological processes underlying language acquisition and competence. Effectively founded by Chomsky (1957, 1965), psycholinguistics suggests that we innately possess a 'language acquisition device' (LAD), which is a rule-like representation of the fundamental rules of grammar of any language. Psycholinguistics also proposes a set of innate concepts which underly the lexicon of any language (e.g. Chomsky 1988; Fodor 1975). These representational systems are the capacities that all humans have for acquiring the ability to speak their mother tongue, which is, in effect 'switched on' (Chomsky 1988) by exposure of the baby to its community language. When the mother tongue is 'switched on', this constitutes the linguistic **competence** of the native speaker. Crucial to the psycholinguistic account is that most of one's language is learned rapidly and without effort. The account is informative because, it is maintained, the LAD explains how the ability to understand and speak new and potentially infinitely long sentences can be acquired through exposure to a few finitely long ones. Psycholinguistics has also been employed to explain how one learns to read (see **reading**).

Although extremely influential, this approach to language learning has come under vigorous attack, notably from philosophers and linguists influenced by Wittgenstein (e.g. Baker and Hacker 1984, but see also Searle 1992). Wittgensteinian critics regard the psycholinguistic identification of mind with brain as nonsensical and the postulation of representations and **rules** in the brain as a category mistake which leads to incoherence in the attempt to explain human linguistic ability.

public schools   To begin with, the title of this section will be understood in the English sense i.e. where 'public' means 'private'. There is actually very little in the literature of the philosophy of education which deals directly with the existence of private schools within the context of a state education system. What little there is tends to either focus on parental rights and a liberal concern for diversity within educational provision. Of late such variety of provision has tended to be seen as one of the strands of **multiculturalism** (see Almond 1991).

This lack of attention to private education as such might be the result of the distaste that many educationalists (and therefore many philosophers of education) feel for it. However, if so, the proper response to distaste may be attack rather than removing one's gaze. Or it may be the case that the silence results from a deep feeling for the dilemma of parents who have to choose between what they think is good for society as a whole – an excellent state schooling system – and what they think is good for their own children – a place in a private school because the local state schools are less than excellent. Again, a proper discussion of the conflict, rather than turning away from it seems desirable.

For it is an important conflict and the context that gives rise to it is both educationally and politically very disturbing. It has been argued (Hollis 1982) that education in many of its aspects is a 'positional good' that is, a good valuable to some people only on the condition that others do not have it. It is certainly true that in Rawls's terms (Rawls 1971) education is both a primary good (something that every rational person would want), but is also an excellent indicator, once you've got it, of your chances of acquiring and keeping other primary goods such as health, wealth and self respect. Given both of these notions of goods, it is obviously the case that education is of enormous social and political (and moral) concern.

It becomes even more of a concern in a system such as the English one where there is provision of places in Higher Education for only a third of a relevant section of the population and where the 'league tables' of educational performance are fittingly so titled because they show that it is indeed the case that different schools are in different leagues. So for instance, the last league tables (1997) indicated that, although private education by no means guaranteed good educational outcomes, attendance at the best private schools – and the best were by no means confined to the old 'greats' such as Eton, Westminster, Harrow – gave you opportunities for educational outcome which were very significantly better than the opportunities on offer at the best state schools. The gap between the best state schools and even moderately successful state schools was at least as great as the gap between private and state system. And the gap between the best and the worst of either system was of Grand Canyon scale. With approximately 10 per cent of children in private education and a system manipulated by the middle classes to ensure that their children (a) attended private schools, or (b) the best state schools, or (c) had significant educational help at home to become educationally successful, we have a recipe for potential educational and social disaster. Our system seems designed to deny social justice rather than promote it and to ensure that education with all the goods attached to it is the province of a minority – albeit a large one – of the population.

A warning has been sounded by someone writing about public schools in the American sense. After arguing that both liberals and conservatives in America have, in their different ways, undermined the notion of the common school, Reese (1988: 440) writes:

> Democracy is a sham without a system of public schools that introduce everyone to a world of ideas, values and knowledge that takes all children beyond their own narrow and private worlds.

and

> The enemies of the common culture are those who think the poor or culturally different are so different that they, cannot share in a common bounty.

If education, in either place, really is contributing to these divisions then we all may be in serious trouble.

punishment   The usual opening move in discussions of punishment in schools is to distinguish punishment from **discipline** and then to discuss the type of consideration that might be thought to justify punishment within schools. Following

Peters's treatment (1966) 'discipline' is usually defined as the submission to **rules** – whether these rules be those of a subject such as English, those of a context or institution such as a classroom or school, or moral rules – and punishment explained as that which may happen when such rules are broken.

The definition of 'punishment' often taken for a starting point derives from Hart's seminal work on the subject (Hart 1970). Hart defines punishment as the deliberate infliction of pain or unpleasantness, by someone in **authority**, upon an offender, for an offence. (There are provisos in Hart's account for slightly substandard cases, for example, it can be something usually supposed to be painful or unpleasant; and the notion of 'offence' – and therefore 'offender' – is tied to voluntary wrongdoing.)

Whilst Hart offers the standard case of punishment it is obvious that it needs amendment when applied to schools and children. Partly, this is because school rules are, in many ways, unlike the laws of the land; they often involve customary practice rather than published statute. Partly, because in schools, but not in society, there is no separation of powers, so that the teacher can be judge, jury and gaoler. Partly, because the fact that we are dealing with children complicates the notions of 'offence' and 'offender'. (Can we really talk in these terms of a small child? See Peters 1966 and Richard Smith 1985.) One might also mention in this context – and following on from the above points – the scale of penalties used in schools. Although there are obvious formal penalties used by schools such as detention and suspension (and, when Peters first addressed the issue, corporal punishment) the most likely form of punishment is a reprimand. The realisation that this is the sort of thing we are talking about in this context, might reassure those who think that it is simply inappropriate to talk of 'pain and unpleasantness' in a school setting, and that any talk of punishment here is simply a confession of failure.

The main argument among philosophers of education concerns the role of punishment in schools. There are those, following Peters, who see punishment as, at best, a 'necessary nuisance' in schools. The idea here being that if children

understand the rules and the penalties attached to infringe-
ments then the best outcome would be simple compliance
and no necessity for punishment. For, in punishing, the
teacher may erode the relationship with the child which is
necessary for successful schooling. There are those, influenced
by P. S. Wilson (1971) who see punishment as a vital part
of introducing children to the moral dimension of life. The
thought here is that if we do not respond in appropriate ways
to children's actions, such as reacting with gratitude when
they do something for us, then children will never learn the
meaning of moral terms. Punishment is the appropriate
response to wrongdoing.

The Wilson case is rather spoiled by a dubious distinction
between punishment and penalisation, but also by a rather
glaring *non sequitur*. In the first of these Wilson tries to argue
that mere penalties such as a parking fine, do not carry a
moral impact whereas punishments proper, like detention for
bullying, do. However, his distinction between the moral and
non-moral seems distinctly odd (see R. Smith 1985). The
non sequitur occurs because Wilson argues that punishment is
a way of *introducing* children to the moral dimension of life.
However, given that the standard definition of 'punishment'
implies that you can only punish voluntary offenders for
particular offences, and given the fact that usually built into
the notion of 'voluntary offender', is the idea that the person
concerned knows that they are doing wrong, then Wilson's
argument must be mistaken. Either children do not know
they are doing wrong, and therefore you cannot, logically,
punish them; or, they do know they are doing wrong, and
therefore they do not need punishment to *introduce* them to
a realisation of this.

However, faults in argumentation apart, Wilson seems to
be driving towards an important point. If we do not in some
way, respond differently to a moral offence than to, say, an
error of procedure in mathematics, then how are children to
learn the difference betwen the two?

The answer here, perhaps, lies in noting two things. First,
in moral education as elsewhere, practice is of vital importance

and whereas punishment cannot introduce children to morality it can help to reinforce moral practice. Second, the same words – or almost the same words – spoken in a different tone of voice – and tone is of the essence here – may serve a different function. The first time they are spoken they may serve as a warning to a child that a certain action is not permitted (hopefully with an explanation as to why it is not permitted). The second time they are spoken they may serve as a reprimand, that is, a punishment.

If punishment in schools does have a function in moral education it is attended by dangers. *Contra* Wilson, it seems perfectly possible to punish for the infraction of rules that are idiosyncratic, stupid or downright nonsensical. If schools punish for such infractions then they run the risk of alienating children from the processes of moral education that punishment is supposed to reinforce. But even if the rules make sense we have to be careful that we send the types of moral message that we deem appropriate. So, for instance, few of us would object to rules against bullying and punishment following the breaking of such rules, and few of us would have difficulty in justifying such rules. However, when it comes to rules about school uniform or types of hair style and the punishments that follow from infractions of these rules, then the matter changes. Partly, because how one wears one's hair does not seem to be a moral matter at all. Partly, because in enforcing such rules, schools seem to be stepping over the private/public boundary which derives from Mill (1974) which many of us would see as crucial to a proper understanding of morality.

This is not to deny that one may have to have procedural rules which, whilst not directly moral, function as part of the social glue which helps the institution to continue and, are, therefore, indirectly of moral concern. It is to deny that some of the issues which schools identify as needing such rules have any such role.

quality   During the 1990s it has become fashionable to talk about 'quality in education'. Part of the reason for this is a renewed interest in **accountability**. Why should the concern for accountability be expressed in terms of quality? One major reason is that concerns about whether or not a particular form of education is worthwhile have been expressed in terms of a paradigm derived from manufacturing industry. 'Quality' in a commercial context strongly connotes product usefulness and reliability. 'Quality assurance' refers to systems that are robust enough to ensure that products that are defective or unreliable simply do not get made. The idea, as one quality guru has said, is to 'get it right first time'. Of course, an artefact can be scrapped or reworked if it is defective, but a service cannot. If it is not 'right first time' then it is not right. So effective quality assurance systems ought to be particularly relevant to service areas of economic activity.

Whether or not it is in the private or the public sector of the economy, it is sometimes maintained that **education** has the characteristics of a service industry. In particular, if education is poorly provided then there is no second chance for the recipient. A diner at a restaurant who has a badly cooked meal will feel disgruntled but will suffer no permanent damage. On the other hand, the pupil who receives a poor education may not even feel disgruntled but may suffer permanent damage in terms of future life prospects. It is, then, not

surprising to hear that a key feature of educational accountability is the provision of quality assurance systems.

The question then arises of how one assures the quality of
education. There are two answers which are not necessarily
incompatible with each other. The first focuses on *processes*,
the second on *outcomes*. Process-based quality assurance relies
on observation of teaching and learning and the activities that
support it, to be the key determinant of whether the education
being offered is worthwhile. **Inspection** is the most common
form of process quality assurance. Outcome-based quality
assurance relies on the **assessment** of the outcomes against
certain pre-agreed standards. Examination and testing are the
most common forms.

Both these approaches are widely employed and both have
their critics (for a comprehensive account of the issues see
Winch 1996). Inspection is criticised for employing subjective ideas about what constitutes **good practice** as criteria
for the assessment of processes (Alexander 1992). Testing is
criticised for lack of reliability and validity and for distorting
the curriculum (Davis 1995). Beyond this, there are value
questions: are certain forms of teaching inherently damaging
irrespective of results? Are certain educational **aims** unavoid-
ably compromised through a regime of measuring results
through testing? One approach now thought to be disastrous
is a combination of both approaches through the use of an
inspectorate to test outcomes. This underlay the 'payment by
results' approach to teachers adopted in the latter half of the
nineteenth century (Silver 1994). This example suggests that
any approach to quality assurance, when employed dogmati-
cally and insensitively, is liable to prove a poor indicator of
quality.

racism It might be thought that the definition of 'racism' is relatively straightforward and would involve something like the idea of discriminating against a racial group in a particular situation upon grounds that are not relevant to the matter in hand. With this kind of definition we seem to capture the unfairness, prejudice, offence against impartiality, involved in refusing to consider certain people for a non-racially sensitive job – whilst at the same time not considering as racist those practices of discrimination, such as screening babies of African ancestry for sickle cell anaemia, where race is a relevant factor given this particular issue.

However – and apart from the fact that 'race' itself may be disputed concept – much recent literature on the subject and its implications for education has objected to the simplicity of this definition because, it is felt, it does not capture all we ought to be concerned about in this area. So, for instance, M. Jones (1985) has argued that we need a definition of racism which focuses on outcomes as well as attitudes and procedures and which is sensitive to the fact that what is non-racist in one condition of society is racist in another (but see Flew 1987). Such a notion of 'institutional' racism has been extended by other authors to include more or less everything about the present status quo. So, for instance, Nixon (1985) and Troyna (1987) seem to argue that racism is about domination and power in a capitalist society and that unless this is recognised very little can be done within education to change the situation (but see Short 1991).

Whatever the pros and cons of the above debate it is slightly depressing to see it carried out in the empirical vacuum that usually characterises it. It may be the case that we live in an endemically racialist society. It also may be the case that our educational practices contribute to that racialism. However, if this is so then some of the evidence which seems of obvious pertinence to these issues needs to be confronted head on. So, for several years the Inner London Educational Association research unit compiled figures of educational outcomes in terms of racial groupings. Patterns in these findings do emerge but they do little to support any notion of simple or institutional racism. So, for example, one might find in a particular year, that children from an African background do significantly better than children from an Afro-Caribbean background. Children from an Indian background both outperform white British children and far outperform children of Bangladeshi origins. Children from Turkish and Irish backgrounds do significantly worse than all other groups. Such differential outcomes *may* be the result of schooling and there *may* be something we can do about this, but we cannot even begin to address these problems unless we focus upon them and not – either theoretically and practically – upon racism as such – in either its simple or institutional forms and as long as we keep talking about the problems of 'black' children.

rationality   The achievement of rationality has been a declared **aim** of liberal education at least since the time of Plato. The Platonic tradition has stressed the importance of rationality in mastering the passions and achieving a detached view of reality. Since the time of Kant, the emphasis has shifted to seeing rationality as (a) a necessary condition for the achievement of **autonomy** and (b) in a more immediately practical way, as a means of achieving one's everyday goals. In the work of Peters (1966) and his immediate successors, rational autonomy has become the main aim of liberal education. In the work of

Peters, Hirst (1965a) and, to some extent, J. P. White (1973, 1982), rationality had to be undergirded by a substantial degree of propositional knowledge. Modern **progressivism** retains autonomy as an aim but is much less insistent on the under-girding knowledge. Achievement of one's own ability to rationally choose ends in life has come to be seen as the criterion of a successful liberal education. The achievement of highly specific practical rationalities, on the other hand, has come to be seen as the proper goal of **vocationalism**. In the US, the Deweyan tradition has tended to emphasise the role of education in providing a critique of existing knowledge and values and, consequently, the theoretical faculty of critical rationality has been highly prized. This concern with the development of critical rationality as the principal educational aim has provided much of the impetus behind the **critical thinking** movement.

In the last two centuries, Plato's influence has made itself felt in another way. In the *Republic*, only a small number of carefully selected men and women were capable of achieving theoretical rationality. The work of Galton (1973) and his followers gave rise to the psychometry movement, one of whose major claims was that intelligence (conceived as capa-bility for rational thought) was innate, measurable and unalterable. These Platonic tenets were put into effect by Burt in the UK and underlay selection for secondary schooling from 1944 until the beginning of the 1970s. In the US the testing movement was associated with Terman (1917) and later, with Jensen (1973), and Murray and Herrnstein (1994), where it became influential in debates about the innate rational capacity of different racial groups. Needless to say, there were many critiques of this movement, among the most effective is that of Gould (1981).

Claims concerning alleged different levels of rationality for different ethnic and social groupings can also be found in verbal deficit theories (associated with Bernstein 1973 and Bereiter and Engelmann 1966). In these theories, it is the language of lower-class groups that has a limited capacity for the expression of rationality. A celebrated, although exaggerated, rebuttal of these claims can be found in Labov (1972). Mainstream philosophical work on the concept of rationality has continued apace. Bennett (1964) provides a useful conceptual basis for examining the claims of the psychometric and verbal deficit movements. C. Winch (1990) surveys the debates over these movements. More recently still, game theoretic models of practical rationality have been used to explore political issues concerning the provision of education (e.g. Tooley 1995).

reading There have been many different attempts to explain the ability to read. Some focus on the alphabetic nature of **writing** and maintain that one learns to read through the recognition of letter–sound correspondences and the phonic complexity of words; an approach known as *phonics* (e.g. Bryant and Bradley 1985). Others maintain that one learns to recognise words as indecomposable wholes. One of the most influential recent approaches is based on **psycholinguistics** and **constructivism** (F. Smith 1985). The psycholinguistic approach maintains that the 'reading process' is really a process of interpreting authorial intentions and that there is no literal meaning to be gained from text. This process takes place at a level beyond consciousness and does not, therefore, require conscious effort. Accordingly, children learning to read should be exposed to 'real books' rather than primers based on faulty accounts of how children learn to read and should learn through a form of **apprenticeship** (Waterland 1985), copying adult reading behaviours.

In the most recent period, there has been a backlash against apprenticeship approaches in favour of phonics, due to claims that the former method leads to a decline in reading standards. For example, the two major political parties in the UK have publicly aligned themselves with phonics. Disputes about the correct way to teach children how to read are usually conducted with such passion that one suspects that a larger agenda lies behind the particular quarrel. It is quite likely that the alignment of psycholinguistic approaches with **progressivism** and phonic approaches with more traditional

approaches to **pedagogy** is the motivation for the ferocity
with which debates about reading are usually conducted.

reconstructivism   Reconstructivism was an approach to **education** in America which stressed the social roles of **schools**
in any attempt to change society. It first appeared in the 1930s
after the Great Depression but, perhaps its fullest flowering
was in the work of Brameld in the 1950s (1950a, b). He
identified three major approaches to education in America:
perennialism (the Great Books approach), essentialism (the
social heritage approach) and **progressivism**, which he identified with growth. Whilst dismissing the first two he saw his
own ideas as a completion of the third. His work was unusu-
ally ambitious in its scope, seeking to synthesise the work of
the **pragmatists** with the work of such figures as Freud and
Marx and looking for a conception of truth grounded in social
consensus. Such grand theories, of anything, are always at the
risk of disintegration because of attacks upon their component theories. It is also the case, with this particular grand
theory, that the 1950s in America were hardly propitious times
for someone who cited Marx and was tolerant towards
communism. The movement seems to have ended at the end
of the decade.

Such grand approaches have fallen from favour with the
growth of the analytic movement within philosophy of education but echoes of this type of synthetic understanding of
education can, perhaps, be seen in the work of Egan and his
'recapitulation' theory (1988).

reductionism   Reductionism is the doctrine that one kind of
thing is really another (for example, the mind is really nothing
more than the brain) or one kind of event can be *explained*
as another kind (for example, all mind activity can be
explained as brain activity; for a critique, see Taylor 1964).
The first of these is called *ontological* and the second *epistemological* reduction. Reductionism has been popular in certain
areas of education because it promises to impose simplicity

of explanation on what appears to be complex. For example, learning can be described as training the brain (Evers 1990), or learned abilities can be redescribed as a series of **competences** (Jessup 1991). While it might be tempting to think that education could consist of nothing more than brain-training or competence-inculcation there are factors that should make us suspicious. The most important of these is the possibility that the reduction is spurious, that the mind is not to be identified with the brain or ability with a set of discrete competences. If the reduction is spurious, then so is an explanatory reduction based on the ontological one. Reductionism will always be a temptation in education. This is partly because of the general influence of philosophical ideas on educational ones, partly because reductionism offers a Holy Grail to teachers and policy-makers, namely the possibility of showing that something highly complex is really rather simple. Unfortunately, it has too often been shown that complexity is an irreducible feature of human life and cannot be explained away.

reflective teaching   A recent survey of teacher training courses in England and Wales asked whether there was an agreed model of the teacher involved in such courses. Of the course leaders who answered 'yes' to this question, the vast majority described this model as that of the 'reflective practitioner' (Whitty 1992). But, as McLaughlin (in an unpublished paper) has shown, there is a vast difference between using this kind of description as a slogan and unpacking it in a way that is both sensible and useful. One of the problems here is that the literature on 'reflective practice' presents us with different and competing models of the meaning of the term. At one end of the 'reflective practice' continuum are notions of technical rationality derived from Aristotle and Dewey, where emphasis is placed upon approaching educational problems in a systematic, scientific manner. At the other end, where reflection deals with the implicit and the intuitive, there are models derived from Schon (1983, 1987), which focus on the type of mastery which is embodied, for example, in a group of jazz musicians improvising together. Both halves of the continuum invite questions concerning the scope and objects of reflection and the assessment of the quality of such reflection. As with Aristotle's *phronesis* or practical wisdom, it may be much easier to gesture towards someone who exhibits this quality than to give any compelling account as to how the quality can be developed and judged.

relativism Relativism is the idea that there are belief systems – whether factual or ethical – which are somehow constitutive of a given society or social group; which conflict in some way with the belief systems of other societies or social groups, and for which there is no objective decision procedure when such a conflict occurs. In the case of values this means that what is taken as valuable by one social group may be taken as either valueless or wicked by another social group and there is no way of rationally resolving this difference of valuation. In the case of factual or cognitive relativism it is held that what is true or rational for one social group may not be true or rational for other social groups and given that truth and rationality can only be applied relative to some social group – that is, something is only true or rational *for someone* – then there is no way of deciding what is really true or rational.

Both types of relativism have their basis in the obvious fact that societies and social groups have differed and do differ in their ethical and factual outlooks. However, such true descriptions of the world do not, in themselves, sanction the type of relativistic positions drawn above. For these to follow, we would have to assume that each of the differing belief systems were subscribed to by equally enlightened, knowledgeable, conceptually clear and reflective people, that is, that they are not the result of ignorance, prejudice, pig-headedness and lack of vision; and there seems to be no reason to make these assumptions. Certainly, the moral and cognitive recommendations that are often tacked on to relativistic theories, for example, that we should be tolerant of other belief systems, seem often to be either mistaken or incoherent. If I believe, for instance, that taking innocent life is wrong then this must mean that I condemn societies that practise some forms of human sacrifice (Distance here adds a dubious gloss to the thesis. 'Cannibalism is right for cannibals but not for us' ignores the fact that in certain circumstances it is us that the cannibals want to eat.) If I believe that science gives us knowledge then I must disbelieve that the same is true for magic. Besides the recommendation of **toleration** seems a poor attempt to smuggle in one universal value into a world which, according to the relativists, can harbour no such thing. Cognitive relativism typically (a) can give no account of its own thesis – how can it be true *for everyone* that there are no universal truths? and (b) routinely includes within its descriptions items that are barred by its thesis, for example, if it really is true that the only rationality and truth that I can recognise is that of my own social group then how can I possibly discern that other social groups have *any* notion of rationality and truth?

Relativism, from time to time, becomes a force to be reckoned with in education. It surfaced within the Sociology of Knowledge (see **sociology of knowledge**) and has resurfaced within **postmodernism**. However, it has never been and is not the orthodox position in philosophy as such and, despite the claims of some of its supporters, it does not represent the received wisdom of the end of the twentieth century. Good discussions of various forms of relativism are to be found in B. Wilson (1970), Hollis and Lukes (1982), and B. Williams (1972).

Religious Education (RE) RE raises a number of important philosophical, political and educational issues. First, the nature of religion; second, the nature of religious education; and third, questions of **accountability** and freedom. Religion is described both as a set of beliefs and as a practice. Some maintain that religious belief is the most important thing

205

about religion, so that the distinctive characteristic of reli-
giously-minded people is that they believe certain propositions
about deities, prophets, cosmology and miracles to be true.
In addition, they subscribe to a code of moral beliefs that is
closely related to the first set of beliefs mentioned above. The
second approach to religion maintains that practice is most
important. The distinctive characteristic of religious life,
according to this account, is prayer, worship, singing and cere-
mony. Religion is a primarily expressive activity, with a
significant emphasis on abiding features of human life, such
as birth, procreation and death, together with a close relationship with a moral code.

The major point of difference between literal and expressive
conceptions of religion lies in the interpretation of indicative
mood statements. Subscribers to the first point of view hold
that these statements are either true or false and that religious
believers take them to be true in the case of their own beliefs
and false in the case of others. Statements like 'Christ has
risen', would be taken by Christians for example, to refer to
events concerning a real person which are true. The contrary,
expressive view interprets such statements not as true or false
but as expressive of certain attitudes and emotions. In the
case of the example, the statement should perhaps be interpreted to mean of Christ 'Let Him be exalted' (D. Z. Phillips
1997). This in turn can be interpreted as an expression of
thanksgiving for the life of Christ and an exhortation to
prayer.

It might be thought that it is not possible for both of these
accounts to be true; it cannot be possible for a statement to
be both true and expressive, any more than one can ask a
question and issue a command with the same utterance. But
this need not be the case. It is an oversimplified view of
language to hold that utterances must have only one aspect.
When someone says, in an appropriate context, 'There are
no circumstances under which I will betray you', he can be
taken to be saying something that he thinks is true and to
be giving a solemn promise. The former aspect is assertoric,
the latter is expressive. Likewise, there is no reason to suppose

that one could not utter 'Christ has risen' and mean *both* that an event had occurred which involved a real person *and* that such a person and such an event should be given thanks for. Indeed, it might be claimed that a distinctive feature of religion was that it combines assertoric and expressive practices in such a manner that they cannot readily be disentangled.

RE is usually classified either as *confessional* or as *non-confessional*. In the former case, the aim is to encourage participation by engendering belief in the tenets of the religion or through full-hearted participation in religious practices or both. The latter aims to teach about the beliefs and practices of a religious community without engendering belief or a desire to participate. Secularists usually maintain that non-confessional forms of religious education are the only kind compatible with the aim of **autonomy**, anything else is **indoctrination**. Believers, on the other hand, hold that the only way in which one can bring up a new generation of believers is by giving them a confessional religious education from birth (*ab initio* RE). Hirst (1965b) argued that religion is not, properly speaking, a form of **knowledge** and so should not be taught confessionally. D. Z. Phillips (1970) argued, in opposition, that religion was not primarily assertoric but expressive and that it was a misunderstanding of religion simply to see it as a set of beliefs, either true or false. The aim of religious education on this account is to elucidate religious belief and practices in order to show how they work for religious believers. Neither of these accounts addresses the issue raised by the claim that *ab initio* confessional religious education is necessary for the transmission of religious belief. Those who hold the necessity of confessional RE would also argue that neither kind of the above would give children an insight into the nature of religion. Both the approaches advocated by Hirst and Phillips can only work if they are a secondary form of RE, building on the earlier work of confessional religious educators. Otherwise RE threatens to give children a distorted picture of confused and irrational practices and beliefs which obscures, rather than elucidates, the nature of religion.

Confessional RE raises its own problems. Do parents have the right to raise children in their own religion? If they do, should they be supported in their endeavour through public funding? If public funding is made available by a state which is neutral between religions and secular in its constitution, what should the expectations be of the religions, churches and schools to whom funding is made available for confessional RE? There are two problematic areas. The first concerns the **aims** of education. K. Williams (1997) argues that believers have a right to educate their children in their own religion with public funding. However, they cannot expect a secular state to give up its values and they must accept that they need to work within the secular objectives of public education. Specifically, this means that they acknowledge and promote autonomy as a fundamental educational aim alongside the aim of engendering religious commitment. A question arises as to the compatibility of these two aims. The second issue concerns the curriculum. If religious educators wish to see religion permeate all subject areas, to what extent is this compatible with the secular view of those subjects which is adopted in publicly funded secular schools? Again, a question of compatibility arises. It is evident that there are no easy answers that will satisfy everyone concerning the nature and scope of religious education.

research Educational research has tended to have a bad press amongst philosophers of education, who often argue (often rightly) that empirical researchers often mix up conceptual and empirical questions (Ryle 1974), offer banalities or tautologies in place of useful information (J. P. White 1997a), take an inappropriate technicist approach to value questions (D. Carr 1994) or just conduct poorly conceived projects (Barrow 1984).

Is such near-universal disdain appropriate? Given the well-established difficulties of conducting social science research and the value-laden nature of education, it might be justified. However, there are good grounds for not dismissing it so lightly. First, the difficulties of social science research counsel caution rather than abandonment. In particular, one should acknowledge that inferential hazard (Dearden 1979) should always lead researchers to qualify their findings. Second, given aims, one can inquire as to whether an educational practice is likely to succeed in achieving them. Third, philosophers could be active in helping to design better-conceived projects. They should be active in helping researchers to distinguish between conceptual and empirical questions. Finally, if research offers banal results, then researchers should be encouraged to look at more controversial areas where banality is less likely.

Research can also be seen as one means of ensuring **accountability**, through investigating whether public monies for education are being used to good effect. It can also be seen as a possible means of counteracting a certain fatalism that suggests that no educational intervention is capable of disrupting patterns set by the givens of class, ethnic grouping or gender.

rights Both parental and children's rights are central to education. John Locke (1961c: ch. 6) tried to explain the relationship. Children have rights to a proper education which derive from their interests in becoming full members of society. Since their limited **rationality** makes it difficult for them to exercise these rights immediately, their parents have a *duty* to attend to them on their behalf. This means that parents have secondary, derivative, rights to attend to the child's interests. It thus turns out that children's rights are exercised by parents (see **parental**).

There are two important objections to the Lockean argument. One is to question whether children are really of such limited rationality as the argument makes out (Aviram 1990). A key issue is whether or not children can make sensible judgements about their long-term interests and hence can assert their own rights. Aviram's assertion that even young children are capable of Piagetian concrete operations does not alleviate misgivings about this, since being able to perform concrete operations is precisely to be able to reason only in context-bound situations. The second objection maintains that parents cannot be allowed to *interpret* children's best interests. A parent who was prepared to allow her child to die rather than submit to a medical procedure, on the grounds that the child's afterlife was more important than his current health would be widely criticised. This suggests that the determination of rights remains to a large extent in the public, rather than the domestic, sphere.

rules Wittgenstein is largely responsible for contemporary recognition of the philosophical importance of rules and rule-governed behaviour. He argued that human action is socially-based and that it is to be understood in terms of the rules which govern it (for an account, see P. Winch 1958). This insight has led to a growth in attention to rule-governed phenomena. Wittgenstein was particularly interested in the way in which people learn to follow rules and drew attention to the importance of **training**, correction and instruction as conditions for the possibility of such processes as ostensive definition and discovery. More generally, his approach has led to greater attention being paid to rule-governed phenomena in human life in general and in education in particular. For example, Kazepides (1991) has drawn attention to the importance of learning to follow rules in moral education, while C. Winch (1996) has emphasised the normative nature of the **curriculum**.

Rousseau believed that society could only legitimately be constituted on a rule-governed basis through the unconstrained agreement of rational adults through a social contract (Rousseau 1913). Other forms of overt imposition of rules on behaviour were, he held, disastrous for the formation of a child's *amour propre* (see **self-respect**). Rousseau's educational enterprise depends on substituting the constraints of nature for the rules of humans in upbringing (Rousseau 1911a). **Psycholinguistics** has attempted to 'desocialise' the fundamental rules that govern **learning** by locating them in the brain. It is doubtful, however, whether such a fundamental feature of human life as rule-following can be downplayed.

S

schools and schooling   A distinction is often made between **education** and schooling. In most cases, the aim is to distinguish educational from other activities that occur in the same institutional setting. These activities in turn can be categorised as functional (for example, learning to walk rather than run in corridors, how to address teachers, cf. Hamm 1989); valuable but non-educational (for example, vocational preparation, cf. Barrow 1981); without value or even harmful (for example, learning to be docile and obedient, cf. P. S. Wilson 1971).

Before considering this distinction it is helpful to look at what a school is. Etymologically speaking, the term originates from the Greek *schole*. A *schole* was a place of learning or leisure. In contemporary usage a school is an institution dedicated to educational purposes, usually for children and adolescents. It is usually associated with the compulsory phase of education. The association with compulsion is thought by some to be an invidious aspect of schools. On the face of it, it seems odd to distinguish between education and schooling in the compulsory phase, since, if schooling is the main activity that takes place within a school and education is also the main business of a school, there is a strong presumption that education and schooling will be nearly identical activities. Yet this is denied by many philosophers of education; why?

One answer is straightforward enough; any institution like a hospital, factory or school has to have rules and routines that allow it to function efficiently. In the case of a school these will include routines for movement, for orderly and courteous conduct and for the careful use of resources. These rules and routines are necessary means to an educational end, they are not ends that are valuable in themselves. This distinction between education and schooling is straightforward, it is easy to see that, in this sense, 'schooling' is not the main business of a well-run school. What, however, of the claim that schooling *is* part of the main business of a school, to be distinguished from education, its other main business? This is usually based on the view that the most valuable activity, which just happens for convenience sake to take place in a school, is education. Most writers who make this distinction come from a liberal educational tradition. Their motive in making the distinction is to demarcate educational from other activities that take place in schools, such as preparation for citizenship or work. Notice that on this account, both education and schooling are contingently related to schools, both citizenship and vocational preparation could take place in institutions other than schools as could inculcation into a cultural heritage or preparation for autonomy. Indeed, there is a powerful strand within liberal education which maintains that schools are inimical to educational aims. Rousseau (1911a) is the most distinguished exponent of this view, which is also maintained by contemporary **deschoolers**.

The claim of those who wish to separate the two rests on a view about educational **aims**. The most valuable aims, such as introduction to cultural heritage or the promotion of autonomy, are deemed to be 'educational', other, less valuable, or even harmful aims are deemed to be aims of 'schooling'. But if education in its most general sense is a preparation for life then this distinction will not work, for it is easy to see that vocational and citizenship preparation are just as educational in this sense as liberal aims. The issue is that of which particular *conception* of education is going to be dominant and the liberal educator, in making the distinction, is staking his claim for a particular conception of education to be the dominant one. One cannot, however, do this by *fiat* if one hopes at the same time to convince an audience that there are reasons for making the schooling/education distinction. This means demonstrating that certain aims of the processes that take place in schools or other institutions are the most valuable ones and providing conclusive arguments for thinking that one aim or set of aims is more valuable than another. Those who make the distinction are, then, open to the charge of begging the question about the nature of education in their own favour. There is another odd consequence of this position. If vocational preparation is properly 'schooling' rather than 'education', then schools will often not be the best places to carry it out; vocational colleges, workshops, businesses and factories are all better suited.

One element of the liberal tradition does take schools very seriously and that is Deweyan **progressivism**. Dewey saw education as being largely about the promotion of **democracy**, which he understood as the multiplication of social contacts (Dewey 1916: 100). He thought that schools organised on the right lines were a very favourable mode of socialisation and hence promoted democracy. Such schools would, however, have particular characteristics. They would be non-authoritarian and would pay particular attention to the social aspect of their work. It can, therefore, be argued that what takes place in schools is, for Dewey and his followers, non-contingently related to education; 'schooling' in the sense of learning within a particular institutional mode, is part of what is meant by a desirable education. Dewey did not give a *carte blanche* to all schools and many who are sympathetic to his views nevertheless show much hostility to contemporary schools. One complaint often made is that, in addition to the *overt* **curriculum** there is a *hidden* one which permeates the life of the school, whose main purpose is to inculcate obedience and respect for **authority**, aims which are inimical to those of most liberal educators. For people who take this view, schooling is more likely to be the antithesis of education since the aims of each are incompatible.

The distinction between education and schooling is usually made with a purpose in mind, namely to validate a particular

conception of education. Those who make it should, therefore, be asked to justify a distinction which, on the face of
it, is a curious one.

scientific method   The place of scientific method within our
general understanding(s) of the world has been the subject of
extremely important philosophical debate during the last hundred years. Inheriting the work of the empiricist philosophers
such as Locke, Hume, Mill and Russell, and building upon
some remarks of the early Wittgenstein, the philosophers who
made up the Vienna Circle (Schlick, Hempel, Carnap, Popper)
claimed that scientific understanding, far from being one
among many ways of understanding the world was, in fact, *the
only way* of understanding. Thus, traditional philosophical areas
of enquiry such as metaphysics, ethics and aesthetics, were
branded as pointless investigations into pseudo-problems. The
rather breathtaking – but often invigorating – dismissal of large
areas of human endeavour which was the hallmark of this
school did not long survive the investigation of its own presuppositions. However, the work that they began – suitably
modified – continued to be carried on by philosophers such
as Quine and Popper. Quine, for instance, argues over many
years (1953, 1969, 1981) that even areas such as logic and
mathematics are not independent areas of knowledge but are
rather the handmaidens of science. Popper, refining his own
understanding of science tries to show its differences from
pseudo-science (1959, 1961, 1969, 1972).

This debate, whilst it may have influenced science itself, has
had little influence on the teaching of science in schools. There
was a time in the 1970s when some sociologists of education
– perhaps influenced by the work of philosophers of science
such as Kuhn (1970) and Feyerabend (1975) – tried to over-
turn our normal notion of objective knowledge and present
us with a relativised version of knowledge (see **sociology of
knowledge**). However, this had little effect on the curriculum in general and no effect on the science curriculum. More
surprisingly, the influential work of Popper with its insight that

no experiment(s) can possibly confirm the universal general-isations that make up the laws of science – how could you possibly confirm that all metals, past present and future, expand when heated? Therefore scientists, when engaged in experiments, are seeking to disprove theories rather than prove them – so that our present scientific knowledge consists of those scientific hypotheses as yet not disproved – seems to have little effect on the teaching of science in schools. Thus children still seem to be taught that scientists 'prove' theories. Their experiments still focus upon expected results rather than unexpected – and more interesting – results. And their scientific 'education' continues to ignore both the theoretical complexity of science and the vertical discontinuity between scientific understanding and common sense (see Brandon 1987: esp. ch. 3), so that we still have children leaving school who are sure that the Earth goes around the Sun but who have no understanding of the Copernican revolution that led to this conclusion and provides the impetus for modern science.

selection   The idea that children should be selected for different kinds of education can be found in Plato's *Republic* (1970b) Bk. 3. Plato believed that children should be selected for their **intelligence** and this view has persisted in some countries up to the present (e.g. Cooper 1980). There are obvious difficulties in selecting for intelligence, not least the difficulties saying what it is or in assessing it accurately. If children are selected for the best education because of their high intelligence then one may wonder what kind of education is appropriate for those who do not possess it. Plato's answer was to provide **vocational** education for those less well endowed. Modern selectors have often advocated the same kind of education as that provided for the highly intelligent, but of an inferior kind (e.g. Bantock 1965; Cooper 1980).

Another approach is to select according to ability. The idea is that different children have different potentials and that, at an appropriate age, they should be selected for the type of school that is most likely to fulfil their potential (Burt 1973).

This approach avoids the need to define and to test intelligence and leads to the need to carefully devise ways of exploring the developing interests and abilities of a child. Arguably, the German secondary system is of this type, while the UK system up until the 1960s was of the former kind. Selection will always arouse strong opposition so long as it is thought to be inequitable and therefore must be fair if it is to command confidence.

self-respect   Rousseau is the philosopher who elevated self-respect into a key educational concept under the name of *amour propre* in his major work on education, *Emile* (1911a). *Amour propre* encompasses what is normally meant by self-respect but is both a broader and more complex concept. Rousseau maintains that all animals have a love of self or *amour de soi*, which is the desire for physical and animal well-being. *Amour propre* is a feature of the human form of *amour de soi* (Dent 1988) and, as such, has particular characteristics. The most important of these is that it has a social and moral dimension that takes into account the standing of an individual with others. A second point is that it is not static, but changes both in accordance with biological imperatives and with human relationships. Furthermore, it is expressed differently in men and women.

The development of a healthy adult form of *amour propre* depends on the careful regulation of a child's relationships from birth right through to young adulthood, according to Rousseau. There are, in particular, two dangers to be avoided, both of which come about through the overt imposition of one will on another. The first is through the child being allowed its own way through the subordination of its carers to its own will. When this occurs repeatedly, the manifestation of *amour propre* becomes an overwhelming desire to gratuitously dominate others. The second is through the overt subordination of the child's will to that of others, which offends against its natural sense of justice and engenders a paranoid resentment and suspicion of others. Both the spoiled and the repressed child will grow into adult monsters. It is, therefore most important that *amour propre* be carefully managed at all stages of education.

Rousseau's solution is to substitute the domination of things or of nature for the domination of other human beings. A child cannot resent the impersonal obstacles that nature places in its way. A spoiled child should not be told 'I won't let you have that!' as this will lead to paranoid resentment. Instead, he should be told 'There isn't any' ('Il n'y en a pas'), thus pointing out that it is not a human will that is thwarting his wishes, but a lack of something in the world. An upbringing that develops self-respect in a healthy way thus treads a tightrope between suppression and indulgence, either of which lead into the abyss of psychological deformity.

Whatever we may think of the underlying moral psychology, the **pedagogical** strategy developed to deal with it seems to be fraught with risk. The teacher becomes an arch–manipulator hiding the overt expression of his will behind the manipulation of events designed to bring about educational ends without damaging self-respect. However, this shifting around of the scenery of life is unlikely to fool an intelligent child for long. Once he or she realises that there is an omnipresent covert will manipulating events, the danger is that any sense of self-respect will be lost and instead that the enduring sense of paranoid suspicion and resentment that Rousseau was so anxious to avoid will appear in a virulent form.

sex and gender Until recently – very recently in some instances – it was thought obvious that the education of the different sexes should, at some levels at least, have different **aims**. Thus, education should prepare girls for motherhood and domesticity and boys for the cut and thrust of the work place (aristocratic education, although not predicated simply upon the expectations of work and motherhood, made similar assumptions concerning the different interests and aptitudes of the sexes). Even an educational radical such as Rousseau prescribed a very different education for Emile and for Sophie, one in which, it is hardly an exaggeration to say, Emile is prepared for the world and Sophie is prepared for Emile.

Modern philosophies of education, perhaps reacting as much as anything to what many see as the offensive sexism of these prescriptions, for much of the time has endeavoured to remain sex blind. So, for instance, in Peters and Hirst's suggestions for the content of a liberal **education** (See Peters 1966; Hirst 1965a) there is not, and cannot be, any differentiation in the **curriculum** that is offered to boys and girls. Given that the things on offer are intrinsically valuable then they are so for either sex.

Some forms of **progressivism** (e.g. P. S. Wilson) lead to a slightly different situation for curriculum choice. So, for instance, if curriculum choice is driven by the children's interests, it is possible that difference of interests between the sexes will lead to the construction of a different curriculum for boys and girls. (Although we suspect that this would embarrass many progressivists.) But, even here, this is a contingent feature of this view of education and does not follow directly from the view.

Such sex 'blindness' was initially welcomed by radicals, partly because of its implicit egalitarianism; and partly because it seemed to fit in with a distinction between sex – biologically determined – and gender – socially determined which they wished to promote.

However, such a neat picture and its egalitarian educational implications has lately been questioned. Some commentators (Dunlop 1982) have argued for, at least, a partial return to traditional practices. Others, more persuasively, have argued that a 'blind' approach to education conflicts with some of our important beliefs about the social and political world that we live in (Freeman 1977) and that the issues that are raised by sex/gender and education are some of the most complex issues for educational debate and that the key distinctions have hardly begun to be understood (Jonathan 1983).

sex education There is very little on this important topic despite evidence (see R. Jones 1989) that children are ignorant in this vital area of their lives. A. Harris (1974) working from Peters's definition of **education** reaches the conclusion that what sex education should do is to promote rational sexual **autonomy**. Jones, whilst endorsing Harris's aim as part of sex education, also thinks that it can have other, equally important aims. First, it can work towards allaying the fears and unhappiness that children – and adults – experience with regard to sexual matters. Second, it can help to ensure that people, when sexually active, achieve as much sexual satisfaction and pleasure from their lives as is possible. Third, it can foster enquiry into and critical reflection on, sexual issues.

Whilst it seems possible that sex education could serve these aims, it also seems possible that teachers in schools may not be willing to engage in such education. Jones rather ignores the embarrassment factor that often accompanies sex education and he does not mention the fact that teachers may be unwilling to engage in lessons which may reveal rather more than they want to about their personal lives.

skills There has a risen a demand, at least in England, over the last ten to fifteen years that schools impart not merely knowledge but skills. On some levels such a demand seems both understandable and perfectly reasonable. So, for instance, few would cavil at the notion that before a young child can learn to paint or draw properly they have to be taught or develop fine motor skills, for example, how to hold a paintbrush or pencil for maximum effect. At a different level – but still within understanding and reason – professional historians seem split at the moment between those who think that the school's place is simply to deliver 'the facts' – or what passes for the facts at the present moment – and those who think that schools should try to develop the type of skills exemplified by a historian at work; for example, the identification and analysis of primary source material. However, skills talk and prescriptions involved with it has developed far beyond these uncontroversial examples. On the one hand, there has been a tendency to identify every ability or competence with a skill, so we could talk of walking skills or door-opening skills or shoelace-tying skills; where what we mean is that the person in question can walk, open doors and tie their shoelaces. Such a usage seems both strange and redundant. On the other hand there are people who want to insist that we can identify and teach a whole range of very general skills which are supposed to underpin particular performances; so, for instance, **critical thinking** skills, teaching skills, research skills. Even, more extreme have been the claims of some who seem to want to extend skills talk into what would seem to be uncongenial and morally loaded areas e.g. 'caring' skills and 'friendship' skills.

The reactions of philosophers of education to this kind of linguistic imperialism has been, largely, hostile. However, the recommendations as to what to do have differed. A conservative reaction has insisted that the proper use of 'skill' refers to a very narrow set of activities; that skills are 'abilities that are minimally involved with understanding, that are essentially physical, and that are perfected by practice at the activity itself' (see Barrow 1987: 191). Others have objected to this account on various grounds, for instance, that its emphasis on discrete, impersonal performances and the downplaying of understanding cuts the concept of skill away from areas where we happily and fittingly employ it. So talk of a master craftsman lovingly, knowledge-ably and patiently working upon his materials is not, if we use the word 'skilled' to describe his performance, a misuse of language but rather one of the central and important uses of the word (see R. Smith 1987: 197–201).

Others have been even more liberal and, developing points originally made in Ryle's distinction between 'knowing how' and 'knowing that' (see **knowledge**) have suggested that any attempt to insist that skills are necessarily non-intellectual and physical does injustice both to the concept of skill itself and to the proper understanding of the relation-ship between theoretical and practical abilities (see Griffiths 1987: 203–13).

Whatever the rights and wrongs of these analyses it is certainly the case that we can talk of 'skilful' performances which go far beyond the unintellectual and physical; for example, a musician may be a skilful interpreter of Beethoven, a footballer may be a skilful reader of the game, and a historian may be a skilful weaver together of different strands of his narrative, and it would seem a little odd to cut 'skill' away from 'skilful'.

However, the above writers are surely right when they counsel against such things as 'caring' and 'friendship' skills, for what we want in people is not that they exemplify any such set of skills – should they exist – but rather that they care and are friendly, which is a rather different matter.

social cohesion   'Social cohesion' is that property of a society which expresses the ability of its citizens to live together harmoniously and with **self-respect**. Many politicians on the centre-left consider social cohesion to be an important goal. Its promotion is sometimes taken to be one of the **aims** of education. There are a number of ways in which this might be done. One is through citizenship education and the promotion of civic virtue. Another is through a thoroughgoing **vocationalism** that seeks to ensure that no one is economically excluded from society.

It is evident that pursuing social cohesion is difficult to reconcile with the promotion of individualism. Insofar as it is the aim of education to promote the latter, it may be impossible to promote the former at the same time, if by 'individualism' one means the promotion of individual at the expense of social rights (see also M. Phillips 1996). If, on the other hand, one means the cultivation of an individual personality or **individuality**, then this need not be so. The promotion of social cohesion seems to be compatible with weak **autonomy**, the ability of the individual to choose amongst life-goals approved by society. Someone could develop their own individuality in a way that was compatible with or which promoted, social cohesion. This is becoming an important issue in both the US and the UK because both societies are worried about the way in which the unbridled pursuit of strong **autonomy** might undermine them.

socialisation **Education** and **schooling** must, in one sense of the term, as Durkheim (1956) realised, consist of socialisation. That is that, as the process of becoming educated and the institutions that make up schooling can only exist within a society they must transmit to those being educated or schooled, in some way, the norms and beliefs of the given society. Durkheim's use of the term is both wide, in that it includes the sort of cultural transmission that is the point of lessons in maths and history as well as an initiation into some of the customs, institutions and morals of the society. But it is also selective, in that Durkheim did not envisage every norm, belief or practice which exists being passed on during education or schooling.

Others, after Durkheim, have wanted to draw a distinction between the socialising effect of these things and their educational input (see P. White 1972). However, often not enough is done to spell out the manner and matter of this restricted nation of socialisation. Or, if it is clear what is being recommended, such recommendations are morally dubious (ibid.). Of course, some radical theorists have regarded most of what is passed on in schools as dubious in this way (see Goodman 1964).

sociolinguistics Sociolinguistics is the study of language in social context. Because linguistic competence is thought to be a necessary condition of educational achievement, a study of the factors that affect the former may shed light on students' ability to do well at school. Sociolinguistics tends to distinguish between **competence** in the **psycholinguistic** sense and 'sociolinguistic competence', which refers to an individual's ability to use language in social situations. Since the 1950s, a series of studies has purported to show that linguistic competence is social-class related (e.g. Loban 1963; Bernstein 1973) while others have denied this (e.g. Labov 1972; Wells 1987). The former have produced theories of working-class verbal deficit, while the latter have argued that other factors, some connected with material deprivation, others with linguistic factors, also have a significant role to play.

Some researchers take seriously the idea that there is a linguistic element underlying educational achievement. It is sometimes identified with different knowledge of, and attitudes towards, **literacy** amongst the working as opposed to the middle class (e.g. Wells 1981). Others draw attention to the differing roles that story-telling plays in various communities (e.g. Brice Heath 1983). As a discipline, sociolinguistics has suffered from inadequate attention to philosophical issues concerning its basic concepts, but its potential as an empirical discipline, for shedding light on issues of educational achievement, is enormous. Other areas which merit sociolinguistic investigation include the Creole Interference Hypothesis (see Winch and Gingell 1994) and issues concerning the role of conversation in classroom learning processes.

sociology of knowledge   The doctrines associated with the sociology of knowledge briefly erupted into educational debate with the publication of Young (1971), although variants of the main thesis have resurfaced in recent work on **feminism**, **multiculturalism**, and **postmodernism**. The approach to epistemology incorporated within these doctrines was derived from some of the work of Kuhn (1975) within the philosophy of science, distinguishing radically different approaches to science, e.g. Newtonian and Einsteinian physics, and some work in the philosophy of anthropology dealing with the profound differences between the belief systems of modern western man and the systems of some 'primitive' societies (see B. Wilson 1970 and especially the papers by P. Winch).

The central idea developed by the sociologists of knowledge is that because ideas concerning **truth**, **rationality** and **knowledge** are constructed within particular societies at particular times they must only be operative relative to their own particular society. So, for instance, the Azande tribe in the southern Sudan will operate the Azande notion of truth, rationality, etc. whilst western anthropologists will operate with western notions of these things. As such notions are internal to the functioning of particular societies there is no neutral point whereby different notions can be compared one with another e.g. nowhere we can neutrally stand and judge the western notions right and the Azande notions wrong or vice versa.

Several of the authors in Young (1971) (see the introduction and essay by Young and essays by Esland, Blum and Keddie) apply this 'insight' to educational matters. Using social class as the key societal determinant they hold that given that there are no absolute and universal truths or standards of rationality any attempt by middle-class teachers to work with such absolute notions with working-class pupils is bound to fail and that there must be vast cognitive gaps between such teachers and their pupils, e.g. gaps that render any talk of working-class educational 'failure' redundant.

Apart from the fact that in explaining away working-class 'failure' the authors in question are left to explain working-class 'success' (i.e. given that working-class children are working within a system in which they cannot possibly understand the cognitive norms at work, how do some do so well within the system?), the key thesis of sociology of knowledge seems to run into insuperable difficulties. First, it seems that the statement of the theory offends against the theory itself, i.e. that the claim that there are no objective truths seems itself to be a claim to objective truth. Second, as is usual with certain types of **cognitive relativism**, those supporting the theory claim to understand certain things which they cannot possibly understand if their theory is sound. So, for instance, if different social groups have radically different notions of truth etc. which cannot be understood from outside then so be it. But, if this is so, then the most we could say is that *we* have notions of truth, rationality and knowledge but we simply do not know – and can have no way of knowing – whether other social groups have such notions. A humbler variant of this type of objection is contained in the question 'If middle-class teachers cannot understand working-class children then how come middle-class educationalists like Young *et al.* can?' (For these objections and many more see Flew 1976.)

The weight of these objections, plus the sheer extravagance of some of the claims made by the sociologists of knowledge, for example, 'It is easy to see that the methodical character of marriage, war and suicide is only seen, recognized and made possible through the organised practices of sociology' (Blum, in Young 1971: 131) ensured that the *succes de scandale* of the work was short lived.

special education/learning disabilities Special education encompasses a broad range of attributes, including, in the UK, **giftedness**. Learning disabilities fall into a number of categories, each of which merit different approaches. Some are cognitive, but at the limit, these may be difficult to separate from **motivational**. Some of these cognitive difficulties have an organic cause, others not obviously so. Others are affective difficulties expressed in problems in relating to other people. There are also problems of physical delicacy and locomotive impairment. Last, but not least, some children have sensory limitations. The category of special needs is diverse both in respect of the range of cases that it covers and in the degree to which each condition affects learning.

There are two broad approaches to the education of those with special needs, each of which represents the endpoint of a spectrum. The first of these is *complete integration*, the second is *separate provision*. Between are mixed approaches which differentiate between conditions both in respect of type and degree. In the UK, following the Warnock Report of (1978), the tendency since 1981 has been to move a considerable way in the direction of integration. In the US on the other hand, one can see the beginnings of a movement towards separatism in some areas of special education (see Feinberg 1997 for a commentary), on the grounds that special education conditions should not be seen as forms of impairment and that some special groups have a distinct cultural identity that would be lost in a common educational environment.

spiritual education   Spiritual education is thought to be problematic for two reasons. The first is that the concept of the
spiritual is too vague to be of any use. The second is that,
if it has any substance, it is as a religious concept. In this
case, spiritual education is a part of **Religious Education**
and thus unacceptable to many non-religious parents. Are
these two assumptions correct? In order to reject them both,
one would either have to show that there is a substantial
secular interpretation of spirituality or that religious forms of
spirituality can be continued in a secular mode in a post-
religious age (e.g. Newby 1997).

The first reply is difficult to maintain in societies which have
strong traditions of religiously-based spirituality which have permeated all areas of life. The second has two forms. The first is
to maintain that there are transcendent features of the human
condition, such as contingency and mortality that can, nevertheless, be interpreted non-religiously (Blake 1996; Newby
1997). The second is to maintain that spirituality is purely immanent; it is to be found in a heightened awareness of the everyday or in the way in which everyday tasks are carried out. Against
the first possibility it is maintained that there is no significant
secular transcendent spiritual tradition (e.g. Carr 1996). Against
the second it is maintained that, in Christian societies at least,
the immanent and transcendent aspects of spirituality are inter-
nally related and cannot be separated from each other. We thus
become aware of the transcendent at least partly through our
commerce with the immanent. Since our only available concept
of transcendence is the one rooted in indigenous religious
traditions, we cannot coherently form a concept of spiritual
education which does not embody irreducible religious features.

However, this line of argument threatens to prove too
much, because very similar considerations can be advanced
against the possibility of **moral education** in a secular society.
Gaita (1991) has argued that there is a morally significant
sense of transcendence which is not religious. This is not to
claim, of course, that any such sense is uninfluenced by the
religious tradition in which it arose, for that would be futile.
Thus, our commerce with the immanent itself becomes a

spiritual experience, intelligible, say, as an extension of Protestant sensibilities but not identifiable with them. Insofar as the immanent leads us to an awareness of the transcendent, it may do so in terms of the themes addressed in traditional religious thinking, such as human mortality and vulnerability, and the timeless nature of good acts, without doing so in a way that is explicitly tied to any religious belief. It is, therefore, possible to maintain that we can use the materials of our spiritual tradition either to constitute an immanent spirituality which is an end in itself or which leads us towards a non-religious form of transcendent sensibility.

Large issues are at stake in spiritual education, for promoting attention to the way in which we do things and heightening our awareness of their wider significance are vital features of any education worthy of the name. And, to the extent that they involve notions of spirituality, that concept belongs at the heart of any educational practice.

standards Standards are norms against which educational performances can be measured and **assessed** (Pring 1992). Given that standards can be used to compare performances, they have a role in comparing students or schools in respect of the norm that the standard expresses. The ability to measure performances, however, does not entail any ability to compare standards. This leaves open the possibility that it may not be possible to compare the standards of maths in, say, the UK and the US (synchronic comparison), or the standards in Australia now and in the nineteenth century (diachronic comparison).

Pring argues that standard-comparison is logically impossible. In order to compare standard *A* with *B*, one would need a further standard with which to compare them, which would, in turn, require a further standard of comparison and so on *ad infinitum*. However, the argument is invalid. Standards *A* and *B* can be compared using a metastandard *C* in order to determine which of *A* and *B* require higher performances. All that *C* has to do is to compare the *requirements* of *A* and

B. So if *C* is a maths test and if standard *A* requires a student to reach 50 per cent on *C* to pass, and *B* requires 70 per cent then, according to *C*, standard *B* is higher than standard *A* (Winch 1996: ch. 6). The performances are the actual grades that students achieve on *C*, judged either by the standards of *A* or *B*. Comparison of standards either diachronically or synchronically is, therefore, possible.

stereotypes   'Stereotyping' has entered our general vocabulary from its use within the social sciences. A definition of it given there is that it 'denotes beliefs about classes of individuals, groups, or objects which are "preconceived", i.e. resulting not from fresh appraisals of each phenomenon but from routinised habits of judgement and expectation' (see Jahoda 1964). There is also a use of the term which, probably, derives from the above and imports normative considerations into this use so that a stereotype has connotations of the 'ideal', i.e. where what is thought – perhaps mistakenly – to be usual is what is taken to be good (see Shaw 1989).

Stereotyping, in both senses, can be applied to a wide range of things, such as genders, races, cultural groups, classes, and may be offensive to members of such groups when it is applied, for example, when women are depicted as only interested in housework and children, or the working class are depicted as uninterested in education, or when black people are depicted as only being good at sport. However, whilst it is certainly the case that such stereotyping does go on and is offensive, it is also the case that there are problems here. So, for instance, the preconceptions that underly such stereotypes may result from ignorance, stupidity or malice but they may equally derive from more or less reliable empirical generalisation; it might simply be the case that women are more interested in babies than men are; it might be the case that working-class children tend to be less interested in education than their middle-class counterparts.

Even if such stereotypes are based upon well-founded empirical generalisations it would be wrong – both logically

229

and educationally (and, perhaps, morally) – to assume that what is true of the group is true of every example of the group; say, to assume that because working-class children in general do not do well in education that this particular class of working-class children must be doomed to educational failure. However, it surely would be equally wrong, in many cases, not to keep in mind the truth of the generalisation for the sake of those particular groups of individuals which you do have dealings with. So, for instance, it would be little short of negligent, in teaching a group of working-class children, to ignore the fact that they may have particular problems to overcome on the way to educational success. And whilst it would be wrong simply to assume that because girls in general prefer the arts to the sciences that this particular girl must, it would be equally misguided not to pay attention to this particular truth in terms of curriculum provision (and even worse to attempt to coerce girls to break the stereotype).

Of course, individuals within education should be given every chance to develop their own individual talents and interests – whatever the talents or interests of the group to which they belong – but, paradoxically, this may best be ensured not by eradicating all stereotyping as some seem to envisage (see Equal Opportunities Commission 1982) but rather by distinguishing the ignorant judgement from the informed and bearing the latter in mind when confronting members of particular groups.

T

teaching (and its relationship with learning) The reason
that this section has two concepts in its title rather than the
normal one is that discussions of 'teaching' within the philosophical literature focus, almost exclusively, on its relationship
to learning (but see Passmore 1980). It is also true that,
whereas there is a great deal on the former of these terms
within this literature there is a tiny amount on the latter. The
analysis of 'learning' seems to have been left, by and large,
to educational psychologists (but see Hamlyn 1978; C. Winch
1998). Thus, the key question that has been addressed is
whether, if a person is teaching, it must be the case that
someone is learning but, very often, no consideration is given
to what exactly constitutes such learning.

Writers within the philosophy of education dealing with
teaching seem to be in unanimous agreement that 'teaching'
cannot be defined behaviourally so that any act, given an
appropriate context, could be a part of teaching; and that,
contrary to the slogan of the child-centred educationalists,
'We teach children not subjects' that teaching must involve
two objects: that if you are teaching you must be teaching
something to *someone*. However, such agreement evaporates
when the relationship of teaching to learning is considered.

There is a more detailed consideration of this issue in the
American literature than elsewhere (McClellan 1976; Martin
1967; Komisar 1968). This is, probably, because Dewey set

the ball rolling there with an analogy between teaching and learning and buying and selling:

> There is the same exact equation between teaching and learning that there is between selling and buying. The only way to increase the learning of pupils is to augment the quantity and quality of real teaching. Since learning is something that the pupil has to do himself and for himself, the initiative lies with the learner. The teacher is a guide and director; he steers the boat, but the energy that propels it must come from those who are learning.
>
> (Dewey 1933)

Such thoughts, and the explicit reference to learners' responsibilities together with the seemingly implicit notion that if the pupil was not learning then the teacher was not teaching, make the relationship of 'teaching' and 'learning' ripe for analysis. After all, and despite Dewey's acknowledgement of the learner's role, any suggestion that teachers whose pupils do not all learn are not really teaching is rather bad news for a profession which, typically, has rather more modest expectations of its own success rate.

During the 1970s analyses of 'teaching' were put forward in both England (Hirst and Peters 1970) and America (Scheffler 1973) which, by focusing upon the intentions of the teacher, seemed to cut the suggested logical link between teaching and learning. Both sets of analyses maintained that the key criterion was that for someone to be teaching they have to intend to bring about learning. However, this criterion alone does not seem sufficient to guarantee teaching. It would not, for instance, distinguish between someone trying to teach but failing to do so and someone actually teaching. The supporting conditions put forward to buttress the initial criterion were various. Hirst and Peters suggested an indicative criterion, that the intending teacher must be doing things with the subject matter (lecturing on it, illustrating it, demonstrating it, etc.) which indicate their purposes to the learner. They also suggested a 'readiness' criterion, that learners must be ready, for example, in terms of age and capability, to learn the intended subject matter. Scheffler suggested two rather different supporting conditions. First, that the strategies chosen by the teacher must, not unreasonably, be thought likely to achieve the learning aimed at. Second, that what the teacher does must fall under certain restrictions of manner.

As has been recognised (Noddings 1976) the key problem with these analyses is the strength that we assign to these supporting conditions and how this affects the initial condition. Suppose that, what the supporting conditions add up to is that the intending teacher is doing everything possible – with, perhaps, some moral restrictions, for example, torture is not allowed – to ensure that the pupils learn. Surely, if this is the case then the pupils will learn and we no longer need the intention criterion? (Note here that 'everything possible' has to be understood in an objective sense, 'everything that anyone could do', and not in a subjective sense, 'anything that this particular person could do'. The latter would be too weak in that it would allow the well-meaning but totally incompetent person to claim they were teaching.)

The trouble with this move is that, whilst it grasps an important truth, that, given enough time, energy, commitment and ideal circumstances anyone may be taught anything within their own capabilities, it ignores the practicalities of all teaching situations. It is simply not the case, that we can achieve such ideal conditions. Teachers, however good, will never have unlimited time, patience and expertise – in both subject matter and delivery – and pupils are unlikely to have a sole and total commitment to learning. Given that this is the case then even with the best example of teaching it is possible that some pupils will not learn.

A more recent writer who has defended the logically tight connection that we seem to see in Dewey, is Kleinig (1982) Kleinig couches his attack upon the intentionality thesis in terms of responsibility. The teacher is responsible for the pupils' learning and, because this is so, the teacher is responsible if the pupils learn things from him even although he did not intend to teach such things, e.g. that it is permissible to be bad-tempered first thing on Monday morning, and the teacher must have been negligent in some way if the pupils did not learn what they were supposed to learn. The first point is, to a certain extent, well taken. Pupils learn things from their teachers for which the teacher may be held responsible but which do not figure in the direct intentions of the teacher. So, for instance, if the teacher exemplifies moral virtues or vices the pupil may pick these up from the teacher. This is a very important point for **moral education** although whether simple exemplification counts as teaching is, we think, an open issue. However, Kleinig's second point appears again, to be too strong. Negligence typically involves causing harm to a person or persons in a specific set of circumstances. To defend against a charge of negligence you do not have to show that the harm was not caused or that, given totally different circumstances, the harm would not have been caused. It is enough to show that, given these particular circumstances there was nothing more you could have done to prevent the harm, i.e. that the harm was not your fault. Sometimes, it is possible to show simply that. What this means for teaching is that failure to learn may not be the teacher's fault – i.e. that pupils may fail to learn even though teaching was going on. However, if we take Kleinig's emphasis on responsibility seriously it may be the case that when pupils consistently fail to learn we may have a very good reason for asking the teachers in question to demonstrate why such failure is not their fault.

theory and practice If one listens to some teachers the difference between theory and practice seems deep and unbridgeable. Educational theorists are concerned with unrealistic generalisations which have little or no implications for practice; whereas practitioners are concerned with the real and untheoretical problem of, say, getting a particular pupil to pay attention to a particular thing at a particular time. Such a conception of these two areas is misleading, to say the least. Theories, in this and other areas, do not grow like Topsy, but rather come from an attempt to understand various practices.

And practice, whether the practitioner is conscious of this or not, is always at least partially embedded in theory; for instance, about the nature of human learning.

However, it is true that the relationship between theory and practice is often both complicated and subtle and this is especially the case in an area like **education** which necessarily involves values as well as facts. Part of the problem is that different types of theory apply to the practices of education in different ways, so that one might, for instance, have a philosophical theory concerning human learning and the whole overlooked by a moral theory concerning our relationship to children (Barrow 1984). As Dearden (1984b) has shown, the relationship between theory and practice not only turns upon the different types of theory involved, but also how coherent and well-understood such theories are; the type of priority one thinks should be given to various aspects of both theory and practice; the type of practical input one expects; and, above all, the exercise of judgement in dealing with both theory and practice. There are few, if any, easy answers here and one would expect in an area like education where people often disagree about **aims** and where different types of theory intersect, for instance, philosophical, political, psychological, that battles concerning particular theories and their relevance to particular practices will continue to be a feature of the intellectual landscape.

tolerance Tolerance is the liberal virtue *par excellence*. An **equality** of respect for others is built into the great moral traditions. It occurs, at the theoretical level at least, in the Christian notion that we are all, equally, the children of God. It surfaces in **utilitarianism** in the idea that, in moral calculation, one person is to count as one person and not more than one person; and, in Kantian theory in the notion that all rational creatures must be treated as ends-in-themselves. But toleration goes beyond such equal respect, for it involves the idea that we should let alone precisely those we do not respect (at the very least). Thus, for instance, the toleration involved in freedom of speech would hardly merit the name if it only extended to the expression of those ideas we share or approve (Gray 1995). It must, if it is to count as a virtue at all, extend to the expression of ideas that we abhor.

It is sometimes claimed that such tolerance provides benefits for us all in that it is a necessary condition for reaching the truth about the world and that, in encouraging and studying different life-styles we are presented with alternatives which may be open for us or, at the very least, given a deeper understanding of our own choices in the recognition of the different choices of others (Mill 1974). However, within the liberal tradition, there is also a recognition that tolerance must have its limits. Famously Mill (ibid.) draws the line at harm to others. This, of course, necessitates a workable definition of 'harm'. Whilst Mill's 'harm principle' has been profoundly influential in legislation this century concerning sexual relationships and pornography, it is also the case, as a recent prosecution in Britain concerning consenting sado-masochists made clear, that it is not the only basis for legislation concerning personal relationships.

The liberal picture of tolerance and its residual questions, has come under fierce attack recently. It has been suggested, first (by Taylor 1979), that the notion of liberty as freedom from the interference of others, is not strong enough to do the job it is supposed to do; second, that liberalism, with its emphasis upon the autonomy of individuals, ignores the cultural contexts which provide the grounds for individual identity and the basis of individual choice (see Taylor 1979; Sandel 1982).

This still-raging argument is enormously important for education. First, its result will determine what should be included under the name of **multicultural** education. Second, inherent within this struggle is the question as to whether, in being tolerant towards other cultures we are not, in fact, encouraging the intolerance that they show to their individual members (see J. Harris 1982). Third, the relativisation of 'harm' that often seems to be implicit within the work of critics of liberalism (see Giroux 1988; Siegel 1995) seems to threaten the whole idea of a common education system.

The outcome of this battle of ideas cannot, as yet, be predicted. However, two things already seem clear: first, the blithe assumption made by some within the debate that we can uproot liberalism and still easily insist upon basic liberal notions such as freedom of speech, seems very far from well-founded (see Taylor 1994); second, the seemingly 'liberal' idea which often seems to accompany multiculturalism in schools that, to understand differences is to accept them, may be very far from the truth.

training   Training is usually employed as a contrastive concept to **education**. It is associated either with **vocationalism** or with the processes associated with the learning of habits and routines. So, for example, it is customary to speak of job training on the one hand and training children to brush their teeth on the other. Training is also used in the sense of **conditioning** where a repetitive process is applied to someone (or an animal) in order to achieve a desired behavioural result. Thus, rats may be conditioned to run through a maze. The position is further complicated because, while it makes sense to say of both animals and humans that they can be trained, it does not make sense to say that animals can be educated.

If training is associated with conditioning then it is hard to see what its educational value might be or even whether it is ethically desirable when applied to humans, given the lack of **autonomy** that it implies. These considerations are reinforced by reflection on the human role in the workplace in many situations, where production-line work practices and the division of labour require learning of routines so repetitive that there is little scope for autonomy either in their learning or in their application (Dearden 1984a). For these reasons, the idea that training is a desirable component of or alternative to education does not receive much favour in some circles committed to liberal forms of education. Nevertheless there are some who are prepared to allow that training has a role to play in education. Such a position has three identifiable subcategories.

First, there are those who think that training and vocational education are largely the same. Those who take a **competence**-based view of the educational process are such a group and they can be found amongst the adherents of such programmes as National Vocational Qualifications (NVQs) (Jessup 1991). Second, there are those who see the importance of training in **moral education** and think that the inculcation of appropriate reactions and behaviour is a precondition of the later transition to moral autonomy (Kazepides 1991; Strawson 1974). Third, there are those philosophers, largely influenced by Wittgenstein, who hold that not just moral development but some of the more fundamental aspects of early human development presuppose training (Button *et al.* 1995; Baker and Hacker 1984; C. Winch 1995). Some have gone on to argue that training is not incompatible with autonomy nor with a range of educational processes beyond earliest childhood, but is in fact a presupposition of their achievement.

Training is a ramified concept that is apparently applicable to a range of human and animal activities. Its use in educational contexts is, however, severely contested both because of its alleged moral dubiousness and because of its overtones of **authority** (there are trainees and a trainer in an unequal relationship). It is also opposed by educators working in the **progressive** tradition who also object to its apparently authoritarian overtones (Rousseau 1911a).

Are there no circumstances in which education and training are, to all practical purposes, indistinguishable? In order to answer this question it is necessary to look at the nature and scope of vocational education.

transcendental arguments Transcendental arguments are associated with the work of Kant (1963). In the *Critique of Pure Reason*, he tries to show, against pure empiricism, that categories of human thought, such as space and time, are not derived from experience, but rather, are presupposed by the notion of experience as such. Later, in the same work, in attacking the type of **idealism** which would be engendered by Cartesian scepticism, Kant tries to show that the type of internal life that Descartes admits, presupposes the existence of the external world. Thus transcendental arguments are arguments that take a given position and show, simply from the material admitted by that position, that something else must necessarily follow.

> For this concept makes strict demand that something A, should be such that something else B, should follow from it necessarily, and in accordance with an absolutely universal rule.
>
> (Kant 1963: 125)

Transcendental arguments enter the philosophy of education via the work of Peters and Hirst. Peters (1966) seems to use such an argument in two places. First, when he tries to show that the question 'What ought I to do?' presupposes a principle of equality of consideration for persons in that one should not treat people differently without a relevant reason. Second, when talking of worthwhile activities, he tries to show that the question 'Why do this rather than that?' presupposes a commitment to disciplines such as science, philosophy and history, which are relevant to answering such a question.

Hirst (1965a) seems to use such an argument when he tries to show that a person asking for a justification for the pursuit of rational knowledge must be already committed to what he is seeking to justify (crudely, to ask 'why seek knowledge?' is seeking knowledge!).

Whether Peters's or Hirst's arguments are really transcendental in the Kantian sense has been questioned. However, more importantly there have been a number of attacks that seem to show that these particular arguments do not, as they stand, justify what Peters and Hirst think they justify (see Kleinig 1973; Cooper 1993).

truth Educating people involves giving them knowledge and, to the extent that knowledge is a form of justified true belief, in educating people one is, to a large extent, imparting true beliefs. The question arises as to whether it matters what conception of truth an educator should subscribe to. Those who dispute whether truth is a proper goal of **education** would reject the question. They might, perhaps, see education as more concerned with the imparting of values and attitudes or with practical skills. Or, like Plato, they might consider the pursuit of truth to be only appropriate for a small elite.

Few educators reject truth *per se* as an educational goal; it is more common to see it redefined in such a way that a true proposition is no longer validated independently of human purposes. Such writers, largely from **postmodernist**, **constructivist** and **pragmatist** backgrounds, question whether it is ever possible to know objective truths. We cannot be acquainted with propositions that are true for all time, apart from those of mathematics and logic, because we are constantly acquiring new information, more reliable than the old, which also contradicts it. Rather than say that we are constructing the curriculum on the basis of falsehood, it would be better, it is argued, to construct it on the basis of what works for us, or what is viable (James 1910; von Glasersfeld 1989). The tendency to think in this way is strengthened by the belief that learning takes place through hypothesis testing and the view of Popper (1959) that hypotheses can never be proved to be true. The best that can happen, on this view, is that one has access to long-standing but unrefuted positive hypotheses, whose status is not that they are true but that they are *unrefuted* and thus, for present purposes, utilisable.

It is argued that the danger with such proposals is that they cannot avoid making truth subjective. A true proposition is one that is viable for me; it may not necessarily be viable for you. It is then hard to see how education could be a process of introducing people to knowledge that is common to a community. One reply to this is that truth is relative to a conceptual scheme within which propositions are verified. Since conceptual schemes are invariably held in common by members of communities in order that individuals can communicate with each other, these communities have a common stock of viable propositions that ensure a common understanding. On this proposal, truth is relativised to communities rather than to individuals and a distinction is drawn between individual belief and communal knowledge on the basis of the viability-determining procedures of that community. Education as a form of initiation into knowledge still has a place in such a community. An objection to this approach is that conceptual schemes may prove to be unviable and the 'knowledge' held by the community may turn out to be nothing more than communally held falsehoods. The issue then turns on the rigour of the criteria that are used to admit a system of intersubjectively held, communally viable beliefs to the status of a conceptual scheme. At the limit, there is only one unchangeable conceptual scheme. A less extreme position is that even the most viable schemes have to revise opinions of the truth of propositions over time and make changes to their verificatory procedures. On this view, education can still be concerned with objective truth, but not necessarily solely concerned with timeless and universal truths.

utilitarianism Utilitarianism is the doctrine that we ought to act, individually or collectively, so as to promote the greatest happiness for the greatest number of people. It derives from the work of eighteenth-century philosophers such as Hume (1962) and the theory was classically formulated by Bentham (1957) and Mill (1964). The theory is egalitarian: everybody's happiness counts equally; and consequentialist: the theory gives priority to producing good states of affairs over, say, having certain intentions. Although originally couched in terms of pleasure, modern utilitarians tend to define happiness in terms of preference or desire-satisfaction. That is, you are happy when there is some equilibrium between what you desire from the world and the way the world actually is. The theory comes in various forms: act utilitarianism, where every individual act is judged upon its consequences in terms of promoting happiness; rule utilitarianism, where individual actions are subsumed under rules, for example, 'do not lie', and it is the adoption or not of such rules which is judged in terms of consequences; negative utilitarianism, where, in the assessment of consequences, reduction of pain and suffering is given priority over the production of happiness.

It would be difficult to overestimate the importance of utilitarianism both as a theory within moral philosophy and as an influence on social policy. However, despite this importance it is probably fair to say that the theory is un-fashionable today largely because of criticisms raised by philosophers such as B. Williams (1985, and Williams and Smart 1973) and Rawls (1971, 1993).

In the context of **education** and **schooling** the theory has been defended and used over the years by Barrow (1976, 1981) who has taken it as a guide to positive educational practice, for example, concerned with curriculum choice, and as a platform whereby to attack the educational theories of other thinkers. The appeal of utilitarianism as applied to education is not difficult to see. It seems to offer a way of judging the processes and institutions of education in a way that relates them to social life as such and, unlike some versions of liberal education (see Peters 1966) which insist that educa-tion is an intrinsic good, it seems to rest such judgement upon a minimally controversial principle; that education is a good thing if it leads to social well-being.

Utilitarianism has been criticised for offering an **instru-mental** approach to education (Hamm 1989). But such a charge seems often to be based upon a naive version of the doctrine; for example, one in which happiness is simply couched in terms of pleasurable feelings, and it also seems to ignore the fact that the doctrine can perfectly well incorpo-rate the notion that certain types of activity are intrinsically good, for example, that doing history is one of the types of thing that people want to do for its own sake, as long as such intrinsic goodness is, at the same time, couched in terms of personal satisfaction (and it does seem odd to claim that doing history is intrinsically good even if it makes the person doing it thoroughly miserable).

A more sustained criticism of the doctrine as applied to education has been raised by Gutmann (1982) who complains that, because the happiness of individuals over a long period of time is indeterminate, utilitarianism can give no real guid-ance as to what to do in schools. Gutmann's preferred alternative is an education based on rights theory which aims at producing fully autonomous choosers.

utopianism   Utopias are ideal societies which do not necessarily exist. They do, however, exist in the minds of men and women, and express their most deeply-held values and aspirations. Since these differ amongst individuals, it is possible that the same utopia may represent heaven for one person and hell for another. When a utopian vision is actively striven for, **education** is an obvious component in the enterprise, since children need to be prepared for utopian existence and the utopia can, to some extent, be **prefigured** in educational practice. The *Republic* of Plato (1970b) is a utopian vision with educational prescriptions attached, while Rousseau's *Emile* (1911a) is, arguably, an educational prolegomenon to utopia. In modern times utopian educational projects have existed wherever people have thought that there was a prospect of developing a utopia. A socialist utopian project (the kibbutzim movement) started in Israel, while various forms of post-Enlightenment movement in Europe have served utopian projects based loosely on Rousseau's vision of a society founded on equal **self-respect**. A notable example is Robert Owen's New Lanark of the 1840s (Owen 1991).

The problem for educational utopianism is that it must invariably remain outside public education. Public education systems are usually based on pragmatic compromises between groups with different values who cannot fully implement those values without coming into conflict with each other. Educational utopians are by nature intolerant. They require that the full implementation of their value-system takes place in the education of their young. Compromises will destroy the original utopian vision. Those who dislike a world of bland compromises may well find utopianism in education attractive.

virtue theory One of the most popular and influential accounts of **moral education** currently extant is virtue theory, inspired by Aristotle's *Nichomachaean Ethics* (1925) and, latterly by MacIntyre (1981). Virtue theorists maintain that moral concepts are to be explicated in terms of character traits, into which children can be educated, initially through a process of **training** (Kazepides 1991) and subsequently through increasingly reflective practice. Desirable character traits such as courage, kindness or fairness are known as *virtues* and are to be cultivated through moral education.

Virtue theory has been criticised by Kohlberg (1991) for advocating a crude deontological approach to moral education (don't lie, don't cheat, don't steal). This can easily be shown to be a travesty, as virtue education requires deliberation and reflection in situations where complex moral choice is involved (Simpson 1989; D. Carr 1991). It has also been criticised for ethnocentricity, or promoting one particular set of moral imperatives at the expense of equally meaningful alternatives.

This latter criticism ignores the fact that there is both an ethical and a meta-ethical dimension to virtue theory. As a metatheory, it claims that a normative account of character is the best way of clarifying central moral concepts. At the ethical level, it recognises that different kinds and permutations of virtues can be found in different societies and that each should promote those that it values. Thus ancient Greeks particularly valued courage, while medieval Christians valued chastity. A problem occurs when communities with incompatible sets of virtues co-mingle, but we are then back with the need for negotiation about which values a society should implement and to what degree (see **aims**).

vocationalism   Vocationalism is a form of **education** with primarily **instrumental aims**. Vocationalists maintain that the main aim of education, at least for some students, is to prepare them for employment. Such employment need not be paid, for example, preparation for motherhood. There is, however, a serious problem with vocationalism considered as an aim of the part of education that takes place at the compulsory phase. The problem is that this phase of education is not, and could not be, a direct preparation for any kind of vocation. Employment is highly specific in terms of the knowledge and skills that it requires and, furthermore, most of that knowledge and skill can only be acquired contextually, or in the workplace. It follows that any vocational education carried out in schools must be inadequate.

The argument is, however, fallacious because it wrongly assumes that any form of preparation necessarily involves *nothing but* carrying out the tasks for which one is preparing. If this were true, there could not be any education either, since many things that take place in education do not in adult life (e.g. learning times-tables). The vocationalist has to take account of the specific nature of vocations and one way in which it is possible to do this is by distinguishing between the kind of vocational education that takes place at school, and that which takes place in the workplace. The former could deal with knowledge and skill which are required in a range of vocations. For example, a school which specialised in engineering could teach students those generic engineering skills that they are likely to need in any engineering activity (Entwistle 1970). Some knowledge, such as basic literacy and numeracy, is a prerequisite for advanced forms of both liberal and vocational education, and can be taught in the elementary school.

There is, nevertheless, a problem concerning preparation for a vocation, whether it be trade, craft or job because of the specific nature of the knowledge required for each of these. In practice, a variety of solutions are offered. On-the-job training is the most obvious of these. If it is combined with prior pre-vocational education it may be able to provide cognitive depth to complement the breadth provided by the pre-vocational component. One solution, which attempts to ensure that theoretical and broad knowledge are acquired in combination with technical knowledge in depth, is to be found in the German 'dual system' in which school-leavers continue to attend a vocational establishment part-time while following the bulk of their **apprenticeship** at work. Those liberal educators who maintain that there is a complete dichotomy between vocational and liberal education commit the elementary fallacy of thinking that, because two things do not share all the same characteristics they can, therefore, have nothing in common. However, vocational educators may espouse liberal aims like personal fulfilment, while liberal educators may espouse vocational aims like employability as a form of personal fulfilment. Indeed, part of Rousseau's (1911a) liberal programme for Emile was precisely to equip him to be able to earn his living to engender a proper sense of **self-respect** or *amour propre*.

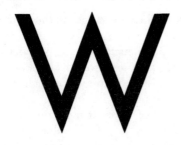

W

work   It is difficult to produce a watertight definition of work which completely contrasts it with **leisure** and **play**. It is likely that the ways in which we distinguish between these various concepts is dependent on purpose and context. The distinction between paid and unpaid work is also important, as is the distinction between work and effort. Insofar as **education** is a preparation for work, it is important to determine its significance in a child's future life. Some commentators have tried to outline education in relation to a work-oriented society (e.g. Entwistle 1970). More recently, J. P. White (1997b) has argued (a) that paid work is on the decline and (b) that education needs to take account of this by preparing children for an adult life of greater leisure.

White's thesis about the demise of work arguably depends on the fallacious 'lump of labour' idea, which maintains that any society has only a fixed and finite amount of work that needs to be carried out. Automation will diminish the amount of work that needs to be done by people. It can be maintained that societies fix the amount of work that they deem to be socially necessary and that there is thus no arbitrary limit on the work to be done or that proportion of it which is to be paid. Even if the end-of-work thesis is true, it still remains the case that children need to be educated into the need to recognise necessity in human life and into a corresponding need to care about what they do. Finally, they need to be educated to make efforts in the achievement of their chosen goals.

writing Writing is the medium of **literacy**. It has different properties from speech: first, it is relatively *permanent*; second it can be taken in spatially as well as temporally (*surveyability*) (C. Winch 1983). These properties allow it to be used for communication across distances of space and time, which make it *non-interactive*. Because it does not rely on the paralinguistic features of context, gesture and facial expression, and because of non-interactivity, writing has to be both explicit and planned so as to take account of the needs and knowledge of readers (*context-independence*).

Traditionally the ability to use writing belonged to a very small elite. Early writing systems were either logographic (based on spoken word/written symbol correspondence – Chinese still is, to a large extent) or syllabic (based on syllable/symbol correspondence). The advent of alphabetic writing (based on phoneme/symbol correspondence) brought a great change. Writing systems only demanded forty or fewer symbols which, concatenated in various ways, could build up all the words used in speech. Writing and **reading** became much easier and potentially accessible to the masses, though until the advent of universal primary education mass literacy was only a dream. However, the structural and functional differences between speech and writing are still poorly understood by many teachers and their pupils, and teaching of the use of writing is inhibited by a lack of understanding of its key function in distance communication and an inability to recognise and exploit its permanence, surveyability, non-interactivity and context-independence.

BIBLIOGRAPHY

Adelstein, D. L. (1972) 'The Wit and Wisdom of R. S. Peters – The Philosophy of Education', in T. Pateman (ed.) *Counter Course*, Harmondsworth, Penguin.

Alexander, R. (1984) *Primary Teaching*, London, Holt.

—— (1992) *Policy and Practice in the Primary School*, London, Routledge.

Almond, B. (1982) *Means and Ends in Education*, London, Allen and Unwin.

—— (1991) 'Education and Liberty: Public Provision and Private Choice', *Journal of Philosophy of Education* 25(2): 193–202.

Althusser, L. (1968) *Reading Capital*, London, New Left Books.

Archard, D. (1993) *Rights and Childhood*, London, Routledge.

—— (1998) 'The Family and the Moral Education of the Citizen', *Proceedings of the International Conference on Philosophy, Education and Culture*, Moray House Institute, Edinburgh (forthcoming).

Aristotle (1925) *Nichomachean Ethics*, trans. Sir David Ross, Oxford, Oxford University Press.

Arnold, M. (1932) *Culture and Anarchy*, first published 1869, Cambridge, Cambridge University Press.

Austin, J. (1962) *How To Do Things With Words*, ed. J. O. Urmson and G. J. Warnock, Oxford, Oxford University Press.

Aviram, A. (1990) 'The Subjection of Children', *Journal of Philosophy of Education* 24(2): 213–34.

Bailey, C., and Bridges, D. (1983) *Mixed Ability Grouping: A Philosophical Perspective*, London, Allen and Unwin.

Baker, G., and Hacker, P. M. S. (1984) *Language, Sense and Nonsense*, Oxford, Blackwell.

—— (1990) 'Malcolm on Language and Rules', *Philosophy* 65: 167–79.

Ball, S. (ed.) (1990) *Foucault and Education: Disciplines and Knowledge*, London, Routledge.

Bantock, G. H. (1963) *Education in an Industrial Society*, London, Faber.

—— (1965) *Education and Values*, London, Faber.

—— (1971) 'Towards a Theory of Popular Education', in R. Hooper (ed.) *The Curriculum: Context, Design and Development*, Edinburgh, Oliver and Begel.

Barnett, R. (1988) 'Does Higher Education Have Aims', *Journal of Philosophy of Education* 22(2): 239–50.

—— (1990) *The Idea of Higher Education*, Buckingham, Open University Press.

Barrow, R. (1976) *Common Sense and the Curriculum*, London, Allen and Unwin.

—— (1978) *Radical Education*, Oxford, Martin Robertson.

—— (1981) *The Philosophy of Schooling*, Brighton, Harvester.

—— (1984) *Giving Teaching Back to Teachers*, Brighton, Harvester.

—— (1987) 'Skill Talk', *Journal of Philosophy of Education* 21(2): 187–96.

—— (1993) *Language, Intelligence and Thought*, Aldershot, Edward Elgar.

Barrow, R. and White, P. (eds) (1993) *Beyond Liberal Education*, London, Routledge.

Bauman, Z. (1997) 'Education: For, Under and in Spite of Modernity', *Annual Proceedings of the Philosophy of Education Society of Great Britain*, 1997.

Beardsley, M. (1958) *Aesthetics*, New York, Harcourt Brace.

Beardsmore, R. W. (1992) 'The Theory of Family Resemblances', *Philosophical Investigations* 15(2): 111–30.

Beattie, C. (1981) 'The Paradigm Case Argument: Its Use and Abuse in Education', *Journal of Philosophy of Education* 15(1): 77–86.

Bedford, E. (1956–7) 'Emotions', *Aristotelian Society Proceedings* 57: 281–304.

Beehler, R. (1985) 'The Schools and Indoctrination', *Journal of Philosophy of Education* 19(2): 261–72.

—— (1990) 'Grading the "Cultural Literacy" Project', *Studies in Philosophy and Education* 10: 315–35.

Bennett, J. (1964) *Rationality*, London, Routledge.

Bentham, J. (1957) *An Introduction to the Principles of Morals and Legislation*, first published 1789, London, Collins.

Bereiter, C., and Engelmann, S. (1966) *Teaching Disadvantaged Children in the Pre-School*, Englewood Cliffs, NJ, Prentice-Hall.

Berkeley, B. (1929) *Selections*, ed. M. W. Calkins, New York, Scribner.

Berlin, I. (1969) 'Two Concepts of Liberty', in *Two Concepts of Liberty and Other Essays*, Oxford , Oxford University Press.

Bernstein, B. (1973) *Class, Codes and Control*, vol. 1, London, Paladin.

Best, D. (1978) *Expression and Movement in the Arts*, London, Lepus.

—— (1985) *Feeling and Reason in the Arts*, London, Allen and Unwin.

—— (1992) *The Rationality of Feeling*, Brighton, Falmer.

Blake, N. (1996) 'Against Spiritual Education', *Oxford Review of Education* 22(4): 443–56.

Blenkin, G. M., and Kelly, A. V. (1987) *The Primary Curriculum*, London, Chapman.

Bloom, A. (1987) *The Closing of the American Mind*, Harmondsworth, Penguin.

Blum, A. (1971) 'The Corpus of Knowledge as a Normative Order', in M. F. D. Young (ed.) *Knowledge and Control: New Directions for the Sociology of Education*, London, Macmillan.

Boot, R. (1987) 'Open Learning: Meaning and Experience', in V. Hodgson, S. Mann, and R. Snell (eds) *Beyond Distance Teaching: Towards Open Learning*, Milton Keynes, Open University Press.

Bowles, S., and Gintis, H. (1976) *Schooling in Capitalist America*, New York, Basic Books.

Bradley, F. H. (1951) *Ethical Studies*, first published 1876, New York, Bobbs–Merrill.

Brameld, T. (1950a) *Patterns of Educational Philosophy*, New York, World Books Co.

—— (1950b) *Ends and Means in Education: A Mid-Century Appraisal*, New York, World Books Co.

Brandon, E. P. (1981) 'Oh, Reason Not the Need', *Development Education*, 6: 18–25.

—— (1987) *Do Teachers Care About Truth?* London, Allen and Unwin.

Brent, A. (1978) *Philosophical Foundations of the Curriculum*, London, Allen and Unwin.

Brice Heath, S. (1983) *Ways with Words*, Cambridge, Cambridge University Press.

Bridges, D., and McLaughlin, T. H. (eds) (1994) *Education and the Market Place*, Brighton, Falmer.

Britzman, D. (1995) 'Is There a Queer Pedagogy? Or, Stop Reading Straight', *Educational Theory* 45: 151–65.

Brown, S. (ed.) (1975) *Philosophers Discuss Education*, London, Macmillan.

Bryant, M., and Bradley, L. (1985) *Children's Reading Problems*, Oxford, Blackwell.

Burt, C. (1973) 'The Structure of the Mind', in S. Wiseman (ed.) *Intelligence and Ability*, Harmondsworth, Penguin, 115–40.

Button, G., Coulter, J., Lee, J. R. E., and Sharrock, W. (1995) *Computers, Minds and Conduct*, Cambridge, Polity Press.

Callan, E. (1997) 'The Great Sphere', *Journal of Philosophy of Education* 31(2): 221–32.

Carlson, D. (1995) 'Making Progress: Progressive Education in the Postmodern', *Educational Theory* 45(3): 337–57.

Carr, D. (1991) *Educating the Virtues*, London, Routledge.

—— (1992) 'Education, Learning and Understanding: The Process and the Product', *Journal of Philosophy of Education* 26(2): 215–25.

—— (1994) 'Wise Men and Clever Tricks', *Cambridge Journal of Education* 24(1): 89–106.

—— (1996) 'Songs of Immanence and Transcendence: Reply to Nigel Blake', *Oxford Review of Education* 22(4): 457–64.

Carr, W. (1995) *For Education*, Buckingham, Open University Press.

Carruthers, P. (1992) *Human Nature and Human Knowledge*, Oxford, Oxford University Press.

Chamberlin, R. (1989) *Free Children and Democratic Schools: A Philosophical Study of Liberty and Education*, Brighton, Falmer Press.

Charmley, J. (1993) *Churchill: The End of Glory*, London, Hodder.

Chazan, B.I., and Soltis, J. (eds) (1975) *Moral Education*, New York, Teachers College Press.

Chomsky, N. (1957) *Syntactic Structures*, North Holland, Dordrecht.

—— (1965) *Aspects of the Theory of Syntax*, Cambridge, Cambridge University Press.

—— (1988) *Language and Problems of Knowledge*, Cambridge, Mass., MIT Press.

Chubb, J. E., and Moe, T. (1990) *Politics, Markets and America's Schools*, Washington DC,The Brookings Institution.

Clark, C. (1979) 'Education and Behaviour Modification', *Journal of Philosophy of Education* 13: 73–81.

Cohen, B. (1978) 'Equality, Freedom and Independent Schools' *Journal of Philosophy of Education* 12: 121–8.

—— (1982) *Means and Ends in Education*, London, Allen and Unwin.

Collingwood, R. C. (1965) *The Principles of Art*, Oxford, Clarendon.

Collins, P. H. (1990) *Black Feminist Thought*, Boston, Unwin Hyam.

Cooper, D. (1980) *Illusions of Equality*, London, Routledge.

—— (ed.) (1986) *Education Values and Mind, Essays for R. S. Peters*, London, Routledge.

—— (1993) 'Truth and Liberal Education', in R. Barrow and P. White (eds) *Beyond Liberal Education*, London, Routledge.

Cope, B., and Kalantzis, M. (eds) (1993) *The Powers of Literacy: A Genre Approach to Teaching Writing*, Brighton, Falmer.

Crittenden, B. S. (ed.) (1967) *Philosophy and Education*, Toronto, Ontario Institute for Studies in Education.

Dancy, J., and Sosa, E. (1992) *A Companion to Epistemology*, Oxford, Blackwell.

Darling, J. (1993) 'Rousseau as a Progressive Instrumentalist', *Journal of Philosophy of Education* 27(1): 27–38.

—— (1994) *Child-Centred Education*, London, Paul Chapman.

Davis, A. (1995) 'Criterion–Referenced Assessment and the Development of Knowledge and Understanding', *Journal of Philosophy of Education* 29(1): 3–22.

—— (1996) 'Who's Afraid of Assessment? Remarks on Winch and Gingell's Reply', *Journal of Philosophy of Education* 30(3): 389–400.

Dearden, R. F. (1965) 'Instruction and Learning by Discovery', in R. S. Peters (ed.) *The Concept of Education*, London, Routledge.

—— (1966) 'Needs in Education', *British Journal of Educational Studies* 14(3): 5–17.

—— (1968) *Philosophy of Primary Education*, London, Routledge.

—— (1972) 'Competition and Education', *Proceedings of Philosophy of Education Society of Great Britain* 4(1): 119–33.

—— (1979) 'The Assessment of Learning', *British Journal of Educational Studies* 27(2): 111–24.

—— (1984a) 'Education and Training', *Westminster Studies in Education* 7: 57–66.

—— (ed.) (1984b) 'Theory and Practice in Education', in R. F. Dearden *Theory and Practice in Education*, London, Routledge.

Dearden, R. F., Hirst, P., and Peters, R. S. (eds) (1972) *Education and the Development of Reason*, London, Routledge.

Delamont, S. (1980) *Sex Roles and the School*, London, Methuen.

Dent, N. (1988) *Rousseau*, Oxford, Blackwell.

Descartes, R. (1966) *Philosophical Writings*, trans. and ed. G. E. M. Anscombe and P. T. Geach, London, Nelson.

Dewey, J. (1916) *Democracy and Education*, New York, Macmillan.

—— (1929) *The Quest for Certainty*, New York, Minton, Balch.

—— (1933) *How We Think*, Chicago, Henry Regnevey.

—— (1938) *Experience and Education*, London, Collier Macmillan.

Dickie, G. (1997) *Introduction to Aesthetics*, New York, Oxford University Press.

Dixon, J. (1987) 'The Question of Genres', in I. Reid (ed.), *Genre and Learning: Current Debates*, Geelong, Typereader Press.

Donaldson, M. (1992) *Human Minds*, Harmondsworth, Penguin.

Downie, R. S. (1988) 'Health Education and Health Promotion', *Journal of Philosophy of Education* 22(1): 3–12.

Doyle, J. F. (ed.) (1973) *Educational Judgements*, London, Routledge.

Dray, W. H. (1967) 'Aims of Education – A Conceptual Enquiry: Reply to R. S. Peters' in B. S. Crittenden (ed.) *Philosophy and Education*, Toronto, Ontario Institute for Studies in Education.

Dunlop, F. (1982) 'The Ideas of Male and Female: a Prolegomenon to the Question of Education Sex Bias', *Journal of Philosophy of Education* 16(2): 209–22.

Durkheim, E. (1956) *Education and Sociology*, New York, Free Press.

Edel, A. (1973) 'Analytic Philosophy of Education at the Crossroads', in J. F. Doyle (ed.) *Educational Judgements*, London, Routledge.

Egan, K. (1983) *Education and Psychology*, New York, Teachers College Press.

—— (1986) *Individual Development and the Curriculum*, London, Hutchinson.

—— (1988) *Primary Understanding*, New York, Routledge.

Egan, K., and Strike, K. (1977) (eds) *Ethics and Educational Policy*, London, Routledge.

Eliot, T. S. (1948) *Notes Towards the Definition of Culture*, London, Faber and Faber.

Elliott, R. K. (1971) 'Versions of Creativity', *Annual Proceedings of the Philosophy of Education Society of Great Britain* 5(2): 139–52.

—— (1977) 'Education and Justification', *Annual Proceedings of the Philosophy of Education Society of Great Britain*, 11: 7–27.

—— (1981) 'Aestheticism, Imagination and Schooling: a reply to Ruby Meager', *Journal of Philosophy of Education* 15(1): 33–42.

The Elton Report (1989) *Discipline in Schools*, London, HMSO.

English, F. W., and Hill, J. C. (1994) *Total Quality Education: Transforming Schools into Learning Places*, Thousand Oaks, Calif., Corwin.

Ennis, R. H. (1962) 'A Concept of Critical Thinking', *Harvard Educational Review* 32: 81–111.

—— (1974) 'Conceptions of Rational Thinking', in J. R. Combs (ed.) *Philosophy of Education*, Normal, Ill., Philosophy of Education Society.

Entwistle, H. (1970) *Education, Work and Leisure*, London, Routledge.

Equal Opportunities Commission (1982) *Do you Provide Equal Educational Opportunities?* Manchester, Equal Opportunities Commission.

Bibliography

Everitt, N., and Fisher, A. (1996) *Modern Epistemology*, London, McGraw-Hill.

Evers, C. (1990) 'Educating the Brain', *Educational Philosophy and Theory* 22(2): 65–80.

Eysenck, H. (1973) *The Inequality of Man*, London, Fontana.

Feinberg, W. (1998) 'Cultural Recognition and Education', *Proceedings of International Conference, on Philosophy, Education and Culture*, Moray House Institute, Edinburgh (in publication).

Feyerabend, P. K. (1975) *Against Method*, London, New Left Books.

Fielding, M. (1976) 'Against Competition: In Praise of a Malleable Analysis and the Subversiveness of Philosophy', *Annual Proceedings of the Philosophy of Education Society of Great Britain* 10: 114–23.

Finnegan, R. (1973) 'Literacy versus Non-literacy: The Great Divide?', in R. Horton and R. Finnegan (eds) *Modes of Thought*, London, Faber.

Flew, A. (1966) 'What is Indoctrination?', *Studies in Philosophy and Education* 4(3): 281–306.

—— (1976) *Sociology, Equality and Education*, London, Macmillan.

—— (1981) *The Politics of Procrustes: Conditions of Enforced Equality*, London, Temple Smith.

—— (1982) 'The Paradigm Case Argument: Abusing and not Using the P.C.A.', *Journal of Philosophy of Education* 16(1): 115–22.

—— (1987) 'Education Against Racism, Three Comments', *The Journal of Philosophy of Education* 21(1): 131–8.

Fodor, J. (1975) *The Language of Thought*, Cambridge, Mass., MIT Press.

Foucault, M. (1970) *The Order of Things*, trans. A. Sheridan, New York, Random House.

—— (1977) *Discipline and Punish*, trans. A. Sheridan, New York, Pantheon.

—— (1978) *History of Sexuality*, vol. 1, trans. R. Hurley, New York, Pantheon.

Frankena, W. (1970) 'A Model for Analysing a Philosophy of Education', in J. R. Martin (ed.) *Readings in the Philosophy of Education*, Boston, Allyn & Bacon.

—— (1973) 'The Concept of Education Today', in J. F. Doyle (ed.) *Educational Judgements*, London, Routledge.

Freeman, H. (1977) 'On Women's Education', *Annual Proceedings of the Philosophy of Education Society of Great Britain* 11: 113–35.

Freire, P. (1972) *The Pedagogy of the Oppressed*, London, Penguin.

Freud, S. (1985) *Sigmund Freud: Art and Literature*, ed. A. Dickson, Harmondsworth, Penguin.

Gaita, R. (1991) *Good and Evil*, London, Macmillan.

Gallie, W. B. (1955–6) 'Essentially Contested Concepts', *Proceedings of the Aristotelian Society*, 56: 167–98.

Galton, F. (1973) 'The Classification of Men According to their Natural Gifts', excerpts from *Hereditary Genius*, in S. Wiseman (ed.) *Intelligence and Ability*, London, Penguin.

Gardner, H. (1993) *Multiple Intelligences: The Theory in Practice*, Port Moody, BC, Pac-Rim Bookservices.

Geach, P. (1957) *Mental Acts*, London, Routledge.

Giglioli, P. P. (ed.) (1972) *Language and Social Context*, London, Penguin.

Gingell, J. (1985) 'Art and Knowledge', *Educational Philosophy and Theory* 17(1): 10–21.

Gingell, J., and Winch, C. (1996) 'Educational Assessment: Reply to Andrew Davis', *Journal of Philosophy of Education* 30(3): 377–88.

Giroux, H. (1988) 'Postmodernism and the Discourse of Educational Criticism', *Journal of Education* 170: 5–30.

Goldstein, H. (1987) *Multilevel Models in Education and Social Research*, London, Griffin, Oxford University Press.

Goodman, P. (1960) *Growing Up Absurd*, New York, Random House.

—— (1964) *Compulsory Miseducation*, New York, Horizon Press.

Goody, J., and Watt, I. (1972) 'The Consequences of Literacy', in P. P. Giglioli (ed.) *Language and Social Context*, London, Penguin.

Gould, S. J. (1981) *The Mismeasure of Man*, London, Penguin.

Grace, G. (1989) 'Education: Commodity or Public Good', *British Journal of Educational Studies* 37: 207–11.

Gramsci, A. (1971) *Selections from the Prison Notebooks*, ed. P. Nowell Smith and Q. Hoare, London, Lawrence and Wishart.

Gray, J. (1993) *Beyond the New Right*, London, Routledge.

—— (1995) *Enlightenment's Wake*, London, Routledge.

Gray, J., and Wilcox, B. (1995) *Good School, Bad School*, Buckingham, Open University Press.

Greene, M. (1988) *The Dialectic of Freedom*, New York, Teachers College Press.

Gregory, I., and Woods, R. (1970) 'Indoctrination', *Annual Proceedings of the Philosophy of Education Society of Great Britain*, 77–105.

Gribble, J. (1969) *Introduction to Philosophy of Education*, Boston, Allyn and Bacon.

Griffiths, M. (1987) 'The Teaching of Skills and the Skills of Teaching: A Reply to Robin Barrow', *Journal of Philosophy of Education* 21(2): 203–14.

257

Gutmann, A. (1982) 'What's the Use of Going to School?', in A. Sen and B. Williams (eds) *Utilitarianism and Beyond*, Cambridge, Cambridge University Press.

—— (1994) (ed.) *Multiculturalism*, Princeton, NJ, Princeton University Press.

Hacking, I. (1986) 'The Archaeology of Foucault', in D. C. Hay (ed.) *Foucault: A Critical Reader*, Oxford, Blackwell.

The Hadow Report (1931) *The Board of Education Consultative Committee Report on Primary Schools*, London, HMSO.

Haldane, J. (1989) 'Metaphysics in the Philosophy of Education', *Journal of Philosophy of Education* 23(2): 171–94.

Hall, N. (1988) *The Emergence of Literacy*, London, Hodder.

Hamlyn, D. W. (1972) 'Objectivity', in R. F. Dearden, P. Hirst and R. S. Peters (eds) *Education and the Development of Reason*, London, Routledge.

—— (1978) *Experience and the Growth of Understanding*, London, Routledge.

Hamm, C. (1989) *Philosophical Issues in Education*, London, Falmer.

Hare, R. M. (1956) *The Language of Morals*, London, Oxford University Press.

—— (1963) *Freedom and Reason*, London, Oxford University Press.

Hargreaves, D. (1996) 'Teaching as a Research-based Profession: Possibilities and Prospects', Teacher Training Agency Annual Lecture.

Harris, A. (1974) 'What Does "sex education" Mean?', in R. Rogers (ed.) *Sex Education*, Cambridge, Cambridge University Press.

Harris, J. (1982) 'A Paradox of Multicultural Societies', *Journal of Philosophy of Education* 16(2): 223–35.

Harris, K. (1979) *Education and Knowledge*, London, Routledge.

Hart, H. L. A. (1970) *Punishment and Responsibility*, Oxford, Clarendon.

Hartshorne, H., May, M., and Shuttleworth, F. (1930) *Studies in the Organisation of Character*, New York, Macmillan.

Hepburn, R. (1960) 'Emotions and Emotional Qualities: Some Attempts at Analysis', *British Journal of Aesthetics* 1: 255–65.

—— (1972) 'The Arts and the Education of Feeling and Emotion', in R. F. Dearden, P. Hirst and R. S. Peters *Education and the Development of Reason*, London, Routledge.

Hirsch, E. D. (1987) *Cultural Literacy. What Every American Should Know*, Boston, Houghton Mifflin.

Hirst, P. (1965a) 'Liberal Education and the Nature of Knowledge', in R. Archambault (ed.) *Philosophical Analysis and Education*, London, Routledge and Kegan Paul.

—— (1965b) 'Morals, Religion and the Maintained School', *British Journal of Educational Studies* 14: 5–18.

—— (1973a) 'Literature and the Fine Arts as a Unique Form of Knowledge', *Cambridge Journal of Education* 3: 118–32.

—— (1973b) 'What is Teaching', in R. S. Peters (ed.) *The Philosophy of Education*, London, Oxford University Press.

—— (1974) *Knowledge and the Curriculum*, London, Routledge.

—— (1986) 'Richard Peters' Contribution to the Philosophy of Education', in D. Cooper (ed.) *Education Values and Mind, Essays for R. S. Peters*, London, Routledge.

—— (1993) 'Education, Knowledge and Practices', in R. Barrow and P. White (eds) *Beyond Liberal Education*, London, Routledge.

Hirst, P., and Peters, R. S. (1970) *The Logic of Education*, London, Routledge and Kegan Paul.

Hobbes, T. (1968) *Leviathan*, first published 1652, ed. C. B. MacPherson, London, Penguin.

Hollis, M. (1982) 'Education as a Positional Good', *Journal of Philosophy of Education* 16(2): 235–44.

Hollis, M., and Lukes, S. (eds) (1982) *Rationality and Relativism*, Oxford, Blackwell.

Holmes, E. (1911) *What is and What Might Be*, London, Constable.

Howe, M. J. A. (1990) *The Origins of Exceptional Abilities*, Oxford, Blackwell.

Hudson, L. (1966) *Contrary Imaginations*, London, Methuen.

Hudson, W. D. (1977) 'Learning to be Rational', *Annual Proceedings of the Philosophy of Education Society of Great Britain* 11: 39–56.

Hull, C. H. (1966) 'Drive as an Intervening Variable in a Formal Behaviour System', in D. Bindra and J. Stewart (eds) *Motivation*, London, Penguin.

Hume, D. (1958) *A Treatise of Human Nature*, first published 1739, ed. L. A. Selby-Bigge, Oxford, Oxford University Press.

—— (1962) *Enquiries Concerning the Human Understanding and Concerning the Principles of Morals*, first published 1751, ed. L. A. Selby-Bigge, Oxford, Oxford University Press.

Hyland, T. (1993) 'Competence, Knowledge and Education', *Journal of Philosophy of Education* 27(1): 57–68.

Illich, I. (1970) *Celebration of Awareness*, New York, Doubleday.

—— (1971) *Deschooling Society*, London, Calder and Boyars.

Jahoda, M. (1964) 'Stereotype', in J. Gould and W. L. Klab (eds) *A Dictionary of the Social Sciences*, London, Tavistock.

James, W. (1910) *Pragmatism*, New York, Longman's Green & Co.

Bibliography

Jensen, A. (1973a) *Educability and Group Differences*, Edinburgh, Constable.

—— (1973b) 'Intelligence, Learning Ability and Socio-economic Status', in S. Wiseman (ed.) *Intelligence and Ability*, London, Penguin.

Jesson, D., and Mayston, D. (1988) 'Developing Models of Educational Accountability', *Oxford Review of Education* 14(3); 321–40.

Jessup, G. (1991) 'Implications for Individuals: The Autonomous Learner', in G. Jessup (ed.) *Outcomes: NVQs and the Emerging Model of Education and Training*, Brighton, Falmer.

Jonathan, R. (1983) 'Education, Gender and the Nature/Culture Controversy', *Journal of Philosophy of Education* 17(1): 5–20.

—— (1990) 'State Education Service or Prisoner's Dilemma: "Hidden Hand" as a Source of Educational Policy', *British Journal of Educational Studies* 38(2): 116–32.

—— (1997) *Illusory Freedoms: Liberalism, Education and The Market*, Oxford, Blackwell.

Jonathan, R., and Blake, N. (1988) 'Philosophy in Schools: A Request for Clarification', *Journal of Philosophy of Education* 22(2): 221–7.

Jones, M. (1985) 'Education and Racism', *Journal of Philosophy of Education* 19(2): 223–34.

Jones, R. (1989) 'Sex Education in Personal and Social Education', in P. White (ed.) *Personal and Social Education: Philosophical Perspectives*, London, Kogan Page.

Kant, I. (1963) *The Critique of Pure Reason*, first published 1781, ed. Norman Kemp Smith, London, Macmillan.

Kazepides, T. (1991) 'On the Prerequisites of Moral Education: A Wittgensteinian Perspective', *Journal of Philosophy of Education* 25(2): 259–72.

Kazmi, Y. (1990) 'On Being Educated in the West: The Disruption in Self as a Narrative and Inauthenticity of Self', *Studies in Philosophy and Education* 10(4): 281–96.

Kleinig, J. (1973) 'R. S. Peters' Use of Transcendental Arguments', *Annual Proceedings of the Philosophy of Education Society of Great Britain*, 7(2): 149–66.

—— (1981) 'Compulsory Schooling', *Journal of Philosophy of Education* 15(2): 191–204.

—— (1982) *Philosophical Issues in Education*, Beckenham, Croom Helm.

Kohlberg, L. (1984) *The Psychology of Moral Development*, San Fransisco, Harper and Row.

—— (1991) 'Stages of Moral Development as a Basis for Moral Education', in C. Beck, B. S. Crittenden and E. V. Sullivan (eds)

Moral Education: Interdisciplinary Approaches, New York, Newman Press.

Komisar, B. P. (1961) '"Need" and the Needs Curriculum' in B. O. Smith and R. H. Ennis (eds) *Language and Concepts of Education*, Chicago, Rand MacNally.

—— (1968) 'Teaching: Act and Enterprise', in C. J. B. Macmillan and T. W. Nelson (eds) *Concepts of Teaching*, Chicago, Rand McNally.

Kress, G. (1998) 'The Future Still Belongs to Boys', *The Independent*, 11 June, pp. 4–5.

Krimerman, L. J. (1978) 'Compulsory Education: a moral critique', in K. Strike and K. Egan (eds) *Ethics and Education*, London, Routledge.

Kuhn, T. (1975) *The Structure of Scientific Revolutions*, Chicago, University of Chicago Press.

Kymlicka, W. (1989) *Liberalism, Commmunity and Culture*, Oxford, Clarendon.

Labov, W. (1972) '*The Logic of Non-Standard English*', in P. P. Giglioli (ed.) *Language and Social Context*, London, Penguin.

Laird, S. (1994) 'Rethinking Co-education', *Studies in Philosophy and Education*, 13(3–4): 361–78.

Lasch, C. (1995) *The Revolt of the Elites and the Betrayal of Democracy*, New York, Norton.

Laura, R. S., and Heaney, S. (1990) *Philosophical Foundations of Health Education*, New York, Routledge.

Lebedeva, N. (1993) 'Pedagogy and Educational Democratisation', *Studies in Philosophy and Education* 12(1): 95–101.

Lerner, L. (1972) *Times Higher Education Supplement*, 27 October.

Letwin, O. (1988) *Education: the Importance of Grounding*, London, Centre for Policy Studies.

Levi-Strauss, C. (1966) *The Savage Mind*, London, Weidenfeld and Nicolson.

Lieberman, D. (1990) *Learning*, California, Wadsworth.

List, F. (1991) *The National System of Political Economy*, first published in 1841, New Jersey, Augustus Kelley.

Loban, W. (1963) *The Thinking of Elementary School Children*, Champaign, Ill., National Council for the Teaching of English.

Locke, D. (1979) 'Cognitive Stages or Developmental Phases? A Critique of Kohlberg's Stage-Structural theory of Moral Reasoning', *Journal of Moral Education* 8(3): 168–81.

—— (1980) 'The Illusion of Stage Six', *Journal of Moral Education* 9(2): 103–9.

Locke, J. (1961a) *An Essay Concerning Human Understanding*, first published 1690, London, Dent.

—— (1961b) *First Treatise of Government*, first published 1694, Oxford, Oxford University Press.

—— (1961c) *Second Treatise of Government*, first published 1694, Oxford, Oxford University Press.

—— (1964) *Some Thoughts Concerning Education*, ed. F. W Garforth, Heinemann, London.

Lytton, H. (1971) *Creativity and Education*, London, Routledge and Kegan Paul.

McClellan, J. (1976) *Philosophy of Education*, Engelwood Cliffs, NJ, Prentice-Hall.

Macedo, S. (1996) 'Tranformative Constitutionalism and the Case of Religion', *Annual Proceedings of the Philosophy of Education Society of Great Britain*.

MacIntyre, A. (1981) *After Virtue*, London, Duckworth.

—— (1990) *Three Rival Versions of Moral Inquiry*, London, Duckworth.

Mackie, J. (1977) *Ethics: Inventing Right and Wrong*, New York, Penguin.

—— (1982) *The Miracle of Theism*, Oxford, Oxford University Press.

Macmillan, C. J. B., and Garrison, J. W. (1983) 'An Erotetic Concept of Teaching', *Educational Theory* 33(3–4): 157–66.

McPeck, J. (1981) *Critical Thinking and Education*, Oxford, Martin Robertson.

—— (1992) 'Thoughts on Subject Specificity', in S. Norris (ed.) *The Generalizability of Critical Thinking*, New York, Teachers College Press.

McPhail, P., Ungoed-Thomas, J. R., and Chapman, H. (1972) *Moral Education in the Secondary School*, Harlow, Longman.

Malcolm, N. (1968) 'Moore and Ordinary Language', in P. A. Schilpp (ed.) *The Philosophy of G. E. Moore*, Chicago, Northwestern University Press.

—— (1977) *Memory and Mind*, Ithaca, NY, Cornell University Press.

—— (1989) 'Wittgenstein on Language and Rules', *Philosophy* 64: 5–28.

Marshall, J. D. (1990) 'Asking Philosophical Questions about Education: Foucault on Punishment', *Educational Philosophy and Theory* 22(2): 81–92.

Martin, J. R. (1967) *Explaining, Understanding and Teaching*, Boston, Allyn and Bacon.

—— (1985) *Reclaiming a Conversation*, New Haven, CT, Yale University Press.

—— (1992) 'Critical Thinking for a Humane World', in S. Norris (ed.) *The Generalizability of Critical Thinking*, New York, Teachers College Press.

—— (1993) 'Curriculum and the Mirror of Knowledge', in R. Barrow and P. White (eds) *Beyond Liberal Education*, London, Routledge.

Marx, K., and Engels, F. (1970) *The German Ideology* pt.1, first published 1846, ed. with intro. by C. J. Arthur, London, Lawrence and Wishart.

Maw, J. (1995) 'The Handbook for the Inspection of Schools: A Critique', *Cambridge Journal of Education* 25(1): 75–87.

Meager, R. (1981) 'The Dangers of Aestheticism in Schooling', *Journal of Philosophy of Education* 15(1): 23–32.

Mendus, S. (1992) 'All the Kings Horses and All the Kings Men: Justifying Higher Education', *Journal of Philosophy of Education* 26(2): 165–72.

Mill, J. S. (1964) *Utilitarianism*, first published 1861, London, Dent.

—— (1974) *On Liberty*, first published 1859, London, Dent.

Miller, D. (1993) 'In Defence of Nationality', *Journal of Applied Philosophy* 10(1): 3–16.

Millet, K, (1971) *Sexual Politics*, London, Hart Davis.

Montefiore, A. (1975) 'The Neutral Teacher: Chairman's Remarks', in S. Brown (ed.) *Philosophers Discuss Education*, London, Macmillan.

Moore, W. (1966) 'Indoctrination as a Normative Conception', *Studies in Philosophy and Education* 4(4): 396–403.

Mortimore, P., Sammons, P., Stoll, L., Lewis, D., and Ecob, R. (1988) *School Matters: The Junior Years*, Wells, Open Books.

Mounce, H. O. (1996) *The Two Pragmatisms*, London, Routledge.

Moyles, J. (1989) *Just Playing*, Buckingham, Open University Press.

Murdoch, I. (1992) *Metaphysics as a Guide to Morals*, London, Penguin.

Murray, C., and Herrnstein, R. (1994) *The Bell Curve*, London, London Free Press.

Nagel, T. (1997) *The Last Word*, Oxford, Oxford University Press.

Neill, A. S. (1965) *Summerhill*, London, Penguin.

Nelson, C. J. B., and Nelson, T. W. (eds) (1968) *Concepts of Teaching*, Chicago, Rand McNally.

Newby, M. (1997) 'Literary Development as Spiritual Development', *Journal of Philosophy of Education* 31(2): 283–94.

Newton-Smith, W. (1981) *The Rationality of Science*, London, Routledge.

Nielson, K. (1971) *Contemporary Critiques of Religion*, London, Macmillan.

Nixon, J. (1985) *A Teacher's Guide to Multi-Cultural Education*, Oxford, Blackwell.

Bibliography

Noddings, N. (1976) '"Reasonableness" as a Requirement of Teaching', in K. Strike (ed.) *Philosophy of Education*, Urbana, Ill., Educational Theory Press.

—— (1984) *Caring: A Feminine Approach to Ethics and Moral Education*, Berkeley, University of California Press.

—— (1992) *The Challenge to Care in School*, New York, Teachers College Press.

—— (1995) *Philosophy of Education*, Boulder, Colo., Westview Press.

Norman, R. (1975) 'The Neutral Teacher?', in S. Brown (ed.) *Philosophers Discuss Education*, London, Macmillan.

—— (1994) '"I Did it My Way" Some Thoughts on Autonomy', *Journal of Philosophy of Education*, 28(1): 25–34.

Norris, S. (ed.) (1992) *The Generalizability of Critical Thinking*, New York, Teachers College Press.

Nozick, R. (1974) *Anarchy, State and Utopia*, Oxford, Blackwell

Office for Standards in Education (OFSTED), (1994a) *Primary Matters: A Discussion on Teaching and Learning in Primary Schools*, London, OFSTED.

—— (1994b) *Handbook for the Inspection of Schools*, and subsequent editions, London, OFSTED.

O'Hear, A. (1981) *Education, Society and Human Nature*, London, Routledge and Kegan Paul.

Olson, D. (1977) 'From Utterance to Text: The Bias of Language in Speech and Writing', *Harvard Educational Review* 47: 257–81.

—— (1994) *The World on Paper*, Cambridge, Cambridge University Press.

Owen, R. (1991) *A New View of Society*, first published 1813–16, London, Penguin.

The Oxford Paperback Dictionary (1988) Oxford, Oxford University Press.

Passmore, J. (1980) *The Philosophy of Teaching*, London, Duckworth.

Pateman, T. (ed.) (1972) *Counter Course*, Harmondsworth, Penguin.

Paul, R. (1990) *Critical Thinking: What Every Person Needs to Survive in a Rapidly Changing World*, Rohnert Park, Calif., Center for Critical Thinking and Moral Critique.

Peters, R. S. (1966) *Ethics and Education*, London, Allen and Unwin.

—— (1967) 'Authority', in A. Quinton (ed.) *Oxford Readings in Political Philosophy*, Oxford, Oxford University Press.

—— (1970a) 'The Education of the Emotions', collected in M. Arnold (ed.) *Feelings and Emotions*, New York, Academic Press.

—— (1970b) 'Education and Educated Man', *Proceedings of the Philosophy of Education Society of Great Britain* 4(1): 5–20.

—— (1971) 'Reason and Passion', collected in G. Vesey (ed.) *A Proper*

Study of Mankind, London, Macmillan.

—— (1973) 'The Justification of Education', in R. S. Peters (ed.) *The Philosophy of Education*, Oxford, Oxford University Press.

—— (1977) 'Ambiguities in Liberal Education and the Problem of its Content', in K. Egan and K. Strike (eds) *Ethics and Educational Policy*, London, Routledge.

—— (1979) 'Democratic Values and Educational Aims', *Teacher's College Record* 80(3): 463–82.

Phillips, D. Z. (1970) 'Philosophy and Religious Education', *British Journal of Educational Studies* 18(1): 5–17.

—— (1979) 'Is Moral Education Really Necessary?', *British Journal of Educational Studies* 27(1): 42–68.

—— (1997) 'Wittgenstein, Religion and Anglo-American Philosophical Culture', in *Wittgenstein and Culture*, Vienna, Wittgenstein Vienna Society.

Phillips, M. (1996) *All Shall Have Prizes*, London, Little and Brown.

Piaget, J. (1953) *Logic and Psychology*, Manchester, Manchester University Press.

Pitcher, G. (ed.) (1968) *Wittgenstein*, Oxford, Blackwell.

Plato (1970a) *Meno, The Dialogues of Plato*, ed. and trans. B. Jowett, London, Sphere Books.

—— (1970b) *The Republic, The Dialogues of Plato*, ed. and trans. B. Jowett, London, Sphere Books.

—— (1970c) *The Laws, The Dialogues of Plato*, ed. and trans. B. Jowett, London, Sphere Books.

The Plowden Report (1967) *Children and their Primary Schools*, London, HMSO.

Popper, K. (1959) *The Logic of Scientific Discovery*, first published 1936, London, Hutchinson.

—— (1961) *The Poverty of Historicism*, London, Routledge.

—— (1969) *Conjectures and Refutations*, London, Routledge and Kegan Paul.

—— (1972) *Objective Knowledge*, Oxford, Clarendon Press.

Postman, N. (1970) 'The Politics of Reading', in N. Keddie (ed.) *Tinker, Tailor . . . the Myth of Cultural Deprivation*, London, Penguin.

Prais, S. J. (1991) 'Vocational Qualifications in Britain and Europe', *National Institute Economic Review*, May, 86–9.

Pring, R. (1992) 'Standards and Quality in Education', *British Journal of Educational Studies*, 40(1): 4–22.

—— (1995) *Closing the Gap: Liberal Education and Vocational Preparation*, London, Hodder and Stoughton.

Quine, W. V. O. (1953) *From a Logical Point of View*, Cambridge, Mass., Harvard University Press.
—— (1969) *Ontological Relativity and Other Essays*, New York, Columbia University Press.
—— (1981) *Theories and Things*, Cambridge, Mass., Harvard University Press.
Rawls, J. A. (1971) *A Theory of Justice*, Oxford, Oxford University Press.
—— (1993) *Political Liberalism*, New York, Columbia University Press.
Reese, W. (1988) 'Public Schools and the Common Good', *Educational Studies* 38(4): 431–40.
Reid, I. (ed.) (1987) *Genre and Learning: Current Debates*, Geelong, Typereader Press.
Reimer, E. (1971) *School is Dead*, New York, Doubleday.
Rhees, R. (1968) 'Can There be a Private Language?', in G. Pitcher (ed.) *Wittgenstein*, Oxford, Blackwell.
Richards, J. R. (1980) *The Sceptical Feminist*, London, Routledge.
Rogers, C. (1990) *The Carl Rogers Reader*, ed. H. Kirschenbaum and V. Land Henderson, London, Constable.
Rogers, R. (ed.) (1974) *Sex Education*, Cambridge, Cambridge University Press.
Rooke, P. (1993) 'The Centre of Everyone's Haunting Nightmare? Reflections on J. Martin Stafford's *Homosexuality and Education*', *Studies in Philosophy and Education* 12(2–4): 273–84.
Rorty, R. (1980) *Philosophy and the Mirror of Nature*, Oxford, Blackwell.
—— (1989) *Contingency, Irony and Solidarity*, Cambridge, Cambridge University Press.
—— (1991) *Objectivity, Relativism and Truth, Philosophical Papers*, vol. 1, New York, Cambridge University Press.
Ross, G. M. (1988) 'Philosophy in Schools', *Journal of Philosophy of Education* 22(2): 229–38.
Rousseau, J. J. (1911a) *Emile or Education*, first published 1762, trans. Barbara Foxley, London, Dent.
—— (1911b) *A Discourse on Inequality*, first published 1755, London, Dent, London.
—— (1913) *The Social Contract*, first published 1762, London, Dent.
Ryle, G. (1949) *The Concept of Mind*, London, Hutchinson.
—— (1972) 'Can Virtue by Taught?', in R. F. Dearden, P. Hirst and R. S. Peters (eds) *Education and the Development of Reason*, London, Routledge.

—— (1974) 'Intelligence and the Logic of Nature – Nurture issue: Reply to J. P. White', *Annual Proceedings of the Philosophy of Education Society of Great Britain* 8(1): 52–60.

Sadker, M. P., and Sadker, D. M. (1977) *Now Upon A Time*, New York, Harper and Row.

Sandel, M. (1982) *Liberalism and the Limits of Justice*, Cambridge, Cambridge University Press.

Scheffler, I. (1960) *The Language of Education*, Springfield, Ill., Charles C. Thomas.

—— (1973) 'The Concept of Teaching', in I. Scheffler (ed.) *Reason and Teaching*, London, Routledge and Kegan Paul.

—— (1991) 'In Praise of the Cognitive Emotions', in I. Scheffler (ed.) *In Praise of the Cognitive Emotions*, New York, Routledge.

Scheman, N. (1993) 'Though This Be Method, Yet There is Madness In It', in L. Anthony and C. Witt (eds) *A Mind of One's Own*, Boulder, Colo., Westview Press.

Schon, D. (1983) *The Reflective Practitioner: Professional Thinking in Action*, New York, Basic Books.

—— (1987) *Educating the Reflective Practitioner*, San Francisco, Jossey Bass.

Schweinhart, L. J., and Weikart, D. P. (1980) *Young Children Grow Up*, Ypsilanti Mich., Monographs of the High/Scope Educational Research, Foundation No. 7.

Sealey, J. (1985) *Religious Education: Philosophical Perspectives*, London, Allen and Unwin.

Searle, J. R. (1964) 'How to Derive "Ought" from "Is"', *Philosophical Review* 73: 43–58.

—— (1969) *Speech Acts, An Essay in Philosophy of Language*, New York, Cambridge University Press.

—— (1992) *The Rediscovery of the Mind*, London, MIT Press.

Sen, A., and Williams, B. (eds) (1982) *Utilitarianism and Beyond*, Cambridge, Cambridge University Press.

Shackleton, J. R. (1976) 'Adam Smith and Education', *Higher Education Review*, Spring, 80–90.

Shaw, B. (1989) 'Sexual Discrimination and the Equal Opportunities Commission: Ought Schools to Eradicate Sex Stereotyping?', *Journal of Philosophy of Education* 23(2): 295–302.

Short, G. (1991) 'Prejudice, Power and Racism: Some Reflections on the Anti-Racist Critique of Multi-Cultural Education', *Journal of Philosophy of Education* 25(1): 5–15.

Siegel, H. (1988) *Educating Reason*, New York, Routledge.

—— (1995) '"Radical" Pedagogy Requires "Conservative" Epistemology', *Journal of Philosophy of Education* 29(1): 33–46.

—— (1997) 'Multiculturalism and the Possibility of Transcultural Ideas', *Proceedings of the International Conference on Philosophy, Education and Culture*, Moray House, Edinburgh.

Silver, H. (1994) *Good Schools, Effective Schools*, London, Cassell.

Simpson, E. (1989) *Good Lives and Moral Education*, New York, Peter Lang.

Smith, A. (1981) *The Wealth of Nations*, first published 1776, ed. R. H. Campbell, A. S. Skinner, and W. B. Todd, Indianapolis, Liberty Fund.

Smith, F. (1985) *Reading*, Cambridge, Cambridge University Press.

Smith, R. (1985) *Freedom and Discipline*, London, Allen and Unwin.

—— (1987) 'Skills: The Middle Way', *Journal of Philosophy of Education* 21(2): 197–202.

Snook, I. (ed.) (1972a) *Concepts of Indoctrination*, London, Routledge and Kegan Paul.

—— (1972b) *Indoctrination and Education*, London, Routledge and Kegan Paul.

Stafford, M. (1988) *Homosexuality and Education*, Manchester, Martin Stafford.

Stainthorp, R. (1989) *Practical Psychology for Teachers*, Brighton, Falmer.

Stenhouse, L. (1975) *Introduction to Curriculum Research and Development*, London, Heinemann.

Stewart, D. (1978) 'An Analysis of Advising', *Educational Theory* 28(2): 202–13.

Straughan, R. (1982) *Can We Teach Children to be Good?* London, Allen and Unwin.

Strawson, P. F. (1974) 'Freedom and Resentment', in P. F. Strawson (ed.) *Freedom and Resentment and Other Essays*, London, Methuen.

Streeck, W. (1992) *Social Institutions and Economic Performance*, London, Sage.

Strike, K. (1983) 'Fairness and Ability Grouping', *Educational Theory* 33(3–4): 125–34.

Suchting, W. A. (1992) 'Constructivism Deconstructed', *Science and Education* 1(3): 223–54.

Taylor, C. (1964) *The Explanation of Behaviour*, London, Routledge.

—— (1979a) *Hegel and Modern Society*, Cambridge, Cambridge University Press.

—— (1979b) 'What's Wrong with Negative Liberty', collected in A. Ryan (ed.) *The Idea of Freedom*, Oxford, Oxford University Press.

—— (1985) 'Foucault on Freedom and Truth', in C. Taylor (ed.) *Philosophy and the Human Sciences, Philosophical Papers 2*, Cambridge, Cambridge University Press.

—— (1991) *The Ethics of Authenticity*, Cambridge, Mass., Harvard University Press.

—— (1994) 'The Politics of Recognition', reprinted in A. Gutmann (ed.) *Multiculturalism*, Princeton, NJ, Princeton University Press.

Terman, L. (1917) *The Intelligence of Schoolchildren*, Boston, Houghton Mifflin.

Thurstone, L. L. (1957) *Multiple Factor Analysis*, Chicago, University Chicago Press.

Tizard, B., and Hughes, M. (1984) *Young Children Learning*, London, Fontana.

Tolstoy, L. (1930) *What is Art?* First published 1898, Oxford, Oxford University Press.

Tooley, J. (1995) *Disestablishing the School*, Aldershot, Avebury.

Troyna, B. (1987) 'Beyond Multiculturalism: Towards the Enactment of Anti-Racist Education in Policy, Provision and Pedagogy', *Oxford Review of Education* 13(3): 307–20.

Turner, M. (1990) *Sponsored Reading Failure: An Object Lesson*, Warlingham Park School Education Unit.

Vico, G. (1968) *The New Science*, first published 1725, Ithaca, NY, Cornell University Press.

von Glasersfeld, E. (1989) 'Cognition, Construction of Knowledge and Teaching', *Synthese* 80: 121–40.

Vygotsky, L. (1962) *Thought and Language*, Cambridge, Mass., MIT Press.

—— (1978) *Mind and Society*, Cambridge, Mass., Harvard University Press.

Wain, K. (1995) 'Richard Rorty, Education and Politics', *Educational Theory* 45(3): 395–409.

—— (1996) 'Foucault, Education, the Self and Modernity', *Journal of Philosophy of Education* 30(3): 345–60.

Waltzer, M. (1994) Comment on 'The Politics of Recognition', A. Gutmann (ed.) *Multiculturalism*, Princeton, NJ, Princeton University Press.

Warnock, M. (1975) 'The Neutral Teacher' in S. Brown (ed.) *Philosophers Discuss Education*, London, Macmillan.

—— (1977) *Schools of Thought*, London, Faber.

The Warnock Report (1978) *The Committee of Enquiry into the Education of Handicapped Children and Young Persons*, London, HMSO.

269

Bibliography

Waterland, L. (1985) *Read with Me*, Stroud, Thimble Press.

Wegener, A. (1952) 'The Ontology of Reconstructionism', *Educational Theory* 2(1): 47–57.

Wells, C. G. (1981) 'Some Antecedents of Early Educational Attainment', *British Journal of the Sociology of Education* 2(2): 181–200.

—— (1987) *The Meaning Makers*, London, Hodder.

White, J. P. (1967) 'Indoctrination', in R. S. Peters (ed.) *The Concept of Education*, London, Routledge and Kegan Paul.

—— (1968) 'Creativity and Education', *British Journal of Educational Studies* 16(2): 123–34.

—— (1973) *Towards a Compulsory Curriculum*, London, Routledge and Kegan Paul.

—— (1974) 'Intelligence and the Logic of the Nature-Nurture Issue', *Annual Proceedings of the Philosophy of Education Society of Great Britain* 8(1), 30–51.

—— (1982) *The Aims of Education Restated*, London, Routledge.

—— (1990) *Education and the Good Life*, London, Kogan Page.

—— (1994) 'The Dishwasher's Child: Education and the End of Egalitarianism', *Journal of Philosophy of Education* 28(2): 173–82.

—— (1996) 'Education and Nationality', *Journal of Philosophy of Education* 30(3): 327–44.

—— (1997a) 'Philosophical Perspectives on School Effectiveness and School Improvement', in J. P. White and M. Barber (eds) *Perspectives on School Effectiveness and School Improvement*, London, Institute of Education.

—— (1997b) *Education and the End of Work*, London, Kogan Page.

White, J., and Barber, M. (eds) (1997) *Perspectives on School Effectiveness and School Improvement*, London, Institute of Education.

White, J., and Gordon, P. (1979) *Philosophers as Educational Reformers*, London, Routledge.

White, P. (1972) 'Education and Socialisation', *Personal and Social Education: Philosophical Perspectives*, London, Kogan Page.

—— (1989) (ed.) *Personal and Social Education: Philosophical Perspectives*, London, Kogan Page.

Whitehead, A. N. (1967) *The Aims of Education*, New York, Free Press.

Whitfield, R.C. (1971) (ed.) *Disciplines of the Curriculum*, New York, McGraw-Hill.

Whitty, G. (1992) 'Quality Control and Teacher Education', *British Journal of Educational Studies* 40: 38–50.

Williams, B. (1972) *Morality: An Introduction to Ethics*, Cambridge, Cambridge University Press.

—— (1985) *Morality and the Limits of Philosophy*, London, Fontana.

Williams, B., and Smart, J. J. C. (1973) *Utilitarianism: For and Against*, Cambridge, Cambridge University Press.

Williams, K. (1990) 'In Defence of Compulsory Education', *Journal of Philosophy of Education* 24(2): 285–96.

—— (1997) 'Education and Human Diversity: The Ethics of Separate Schooling Revisited', *Annual Proceedings of the Philosophy of Education Society of Great Britain*: 127–35.

Wilson, B. (ed.) (1970) *Rationality*, Oxford, Blackwell.

Wilson, J. (1964) 'Education and Indoctrination', in T. H. B. Hallins (ed.) *Aims in Education: The Philosophic Approach*, Manchester, Manchester University Press.

—— (1973) *The Assessment of Morality*, Windsor, Berks., NFER.

—— (1977) *Philosophy and Practical Education*, London, Routledge and Kegan Paul.

—— (1993) 'Equality Revisited', *Journal of Philosophy of Education* 27(1): 113–14.

Wilson, J., Williams, N., and Sugerman, B. (eds) (1967) *Introduction to Moral Education*, Harmondsworth, Penguin.

Wilson, P. S. (1971) *Interest and Discipline in Education*, Routledge, London.

Winch, C. (1983) 'Education, Literacy and the Development of Rationality', *Journal of Philosophy of Education* 17(2): 187–200.

—— (1990) *Language, Ability and Education Achievement*, London, Routledge.

—— (1993) 'Should Children's Books be Censored?', *Westminster Studies in Education* 16: 41–51.

—— (1995) 'Education Needs Training', *Oxford Review of Education* 21(3): 315–26.

—— (1996) *Quality and Education*, Oxford, Blackwell. Also published as a special edition of the *Journal of Philosophy of Education* 30(2).

—— (1998) *The Philosophy of Human Learning*, London, Routledge.

Winch, C., and Gingell, J. (1994) 'Dialect Interference and Difficulties Writing: An Investigation in St Lucian Primary Schools', *Language and Education* 8(3): 157–82.

Winch, P. (1958) *The Idea of a Social Science*, London, Routledge.

Wiseman, S. (ed.) (1973) *Intelligence and Ability*, London, Penguin.

Wittgenstein, L. (1953) *Philosophical Investigations*, Oxford, Blackwell.

—— (1967) *Zettel*, Oxford, Blackwell.

—— (1980) *Culture and Value*, trans. P. Winch, Oxford, Blackwell (2nd edn, 1998).

Woods, J. (1967) 'Aims of Education – A Conceptual Enquiry: Reply to R. S. Peters', in B. S. Crittenden (ed.) *Philosophy and Education*, Toronto, Ontario Institute for Studies in Education.

Woods, R., and Barrow, R. (1975) *An Introduction of Philosophy of Education*, London, Methuen.

World Health Organization founding document, 1946.

Yates, F. (1984) *The Art of Memory*, London, Ark.

Young, M. F. D. (ed.) (1971) *Knowledge and Control: New Directions for the Sociology of Education*, London, Macmillan.

NAME INDEX

273

Name index

Brice Heath, S. 35, 224
Britzman, D. 107
Brown, S. 163
Bryant, P. and Bradley, L. 137, 201
Burt, C. 118, 157, 200, 216
Button, G. *et al.* 238

Callan, E. 174
Camillo, G. 143
Carlson, D. 177
Carnap, R. 215
Carr, D. 65, 81, 102, 146, 148, 183, 208, 228, 245
Carr, W. 33, 111
Carruthers, P. 40
Chamberlain, R. 40
Chandler, R. 51
Charmley, J. 164
Chazan, B.I. and Soltis, J. 150
Chippendale, T. 51
Chomsky, N. 30, 35, 41, 121, 142, 185, 190
Chubb J.E. and Moe, T. 5, 138
Churchill, W. 164
Cohen, B. 141
Collingwood, R. 94
Collins, P. 96
Cooper, D. 7, 82, 87, 89, 90, 145–146, 189, 216, 239
Cope, B. and Kalantzis, M. 99, 179

Dancy, J. and Sosa, E. 106
Darling, J. 178–179, 185
Darwin, C. 52, 110
Davis, A. 7, 17, 197
Dearden R.F. 17, 37, 38, 68, 135, 159–161, 173–174, 189, 209, 235, 237
Dent, N. 217

Descartes, R. 17, 40, 83, 90, 237
Dewey, J. 42, 58, 59, 92, 107, 110, 126, 127, 178–181, 183–189, 200, 203, 214, 231–233
Dickens, C. 51
Dickie, G. 4
Dixon, J. 99
Don Quixote 52
Donaldson, M. 62
Dray, W.H. 72
Dunlop, F. 219
Durkheim, E. 50, 223

Edel, A. 72
Edwards, J. 109, 179
Egan, K. 61, 111, 159, 202
Eliot, T.S. 50
Elliot, R.K. 43, 112, 123
Elton Committee 65
Engels, F. 110
English, F.W. and Hill, J.C. 177, 188–189
Ennis, R.H. 47, 48
Entwistle, H. 68, 87, 246, 248
Equal Opportunities Commission 230
Esland, G. 225
Everitt, N. and Fisher, A. 83, 125
Evers, C. 30, 145, 203
Eysenck, H. 157

Feinberg, W. 226
Feyerabend, P. 215
Fichte, G. 109
Fielding, M. 37
Finnegan, R. 136
Flew, A.G.M. 10, 15, 113, 154, 167, 198, 225
Fodor, J. 30, 31, 41, 142, 190

274

Name index

Name index

SUBJECT INDEX

Subject index